OAKTON COMMUNITY COLLEGE LIBRARY

D0162013

HORROR, THE FILM READER

Horror, The Film Reader brings together key articles to provide a comprehensive resource for students of horror cinema. Mark Jancovich's introduction traces the development of horror from *The Cabinet of Dr. Caligari* to *The Blair Witch Project*, and outlines the main critical debates. Combining classic and recent articles, each section explores a central issue of horror film, and features an editor's introduction outlining the context of debates. Sections include:

- *Theorizing horror* – traces attempts to identify the defining features of the genre and account for the enduring appeal of horror films
- *Gender, sexuality and the horror film* – debates masculinity and femininity in horror films, focusing on female victims and heroes, issues of the gaze and the monstrous, and queer readings
- *Producing horrors* – looks at the contexts in which films are made, from James Whale's *Frankenstein* to the Hammer studio, tracing horror's relationship to both 'low culture' and avant-garde cinema
- *Consuming fears* – considers the reception of horror, studying the marketing of classic horror, noting the critical reception of *The Silence of the Lambs*, the exhibition of *Psycho* and the ethnography of female horror fans

Contributors Harry M. Benshoff, Rhona Berenstein, Noël Carroll, Brigid Cherry, Carol J. Clover, Barbara Creed, Paul O'Flinn, Joan Hawkins, Peter Hutchings, Mark Jancovich, Andrew Tudor, Linda Williams, and Robin Wood.

Mark Jancovich is Reader in Film Studies at the University of Nottingham.

In Focus: Routledge Film Readers
Series Editors: Steven Cohan (Syracuse University) and Ina Rae Hark (University of South Carolina)

The *In Focus* series of readers is a comprehensive resource for students on film and cinema studies courses. The series explores the innovations of film studies while highlighting the vital connection of debates to other academic fields and to studies of other media. The readers bring together key articles on a major topic in film studies, from marketing to Hollywood comedy, identifying the central issues, exploring how and why scholars have approached it in specific ways, and tracing continuities of thought among scholars. Each reader opens with an introductory essay setting the debates in their academic context, explaining the topic's historical and theoretical importance, and surveying and critiquing its development in film studies.

Exhibition, The Film Reader
Edited by Ina Rae Hark

Hollywood Musicals, The Film Reader
Edited by Steven Cohan

Horror, The Film Reader
Edited by Mark Jancovich

Marketing, The Film Reader
Edited by Justin Wyatt

Forthcoming titles:

Experimental Cinema, The Film Reader
Edited by Wheeler Winston Dixon and Gwendolyn Audrey Foster

Hollywood Comedians, The Film Reader
Edited by Frank Krutnik

Music, The Film Reader
Edited by Kay Dickinson

Reception, The Film Reader
Edited by Barbara Klinger

Stars, The Film Reader
Edited by Marcia Landy and Lucy Fischer

HORROR, THE FILM READER

Edited by Mark Jancovich

London and New York

First published 2002
by Routledge
11 New Fetter Lane, London EC4P 4EE

Simultaneously published in the USA and Canada
by Routledge
29 West 35th Street, New York, NY 10001

Routledge is an imprint of the Taylor & Francis Group

Designed and typeset in Novarese and Scala Sans by
Keystroke, Jacaranda Lodge, Wolverhampton.
Printed and bound in Great Britain by
Biddles Ltd, Guildford and King's Lynn

British Library Cataloguing in Publication Data
A catalogue record for this book is available
from the British Library

Library of Congress Cataloging in Publication Data
Horror, the film reader/edited by Mark Jancovich.
p. cm. – (In focus–Routledge film readers)
Includes bibliographical references and index.
1. Horror films–History and criticism. I. Jancovich, Mark. II. Series.

PN1995.9.H6 H75 2002
791.43'6164–dc21 2001048569

ISBN 0–415–23561–8 (hbk)
ISBN 0–415–23562–6 (pbk)

Contents

PART FOUR: CONSUMING FEARS 135

Acknowledgements

1. Robin Wood, 'The American Nightmare: Horror in the 70s', from *Hollywood from Vietnam to Reagan* (New York, Columbia University Press, 1986), pp. 70–80. © 1986 Columbia University Press. Reprinted by permission of the publisher.
2. Noël Carroll, 'Why Horror?', from *The Philosophy of Horror Or Paradoxes of the Heart* (New York, Routledge Inc., 1990), pp. 158–95. Reproduced by permission of Taylor & Francis Ltd/Routledge, Inc., *http://www.routledge-ny.com*.
3. Andrew Tudor, 'Why Horror? The Peculiar Pleasures of a Popular Genre', from *Cultural Studies* 11 (3) (1997) (Taylor & Francis Ltd, 1997), pp. 433–63. Reprinted by permission of Taylor & Francis Ltd.
4. Linda Williams, 'When the Woman Looks', from Mary Ann Doane, Patricia Mellencamp and Linda Williams, eds, *Re-Vision: Essays in Feminist Film Criticism* Los Angeles, American Film Institute), pp. 83–99.
5. Barbara Creed, 'Horror and the Monstrous-Feminine: An Imaginary Abjection', from *Screen* 27 (1) January–February (1986), pp. 44–54. Reprinted by permission of Oxford University Press.
6. Carol J. Clover, 'Her Body, Himself: Gender in the Slasher Film', from *Representations* 20 (Fall 1987), pp. 205–28. © 1987 The Regents of the University of California. Reprinted by permission.
7. Harry M. Benshoff, 'Introduction: The Monster and the Homosexual', from *Monsters in the Closet: Homosexuality and the Horror Film* (Manchester University Press, 1997), pp. 1–28. Reprinted by permission of Manchester University Press.
8. Paul O'Flinn, 'Production and Reproduction: The Case of *Frankenstein*', from *Literature and History* (2) (Autumn 1983), pp. 194–213. Reprinted by permission of *Literature and History*.
9. Peter Hutchings, 'The Problem of British Horror', from *Hammer and Beyond: The British Horror Film* (Manchester University Press, 1993), pp. 11–23. Reprinted by permission of Manchester University Press.
10. Joan Hawkins, 'Sleaze Mania, Euro-trash, and High Art: The Place of European Art Films in American Low Culture', from *Film Quarterly* 53 (2) (Winter 1999–2000), pp. 14–29. © 2000 The Regents of the University of California. Reprinted by permission.
11. Rhona Berenstein, 'Horror for Sale: The Marketing and Reception of Classic Horror Cinema', from *Attack of the Leading Ladies: Gender, Sexuality and Spectatorship in Classic Horror Cinema* (New York: Columbia University Press, 1996). pp. 60–77.

12. Mark Jancovich, 'Genre and the Audience: Genre Classifications and Cultural Distinctions in the Mediation of *The Silence of the Lambs*', from Melvyn Stokes and Richard Maltby, eds., *Hollywood Spectatorship: Changing Perceptions of Cinema Audiences* (London, BFI Publishing, 2001), pp. 33–45. Reprinted by permission of BFI Publishing.
13. Linda Williams, 'Learning to Scream', from *Sight and Sound* 15, xxx (1995), pp. 14–17. © *Sight and Sound*/The British Film Institute.
14. Brigid Cherry, 'Refusing to Refuse to Look: Female Viewers of the Horror Film', from Melvyn Stokes and Richard Maltby, eds, *Identifying Hollywood's Audiences* (London, BFI Publishing, 1999), pp. 187–203. Reprinted by permission of BFI Publishing.

Horror, The Film Reader

General Introduction

In recent years, it could be argued, the horror film has taken over from the western as the genre that is most written about by genre critics. In many of these accounts, the horror genre is claimed to be interesting because of its supposedly marginal, and hence subversive, status as a disreputable form of popular culture. While this current academic interest suggests that the genre no longer has such a marginal status, if indeed it ever had one, the importance of horror goes far beyond this current intellectual fad. Like pornography, not only is the horror genre the object of considerable aesthetic criticism, but it is frequently the target of moral panics and calls for censorship. In other words, the horror film raises questions of cultural analysis as well as cultural policy.

However, while most people use generic categories, and refer to films as 'westerns', 'musicals', 'romantic comedies' or 'science-fiction movies', the precise meanings of these terms are not always clear. Certainly such uses try to establish a connection between different films, but the nature of that connection is usually implicit rather than explicit. As a result, the history of writing on the horror genre has been dominated by two key questions. First, there is the question of what one might mean by terms such as 'horror', and this usually becomes a question of how one defines the horror genre and so identifies its essential features. This first question also presupposes a second and more fundamental question: what is a film genre, or more properly, what should be meant by the term 'genre' when it is used in film studies? Even those writings on horror that have not addressed these questions directly are almost invariably – if not inevitably – structured by their definitions of the term 'genre' in general and 'the horror genre' in particular.

More recently, as we shall see, theorists of genre have come to argue that the study of genre should not be concerned with the search for the essential or defining features of a genre, and have proposed alternative ways of thinking about genre. These theorists rightly claim that an individual genre 'has less to do with a group of artefacts than with a discourse – a loose evolving system of arguments and readings, helping to shape commercial strategies and aesthetic ideologies' (Naremore, 1995–6: 14). For James Naremore, genres should not be conceived of as objects that are composed of a series of texts that share similar features; rather it is the process of classification itself which creates 'a relationship of homogeneity, filiation, authentication of some texts by use of others' (p. 14). Indeed, as Naremore has demonstrated, the films associated with a particular genre can change within different contexts. During the 1960s and early 1970s, *The Innocents* (1961), *Repulsion* (1965) and even *Satyricon* (1969) were all discussed as central moments in the history of horror, although more recent accounts rarely even make mention of them. Alternatively, while 'German expressionist' classics such as *The Cabinet of Dr. Caligari* (1919) or *Nosferatu* (1922) were rarely seen as horror films in their own day, they are now frequently cited as seminal examples of the genre.

However, these new approaches to genre have made little impact on the discussion of individual genres. For example, most writing continues to imply that the horror genre is a known and familiar object, or else returns to the job of trying to define its essence. Even in a recent collection dedicated to new theoretical approaches to the study of genre, David J. Russell dismisses the 'widespread critical indifference to and suspicion of a working definition of the genre as if a consistent critical vocabulary might be, somehow, a bad thing' (Russell, 1998: 233). He therefore tries to 'reintegrate the horror genre' through the following claim:

> The basic definition of any horror film may be centred around its monster character, and the conflict arising in the fantastical and unreal monster's relationship with normality – as represented through a pseudo-ontic space constructed through filmic realism – provides the necessary basic terms for its (filmic) existence.
>
> (p. 252)

Furthermore, most studies still tend to focus on the textual interpretation of classic instances of horror, rather than to examine the historically specific contexts of production, mediation or consumption through which texts are generically categorized or recategorized (Clover, 1992; Crane, 1994; and Creed, 1993).

The aim of this book is to shift the focus of discussion towards these latter issues, but an examination of earlier work is also important for a number of reasons. First, this earlier work establishes the context for later studies: it provides indispensable tools for analysis, but also the positions from which later critics have sought to distance themselves. It is therefore impossible to understand the importance of later work, and the reasons why critics took the path that they did, unless one knows the context from which they were both drawing ideas and differentiating themselves. Second, as has already been suggested, earlier approaches are rarely simply dead but, on the contrary, have often passed into the realm of taken-for-granted assumption. It is only by re-examining the various approaches to the study of the horror genre that one can test one's own unacknowledged assumptions about the genre. In other words, without an awareness of the past, one is often condemned to repeat it.

A brief history of the horror film

However, before we move on to a history of academic approaches to horror, it is important to understand the constructions of horror-film history that inform these approaches. Nor is this simply important for those unfamiliar with the horror genre. Even those who have an extensive and developed knowledge of the genre often find that they have a very different sense of its history from those that are dominant in academic film criticism. It is therefore important to gain a sense of how academics have understood that history in order to make sense of their more general arguments and claims.

As a result, the history that follows should not be seen as *the* history, but only as *a* history, and it is one that has been constructed out of the elements most commonly referenced in academic histories of the genre. This process was not an easy one: there remains little consensus over the shape of this history amongst academics – each account emphasizes some features and ignores others – and I was therefore forced to steer a course between deeply opposed and contradictory constructions of the field.

Many histories connect the horror film with the forms of literary and theatrical horror that pre-existed the emergence of the cinema, but those accounts that set out to identify the cinematic roots of the horror genre make reference to the films of Méliès and his contemporaries. These films often used fantastic scenarios such as *A Trip to the Moon* (1902) to showcase feats of trick photography. In this way, Méliès, who had originally been a magician, is credited with the creation of a cinema of fantasy in which he did not simply seek to document 'reality' as did many of his contemporaries but, on the contrary, used the potentials of film to present images of things that could not be, except in the imagination.

This concern with worlds of the imagination is also central to what is often seen as the next key moment in the development of the horror film, German expressionism. This movement, however, was not intended as a form of popular entertainment, but was a self-conscious attempt to 'make the cinema respectable for bourgeois audiences, and give it the status of art' (Elssaeser, 1989: 32). Again, the key feature of German expressionism was its anti-realist aesthetic: it used lighting effects and set design to create a world that was, 'by comparison with the then-established conventions of film imagery, a world internally awry' (Tudor, 1989: 28). The list of classics associated with the movement is particularly impressive and it includes: Stellan Kye's *The Student of Prague* (1913), Robert Weine's *The Cabinet of Dr. Caligari* (1919), Paul Wegener's *The Golem* (1920), F. W. Murnau's *Nosferatu* (1922), and both Fritz Lang's Dr. Marbuse films and his nightmarish *Metropolis* (1926).

This period is then followed by that of the Hollywood productions of the 1930s. Although some histories include RKO's *King Kong* (1933) as a horror film, most histories concentrate on the films produced by Universal Pictures, most notably James Whale's *Frankenstein* (1931) and *Bride of Frankenstein* (1935), and Tod Browning's *Dracula* (1931). These films are often used to prove the link between horror and the relatively respectable tradition of Gothic literature, but they were, at least initially, produced, mediated and consumed as the film versions of contemporary theatrical hits. None the less, these films drew on some of the techniques from German expressionism and established the now familiar images of both Dracula and Frankenstein's monster. Indeed, it was these films that made the monster their central concern, and made stars of Boris Karloff and Bela Lugosi. Those critics who therefore see horror as centrally organized around the sympathetic and ambiguous figure of the monster generally do so though reference to these films.

A similar concern is also present in the films that Val Lewton produced at RKO during the 1940s, but they are also credited with significance for two other reasons. First, despite their Gothic elements, these films often located their narratives within a recognizably modern world. Although they might, as in the case of *Cat People* (1942), present a conflict between modern rational America and a traditional and superstitious old world, the drama often takes place within the modern American city, and calls into question the very certainties on which this world depends. In other words, the horror no longer takes place in some exotic never-never land but erupts within the normal and everyday. Second, these films self-consciously flaunt their artistic and literary credentials, even while they were largely produced as low-budget shockers. For example, *I Walked with a Zombie* (1943) was a reworking of Charlotte Brontë's *Jane Eyre*, and *Bedlam* (1946) was 'based on the eight pictures in Hogarth's *The Rake's Progress*' (Butler, 1967: 80).

If Lewton's films brought the horror closer to home, the 1950s introduced a series of monsters that were clearly associated with the world of modern scientific America. There is, of course, a lot of disagreement as to whether these films are actually horror or science fiction, but they often involved an alien invading force from outer space, or else a horde of invaders caused by human science itself. On the one hand, films like *The Thing from Another World* (1951) and *Invasion of the Body Snatchers* (1956) concerned alien invaders from outer space, although in the first case the alien proceeded through violence and in the second it spread by insidiously 'replacing' humans with alien copies. On the other hand, in films such as *Them!* (1954) and *Tarantula* (1955), normally harmless animals grew to fantastic size because of nuclear radiation or human experimentation, and so threatened to destroy humanity.

These films were often popular with teenagers, and in its initial years, AIP (American International Pictures) produced a number of alien-invasion narratives that were aimed directly at teenage audiences. However, they also slowly began to return to the Gothic elements of the genre. For example, it had a huge hit with *I Was a Teenage Werewolf* (1957), in which a modern American teenager is 'regressed' by a scientist and becomes a bloodthirsty monster, and, by the end of the decade, Roger Corman was directing the first of a cycle of films that were loosely based on the literature of Edgar Allan Poe. These films were made on a small budget but were lavish colour films that used visual excess to create a nightmarish world of melodramatic fantasy, and were clearly made in response to developments overseas.

At the same time as AIP was enjoying success with *I Was a Teenage Werewolf*, a small British company called Hammer had a phenomenal success with its own film versions of Frankenstein and Dracula. These films were again cheaply made, but used colour and careful set design to create a vividly realized Gothic world that initially shocked audiences with its gore. However, Hammer was not alone in producing Gothic horrors, and throughout the 1960s, a whole series of national popular cinemas made horrors of their own. For example, while Mario Bava and others made a series of horror films in Italy, Jess Franco and others were developing their own breed of horror films in Spain.

Unfortunately, despite this startling resurgence of Gothic horror in the late 1950s, 1960 also saw the release of Alfred Hitchcock's *Psycho*, which has been credited with single-handedly transforming the horror genre in two ways. First, it is claimed to have placed the horror firmly within the context of modern American society and second, it is supposed to have located its origins within the modern American family more specifically (Wood, 1986). Obviously, there are problems with this account. As we have seen, earlier films had already placed the horror within the context of modern American society, and had located the cause of the horror within that context. Furthermore, when one places *Psycho* back into the broader context of horror fiction within the period one finds that it is the product of a far longer tradition of films that are concerned with a crisis of identity within modern society (Jancovich, 1996). In *Psycho*, the monster is not a supernatural being but an apparently ordinary teenager, Norman Bates, who is psychologically disturbed and not only unable to control his murderous impulses, but virtually unaware of them. He believes the murderer to be his mother, a woman who died years earlier, but whose death he can't acknowledge. He is therefore a split personality: the gentle victimized son, Norman; and the vicious killer, Mother.

The focus on the family in *Psycho* is, none the less, seen as initiating a cycle of 'family horror films', although this cycle does not seem to have started until eight years later with the release of *Night of the Living Dead* (1968), a film that involved a feuding group of humans who are besieged by a horde of flesh-eating zombies. The film largely concentrates on the tensions between the humans, and features a shocking moment in which a young girl becomes a zombie, murders her mother with a trowel and eats her father's body. The film launched the career of George Romero, who was soon joined by a series of other horror auteurs in the 1970s: Tobe Hooper (*The Texas Chainsaw Massacre* (1974)), Wes Craven (*The Hills Have Eyes* (1978)), Larry Cohen (*It's Alive* (1974)), Brian DePalma (*Sisters* (1973), *Carrie* (1976)), David Cronenberg (*Shivers* (1975), *Rabid* (1977)) and John Carpenter (*Assault on Precinct 13* (1976), *Halloween* (1978)).

However, the supposedly radical potential of this period is, for some, betrayed by the emergence of the slasher film, after the success of *Halloween* in 1978. The films of this subgenre are supposedly concerned with a process of terrorization in which a serial killer methodically stalks a group of teenagers who are killed off one by one, and it has been presented as deeply conservative, particularly in its attitudes towards women. First, it is argued that these films encourage the audience to identify with the killer and his violence, rather than his female victims. This is supposedly accomplished through the use of the point-of-view camera shots, most famously used at the opening of John Carpenter's *Halloween*, in which we see the action as though through the killer's eyes. Second, it is claimed that the most graphic attacks are directed against women, and particularly ones who have just had sex. These films are therefore argued to be part of a violent reaction against feminism in which 'the women who are terrorized and slaughtered tend to be those who *resist* definition within the virgin/wife/mother framework' (Wood, 1986: 197). These claims have been seriously challenged on a number of grounds, and it has even been argued that one of the distinctive features of these films is both the general absence of male heroes and the presence of what Clover has called the Final Girl, a female hero who does not rely on male action to be saved but takes on the monster herself (Clover, 1992; Jancovich, 1992; and Tudor, 1989).

Alien (1979) was also released the year after *Halloween*, and while it shared a very similar plot structure to that of many slasher films, it has been central to the development of two different tendencies within the 1980s, both of which were also associated with the work of David Cronenberg from the mid-1970s onwards: the development of the science-fiction/horror film and of body/horror. The first tendency is seen as the product of a more general hybridization of genres within the 1980s, but it should be noted that, as David Bordwell, Janet Staiger and Kristin Thompson point out, most films have always been distinguished by genre hybridization in so far as they usually mixed elements to appeal to a variety of audiences. War films, for example, would often include romantic plots designed to appeal to female viewers (Bordwell, Staiger and Thompson, 1985). Even more problematic is the fact that the very notion of genre hybridity depends on the assumption that genres had previously had clearly defined and separate identities that these films played upon, an assumption that will be directly challenged later in this introduction.

Indeed, almost all of the science-fiction horror films of the 1980s clearly identify themselves as reworkings of 1950s science-fiction horror films. Some, for example, present themselves as remakes, such as *Invasion of the Body Snatchers* (1978), *Invaders from Mars* (1986, original 1953) and *The Blob* (1988, original 1958), while others visually and narratively allude to earlier films. *Aliens* (1986), for example, makes continual and self-conscious references to *Them!* (1954).

Body/horror is associated with these developments not only because many examples were science-fiction/horror films, but also because, like generic hybridity, it was associated with a supposedly postmodern collapse of distinction and boundaries. In these films, the monstrous threat is not simply external but erupts from within the human body, and so challenges the distinction between self and other, inside and outside. In *The Fly* (1986), for example, Seth Brundel has an accident when he uses the teleportation machine that he has created. In the process of teleportation, his body is fused with that of a fly at the molecular level. His DNA has been rewritten and the film concerns the gradual transformation of his body and his inability to maintain a sense of mastery and control over his physicality or identity. Brundel is therefore both victim and monster, and the threat comes from the inside, not from the outside.

Many have therefore complained that these films display a fear of physicality in general and of sexuality in particular (Wood, 1986), but by the mid-1980s a new category would emerge that would become the focus of a series of concerns about the representation of sex and violence. This category was the 'video nasties'. The advent of the domestic video machine had been treated with great suspicion by the major Hollywood studios, which feared that it might finally destroy the cinema altogether. They were therefore originally very cautious about releasing their films on video, and the rental and retail market became dominated by smaller, independent companies, which filled the resulting gap. These companies therefore turned to cheap products, often produced outside Hollywood, frequently including sensational films of sex and violence from a number of different international contexts of production.

In Britain, many of these videos became the focus of a concerted campaign for censorship, which argued that a new breed of film was emerging that was not only unregulated but also shown in the home, where children could gain access to it. As Martin Barker and others have pointed out, however, there was no 'new breed of film' but an eclectic mess of films from different periods and national contexts, and the campaign was the product of political motivations that had little to do with the films themselves (Barker, 1984). None the less, while the campaign was successful in establishing regulation of video releases, it also created a new subculture. As banned objects, these videos became celebrated by fans for whom their illicit status made them desirable.

Ironically, while some were complaining about the viciousness of the genre, this period also saw the emergence of a new form of horror comedy that writers such as Kim Newman have seen as a period of decline. Films such as *An American Werewolf in London* (1981), *Return of the Living Dead* (1985) and *Fright Night* (1985) were highly self-conscious plays with the genre, and while they had powerfully horrific moments, they also affectionately mocked the genre. In *Fright Night*, for example, a teenage fan of horror films becomes obsessed with the belief that his new next-door neighbour is a real vampire and enlists the support of an old horror-movie actor to help him. The film's humour is therefore founded on the film's references to earlier horror films, and on the audience's familiarity with these films.

While many claimed that the genre had become tired and that audiences could no longer take it seriously, the early 1990s saw a quite different development. Starting to a large extent with *The Silence of the Lambs* (1991), a series of big-budget horror films were made with star casts and big-name directors: Anthony Hopkins, Winona Ryder and Keanu Reaves in Francis Ford Coppola's *Bram Stoker's Dracula* (1992), Robert De Niro, Helena Bonham Carter and Kenneth Branagh in the latter's *Mary Shelley's Frankenstein* (1994), Brad Pitt and Tom Cruise in Neil Jordan's *Interview with the Vampire* (1994) and Jack Nicholson, Michelle Pfeiffer and James Spader in Mike Nichol's *Wolf* (1994). The generation who had grown up on 1970s and 1980s horror had entered their thirties and forties, and horror films made a bid for respectability. In the process, these films presented themselves as 'quality' productions not only through their directors and casts, but also through their clear allusions to the 'classic' horror movies of the

1930s. Each film turned back to a classic horror monster: Frankenstein's monster, the vampire, the werewolf. However, both *Bram Stoker's Dracula* and *Mary Shelley's Frankenstein* went one better than this and through their titles and their promotion, they claimed (entirely spuriously) that they were faithful versions of the original classic novels, unlike earlier productions.

This cycle was short-lived, and by the mid-1990s, it was on television that the really interesting developments in horror were taking place in shows such as *The X Files* and *Buffy the Vampire Slayer*. However, 1996 did see the release of the hugely successful *Scream*, which went on to spawn two sequels and a host of imitators. This cycle often picked up on the slasher movie of the late 1970s and early 1980s, but also treated them ironically. In these films, the teenage characters are overly familiar with horror and popular culture in general, and continually comment on generic qualities of the narrative within which they are located.

The success of the cycle did not satisfy everyone, and while the knowing self-referentiality soon lost its charm for some, others saw these films as a complete anathema (Jancovich, 2000). For the latter audiences, the cycle's high production values, largely female casts, and association with teen television hits such as *Friends*, *Party of Five*, *Buffy the Vampire Slayer* and *Dawson's Creek* made it the epitome of a mainstream commercial appropriation of 'authentic' horror, which they identified as a low-budget, underground and potentially subversive genre.

For these fans, *The Blair Witch Project* (1999) became a *cause célèbre*. Supposedly made by unknowns on a virtually non-existent budget, the film concerns a group of teenagers who go off into the woods to make a documentary, and the premise is not only that the teenagers have disappeared but that the film itself is composed out of the footage that they shot before their disappearance. However, despite the huge financial success of the film, and the claims that it represented the birth of a whole new type of horror film as well as new ways of making and promoting films more generally, *The Blair Witch Project* increasingly looks like a one-off gimmick rather than the start of a new cycle of horror production, and as the cycle of post-*Scream* films seems to be coming to an end, it is difficult to say where the genre will go next. At present, Hollywood seems to have turned back to the 1970s and is making a series of films that draw on stories of demonic possession and conspiracy such as *The Exorcist* (1973) and *The Omen* (1976) – *End of Days* (1999), *Lost Souls* (2000) and *Bless the Child* (2000) – but given the concern with shock and surprise within horror films, future developments are likely to be difficult to predict.

Re-examining the history of horror

There are, however, a number of problems with the history of horror. For example, most academic histories include films that were not originally produced or consumed as horror films, and are defined as horror only retrospectively. Thus while Carlos Clarens devotes a chapter to the silent filmmakers such as Méliès and his contemporaries (Clarens, 1967), it is not at all clear that these films were originally understood as horror films. Instead, it is more likely that they were seen as examples of the kinds of magical trick photography that Tom Gunning associates with the 'cinema of attractions' (Gunning, 1990).

Clarens's discussion of Méliès also alerts us to another problem. He rarely actually uses the word 'horror' himself to describe these silent films but talks instead of 'the fantastic film'. It is a similar strategy that allows many science-fiction histories to allude to these films as precursors of the science-fiction film. In other words, there is a slippage of terms in Clarens's work that is similar to that which one finds in most other writers on the genre. For example, there is often a slippage between the term 'horror' and terms such as 'fantasy', 'the Gothic, and 'the tale of terror', terms which are not commensurate with one another but through which differences can be elided. For example, Prawer argues:

> I have not differentiated strictly between 'terror' and 'horror'; to mark the continuity between literary 'tales of terror' and what is popularly known as the horror movie.
>
> (Prawer, 1980: 6)

My intention is not to criticize S. S. Prawer for this slippage, which is made for clearly stated strategic reasons, but rather to highlight a problem about generic definitions.

Films such as *Trip to the Moon* are included within histories because of the ways in which they influenced later developments, and this should alert us to a central problem with writing genre history: many histories impose understandings from the present on the past. Periods rewrite the past and so create their own heritage. For example, *Scream* presents itself as a clever, knowing and ironic reworking of the slasher movie, which is presented as moronic and unselfconscious. It also endlessly references *Halloween* as a central text within the slasher movie. However, Carpenter had little or no sense of making a slasher movie, and many critics at the time saw it as a startlingly clever, knowing and self-conscious play with the genre. Carpenter could not have seen *Halloween* as a slasher movie because there was no such category at the time. His film became the template for the slasher film only retrospectively, after imitators had cashed in on its spectacular success. Furthermore, *Scream* needs to present the slasher movie as moronic and unselfconscious in order to establish its own sense of superiority over it.

It is also the case that critics often take one period as representative of a genre as a whole, and develop their theories of generic essences from these particular instances. For example, Bruce Kawin concentrates on the productions by Universal Pictures in the 1930s and the alien invasion narratives of the 1950s, and he maintains that horror is centrally concerned with an encounter between the known and the unknown, in which the unknown is implicitly dangerous and hostile (Kawin, 1984). This claim works well with the mad scientist narratives of the 1930s, and the perils of progress narratives of the 1950s. They also work well with invasion narratives, whether the invaders are supernatural as in *Dracula* or extraterrestrial as in *The Thing*. However, it seems to have little relevance to films such as *Psycho* or the slasher movies of the late 1970s and early 1980s, in which destructive forces erupt from the familiar everyday world.

In contrast, Stephen Neale's claims about the horror genre seem to be largely defined in relation to the slasher movie. He maintains that the monster is usually male and that its victims are usually female, and this position draws on claims about the slasher movie that Neale and others have made elsewhere (Neale, 1981). As we have seen, according to these claims, the slasher movie involved a male protagonist who attacked sexual women, who were therefore punished for the sexuality that men find both desirable and threatening. This position has been contested by a number of critics (Clover, 1992; Jancovich, 1992; Tudor, 1989), but it was generally taken as common sense in the late 1970s and early 1980s. However, even if it were true of the slasher movie, it would not seem to fit the mad scientist narratives of the 1950s or the perils of progress narratives of the 1950s.

Similarly, Robin Wood argues that the 'true milieu' of horror is the family, which he places at the centre of his analysis. Again this position is largely determined by the intellectual concerns of his period, and by the cycle of 1970s films that he took to be the realization of the genre's radical potential. This identification with a particular period also explains another feature of most histories of horror: the sense of permanent crisis or decline within writing about the genre. Wood, for example, not only champions the horror films of the 1970s, but also uses them to challenge the horror films of the late 1970s and early 1980s, films that he sees as a betrayal of the genre.

Kim Newman even writes his study of the post-1968 horror movie as a reaction to specific claims about the genre's decline, in which critics have seen this period as 'debasing their idea of what the genre should be' (Newman, 1988: xi). However, although Newman acknowledges that the problem is a generational one, he falls into the same trap:

> I've started wondering if I'm turning into Denis Gifford. I'll stick by the opinions expressed here, but I keep coming across enthusiasts acclaiming the *Nightmare on Elm Street* series, *Fright Night* or *Re-Animator* as classics. There are even people out there writing respectfully about the *Friday the 13th* films and *House*. Some of these are pretty good but I don't think they quite stack up against the best of Romero and Cronenberg, or even *Halloween* and *The Texas Chainsaw Massacre*.
>
> (p. xii)

None the less, Newman does recognize the generational politics that is going on here. As Newman acknowledges, his book was an attempt 'to redefine our understanding of exactly what a horror film is' (p. xii) against those who viewed the post-1968 horror film negatively because they judged it by standards set up in relation to the Gothic horrors of Universal and Hammer. He therefore hopes that someone from the generation after him 'will write a book sub-titled "A Critical History of the Horror Film, 1988–2008" that contradicts everything you're about to read' (p. xiii).

One of the main problems with most histories of horror is therefore that they are 'narrative histories', and narratives need not only an end but also a central protagonist. In other words, narratives usually end either in a sense of perfect fulfilment (the happy ending where everything is resolved) or in destruction and failure (the tragic ending where possibilities and promise are frustrated), and they do so because they are the story of someone or something. They have a central protagonist whose fortunes organize the narrative. Narrative histories of a genre therefore usually become the story of something – the horror genre – that exists above and beyond the individual movements or periods, an essence which is unfolding before us, and is either heading towards perfect realization (as in Wood's claim that the 1970s discovered the 'true milieu' of the genre in its focus on the family) or failure or corruption (as with those critics against whom Newman sees himself as writing).

It is for this reason that narrative histories also tend to concentrate on classic moments. For example, critics looking at the 1930s have often taken classics such as *Frankenstein* or *Dracula* as representative examples, when the very features that have resulted in their classic status might not make them representative at all. Alternatively, as we have seen, while critics tend to focus on supposedly 'ground-breaking' texts, such as *Psycho*, these films can be seen very differently if they are resituated within the broader context of the period which they were made. In other words, they can often be seen as the product of general processes, rather than the cause of generic transformation (Jancovich, 1996). As a result, the focus on classic moments and classic films tends to repress the diversity within periods, and it is for this reason that most histories tend to focus on one particular national context. They simply cannot create a clear narrative line if they are forced to deal with the diversity of horror production from across the world.

Finally, of course, another problem with these histories is that they are almost invariably histories of production, rather than histories of mediation or consumption, and they therefore imply that the meaning of a particular film or period is tied to the context of its original production. However, as Barbara Klinger has demonstrated in relation to the director Douglas Sirk, films not only have different meanings within the context of their original production but can radically change meaning over time as they are continually resituated in new contexts of mediation and consumption (Klinger, 1994). This should, of course, be clear to anyone with a familiarity with the horror genre given the tendency of horror films to be viewed as shocking on their original release before gradually becoming seen as restrained or even laughable. This process is also related to one in which many horror films are vilified on their original release but gradually come to be seen as classics.

From horror as formula to horror as structure

These problems are directly related to academic approaches to the study of the horror film. Just as the history of horror often assumed a central protagonist who was the subject of its narrative, approaches to the genre have often seen their task as that of identifying the true subject of horror from within all its disparate and diverse manifestations.

Probably the earliest way of thinking about genres was through the notion of genre films as 'formula' films. This notion can be identified in a whole series of different kinds of writing (see, for example, Cawellti, 1976; Twitchell, 1985), but can be seen most clearly, and was probably most influential, in varieties of mass-culture theory and auteurism. Despite the very significant differences and disagreements between these two approaches, they shared the common claim that popular film was dominated by generic formulas, even though the auteur critics did privilege specific auteurs who were supposed to subvert and ironize these formulaic materials through their visual style (see Sarris, 1976). This notion of genre as formula alludes to the use of the term in scientific discourse to describe genre as a procedure (rather than a process) in which certain elements are put together in a particular order to produce a particular predetermined and invariable result.

To say that a film is the product of a formula is to imply that it conforms to a rigid pattern of combination in which the substitution of specific details is unimportant or irrelevant to the nature of the final product. This kind of argument can be seen, for example, in Adorno and Horkheimer's account of 'types' within Hollywood film in particular and mass culture more generally, a term that not only includes genres but also identifies them as essentially *narrative* formulas:

> Not only are hit songs, stars and soap operas cyclically recurrent and rigidly invariable types, but the specific content of entertainment itself is derived from them and only appears to change. The details are interchangeable. . . . As soon as the film begins, it is quite clear how it will end, and who will be rewarded, punished or forgotten.
>
> (Adorno and Horkheimer, 1979: 125)

Here genres such as 'soap operas' are seen as standardized formulas that are used to ensure the efficient replication of texts whose differences are purely illusory and which are therefore *essentially* all the same. In this sense, genres simply exist to accomplish two goals: first, to provide the 'illusion of choice' or 'pseudo-individualistic differences' between texts which are *really* at some fundamental level supposed to be identical with one another; and second, to provide both standardization in production and familiarity in consumption. Standardization in production allows for the rational and efficient streamlining of the techniques of mass production, while familiarity in consumption creates a situation in which the public

> lacking the taste and knowledge of the old patron class, is not only satisfied with shoddy mass-produced goods but in general feels more at home with them because such goods are standardised and so are easier to consume because one knows what is coming next – imagine a Western in which the hero loses the climatic gun fight or an office romance in which the mousey stenographer loses out to the predatory blonde.
>
> (Macdonald, 1963: 28)

In this way, a genre is seen as an object that is composed of a collection of films that are related to one another through their common possession of an essentially invariant narrative pattern in which we all know 'how it will end' and in which all westerns, for example, will therefore culminate in a 'climatic gunfight' which the hero must inevitably win.

In the process, mass-culture theory frequently presented a political and not simply aesthetic condemnation of this mass culture, and it was argued that the ease of consumption created passivity in the audiences. Films involved a 'Built-In Reaction' in which there was no room for ambiguity or interpretative freedom. Instead, films dictated their audiences' responses, and in the process, these audiences were taught to be passive, not to think for themselves, and to defer to authority. Rather than remaining as individuals with their own thoughts and feelings, mass culture taught people to conform, to become like everyone else, part of an undifferentiated mass that was organized and controlled by centres of power.

This kind of approach can be seen in Siegfried Kracauer's analysis of the silent classics of the 'German expressionist' cinema. Here he reads these films as 'popular films' that 'address themselves, and appeal, to the anonymous multitude' and 'can therefore be supposed to satisfy existing mass desires' (Kracauer, 1947: 5). Here he not only sees the multitude as an undifferentiated mass, but argues that it is the problem of identity that is central to these films. *The Student of Prague* (1913) is therefore seen as setting the tone through the 'brilliant film idea to have the reflection, lured out of the looking-glass by the wizard, transform itself into an independent person' (p. 29). As a result, he claims: '*The Student of Prague* introduced to the screen a theme that was to become an obsession of the German cinema: a deep and fearful concern with the foundations of self' (p. 30). However, for Kracauer, these films did not provide a radical consideration of these problems but rather revealed the mass fantasies and desires that would bring the Nazis to power. Rather than encouraging the autonomous individual who was necessary for the functioning of a democratic society, these films 'glorified authority and convicted its antagonist of madness' (p. 67). In *The Cabinet of Dr. Caligari* (1919), for example, Francis believes that Caligari is using his powers to dominate and enslave others. At the end, however, it is revealed that Francis is actually a paranoid madman and that Caligari is simply a benevolent analyst who is attempting to cure him of his delusions. It is therefore claimed that these films encouraged both a deference to authority and an identification with the undifferentiated mass; and that, in so doing, they both reflected and encouraged a mass desire for authoritarian leadership that the Nazis would eventually satisfy.

This kind of approach can also, to some extent, be identified in Wood's auteurist account of George Romero's *Night of the Living Dead* (1968), which is praised for the ways in which it 'systematically undercuts generic conventions and the expectations they arouse' (Wood, 1986: 114–15). Here the horror genre is implicitly conventional and formulaic, and it is the presence of the auteur director which invests it with interest and radicalism through his subversion of that formula.

Academics are not alone in seeing horror films as formula films, and this assumption can be found not only in reviews, articles and everyday talk, but even within horror films themselves. It is this conception of genre, for example, that *Scream* (1996) both draws upon and reproduces in its supposed self-referential play with the 'rules' of the horror film. Not only does Randy Meeks suggest that there are certain inevitabilities within plot and character, but Sidney Prescott even describes horror films as 'all the same'. What is more, the film was heavily marketed through its association with horror auteur Wes Craven, and it is his presence (along with that of Kevin Williamson) that is supposed to define the film as a knowing subversion of the genre.

It was because of a dissatisfaction with these ways of understanding genre that structuralism and myth criticism were first imported into genre criticism, and they initially seemed to offer great potential. Mass-culture criticism and auteurism had provided little space for an analysis of genre: given that genres were largely seen as inherently simplistic and conservative forms, the implication was that they were too obvious for analysis. However, while auteurism had seen genre as a material in relation to which the director had to establish an antagonistic stance, writers such as Jim Kitses noted that many directors worked best within specific genres. This observation led them to see genres not simply as formulaic narratives against which directors defined their authorial personality, but rather as a resource on which the director drew – something that was therefore at least as enabling as it was constraining – and this led writers such as Kitses to two conclusions. Kitses not only acknowledged that the films associated with a genre were not 'all the same', but he also argued that a genre was not simply 'an empty vessel breathed into by the film-maker [but] a vital structure through which flow a myriad of themes and concepts' (Kitses, 1969: 26); that a genre was a complex and meaningful system in itself, irrespective of what a director might then do with it.

In the process, genre critics drew on the structuralist analysis of myth, an approach usually associated with the work of Claude Lévi-Strauss (Lévi-Strauss, 1968), which enabled them to see genres as more than simple and invariant narrative formulas: like Lévi-Strauss, they attempted to identify the specific recurrent oppositions that defined a specific genre, and constituted its 'deep structure'. This position drew on the distinction between *langue* (the structure of language) and *parole* (the individual speech act) that came from structuralist linguistics. It argued that a genre was defined by certain underlying structural oppositions, while an individual film could be seen as a specific speech act, whose meaning was dependent on those structuring oppositions but was also actively engaged in an attempt to find a resolution to these oppositions. As a result, writers such as Kitses did not see genres as being composed of films that shared an invariant narrative pattern, but rather were able to argue that the western, for example, was 'a loose shifting and variegated genre with many roots and branches' (p. 17) and that it is therefore impossible to 'freeze [it] once and for all in a definite model of the "classical" western' (p. 17).

For Kitses, the western was based on the myth of the West, 'an ambiguous and mercurial concept' (p. 8), which dramatized America's ambivalent attitudes to white American civilization and progress. Hence the western can be about the loss of a way of life as well as about the triumphant story of the taming of the wilderness. Indeed, the significance of the western is, it is argued, that it is set precisely at that moment when 'options [were] still open' (p. 12) or at least are perceived as being so in retrospect.

This structuralist approach to genre can also be identified in work on horror. For example, in 'The Mummy's Pool', Kawin (1984) tries to identify the difference between science fiction and horror through the claim that both are structured by the opposition between the known and the unknown. However, in Kawin's account, like many other applications of structuralism, many of the most interesting features of Kitses' work are forgotten, most particularly the sense that genres involve a 'philosophical dialectic' which might permit ambivalence, ambiguity and heterogeneity. For Kawin, for example, there is little sense that different films within a genre might privilege different values and resolve matters in different ways. On the contrary, Kawin not only identifies different options with different genres, but even identifies these options with the level of narrative, rather than with more underlying ideological contradictions that might give rise to a myriad of narratives. For example, he asserts that while both science fiction and horror are concerned with an encounter between the known and the unknown, these two genres are distinguished 'not by plot-elements so much as by attitudes towards plot-elements' (Kawin, 1984: 5). In science fiction, it is claimed, the unknown is viewed as positive and even potentially liberating, while in horror, the unknown can only be threatening. Horror is therefore said to be a conservative genre that works to justify and defend the status quo.

Kawin's argument is developed in relation to narratives in which humanity encounters extraterrestrial life, and he defines as science fiction those films in which the alien is presented as a positive force (such as *The Day the Earth Stood Still* (1951), *Close Encounters of the Third Kind* (1977) and *E.T.* (1982)). Horror is therefore associated with those films in which aliens threaten to invade and destroy us (*The Thing from Another World*, *Alien* and *Independence Day* (1996)). The problem here is, of course, that while it seems to work for some films, it doesn't seem to work for others. It is difficult to accept that *Independence Day* should be seen as primarily a horror film rather than science fiction simply because the aliens are threatening, and indeed many theories of horror have specifically claimed that many of its monsters were sympathetic victims as much as unsympathetic aggressors (*Frankenstein*, *Cat People* and *Psycho*).

For example, Robin Wood also draws on a structuralist work in his account of the horror genre and argues that 'the true subject of the horror genre is the struggle for recognition of all that our civilization represses or oppresses' (Chapter 1, p. 28 in this volume). For Wood, however, the appeal of horror is primarily due to our identification with the Other, that which our society represses and defines as monstrous. As Wood puts it, 'Central to the effect and fascination of horror films is their fulfillment of our nightmare wish to smash the norms that oppress us' (p. 32). He even goes so far as to criticize 1950s and 1980s horror, which, he claims, did not present the monster as sympathetic. While Kawin maintains that horror is defined by its presentation of otherness as threatening, Wood implies that the general tendency in horror is to present otherness as sympathetic and victimized. However, both see the genre as defined by a central opposition or contradiction between the known and the unknown or normality and otherness.

From genre as structure to genre as consensus

It is this central and defining feature of a genre that Andrew Tudor has referred to as 'factor X', and for Tudor, the major problem with genre criticism has been its obsessive preoccupation with identifying this feature. As we saw in Kitses' account, the western was defined by a deep structure of underlying oppositions between the wilderness and civilization, but the role of the deep structure is different from the structuralist concept of Langue or even Lévi-Strauss's concept of myth.

As was claimed at the start of this introduction, the structuralist attempt to identify the central, fundamental and underlying oppositions of a genre was an attempt to distinguish it from other genres. The aim was to police boundaries; to say that particular films were *really* westerns, musicals or horror films, and that others *really* were not. According to this model, a film could not have more than one deep structure or central oppositions (obviously) and therefore a genre critic's task was to identify the appropriate reading of a film by defining the appropriate intertexts for its interpretation. Thus, we find critics claiming that despite their spaceships or alien life-forms, the *Star Wars* movies are *really* westerns; or that despite their contemporary urban setting, the *Dirty Harry* series are *really* westerns; or that Vietnam movies are *really* westerns. Robin Wood even uses this logic to claim that *Meet Me in St. Louis* (1944) is *really* a precursor of the contemporary horror film. For example, Wood argues that there is a 'remarkable anticipation in *Meet Me in St. Louis* of the Terrible Child of the 70s horror film, especially in the two scenes (Halloween and the destruction of the snow people) in which Margaret O'Brien symbolically kills parent figures' (Wood, 1986: 84–5; and Wood, 1976).

Unfortunately, this approach either ends up excluding everything, so that a film such as *Shane* (1953) ends up being the only *real* western, or else it runs the risk of including everything, so that it is difficult to see what wouldn't fit into a particular genre. Indeed, Lévi-Strauss's original formulation was intended to do just this: he was not attempting to distinguish myths from one another, but rather to identify the underlying structure of all myth. What is more, the western's privileged status, as the genre with which the classic period of structuralist genre criticism was most preoccupied (Hutchings, 1995), illustrates this point nicely. Kitses' opposition between wilderness and civilization, as he himself demonstrates, is therefore about the opposition between Nature and Culture, but there are many films that use this opposition and yet most people would find themselves hard pushed to define them as *real* westerns. For Wood, horror is defined as an encounter between civilization and that which it represses, so that the central oppositions of the horror genre start to seem very similar to those of the western. It is therefore hardly surprising to find that, for Lévi-Strauss, the opposition between Nature and Culture was not the underlying structure of the western as myth but more emphatically, the underlying structure of *all* myth.

Nor are these problems simply present within structuralist accounts. The turn to post-structuralism in the 1970s, which is often referred to as '*Screen* theory', shared many of the same problems, as can be seen in Neale's attempt to produce a theory of the genre from within this context (Neale, 1980). Neale needs to be commended as one of the few theorists to take the issue of genre really seriously within this period, and it should be noted that Neale has also significantly revised his position (Neale, 1990; 1999). However, his classic account of genre, which was published in 1980, displays most of the problems already discussed. In his attempt to break with structuralism, Neale argues:

> Genres are not systems: they are processes of systemization. It is only as such that they perform the role allotted them by the cinematic institution. It is only as such that they can function to provide, simultaneously, both regulation and variety.
>
> (Neale, 1980: 51)

Consequently, not only is his work little different from the original structuralist ambitions discussed in relation to Kitses, but it actually seems to mark a regression to the mass-cultural preoccupation with 'pseudo-individualistic differences' or the 'illusion of choice', despite his use of Lacanian terminology.

For Neale, genres are discourses that are defined by underlying oppositions such as human/nature, law/disorder and human/inhuman, and like the structuralists before him, he sees genres as processes specifically because each film attempts to resolve these oppositions. However, these oppositions are structural, and hence every attempt at resolution is inevitably unsuccessful and therefore requires the continuation of the genre, and of the process of attempting to resolve its defining oppositions. In this way, then, individual genre films display differences, but only to a limited extent. The implication is that the central problematic never really changes and repetition is therefore always emphasized over a difference that is implicitly phenomenal or illusory.

Not only does this return once more to the structuralist preoccupation with the policing of boundaries, but it also, more worryingly, has little or no place for ambivalence. Rather than taking Kitses' option of acknowledging that different films might take very different positions with regard to the underlying oppositions, Neale once more seems to associate particular genres with a singular position. Writing on horror, for example, he claims:

> most monsters tend, in fact, to be defined as 'male', especially in so far as the objects of their desire are almost exclusively women. Simultaneously, it is women who become their primary victims. In this respect, it could well be maintained that it is women's sexuality, that which renders them desirable – but also threatening – to men, which constitutes the *real* problem that the horror film exists to explore, and which constitutes also and ultimately that which is *really* monstrous.
>
> (Neale, 1980: 61)

In this way, horror is not only seen to be *really* about issues of sexual politics, but it is also assumed to be implicitly conservative in this regard.

Like Neale, most studies of horror from within '*Screen* theory' claimed that it is not only primarily produced and consumed by men, but that it is an essentially misogynistic genre. Instead of a genre that dramatized ambivalent attitudes towards gender and sexuality, horror is supposed to construct female sexuality necessarily as that which is really monstrous and hence to accord masculinity a privileged status as that which is normal and dominant. However, this position is frequently constructed on the basis of contradictory evidence. For example, while Neale claims that 'most monsters tend . . . to be defined as "male" [and that] it is women who become their primary victims', Barbara Creed claims that the monster is usually defined as 'female' and that it is men who are her primary victims (Creed, 1993). In both cases, however, they come to the same conclusion: the narrative is organized around fear of and hostility to women either as monsters or victims, and the audience identifies with the male character either as the monster or the victim.

These problems have led to many criticisms of structuralist and post-structuralist accounts of genre. Most pointedly, Andrew Tudor has claimed that the search for 'factor X' was entirely the wrong place to start in an attempt to understand genre. He argues that most viewers are 'untroubled spectators' who do not share the 'neurotic critic's' need to define a particular genre, and that while they may talk in terms of genre, they do so far more loosely. Tudor also demonstrates that the search for 'factor X' places most genre criticism in the 'empiricist dilemma' in which it inevitability ends up pre-selecting a group of films for study, the study of which is supposed to identify the appropriate criteria for their selection. To put it another way, the films which one selects in order to study the western will determine how one eventually defines the genre. Hence the circular nature of arguments in genre studies: these films are horror films and they have X in common; and as a result any film that does not share this factor X cannot be a horror film, while any films that do share this factor X must *really* be horror films, no matter how they have previously been defined and understood.

In response, Tudor shifts the question of genre away from the films themselves and towards the classificatory systems within which films are understood:

> In short, to talk about the western is (arbitrary definitions apart) to appeal to a common set of meanings in our culture. We feel we know a western when we see one, though edges may be rather blurred. Thus in calling a film a western a critic is implying more than the simple statement 'This film is a member of a class of films (westerns) having in common x, y or z.' The critic is also suggesting that such a film would be universally recognized as such in our culture. In other words, the crucial facts that distinguish a genre are not only characteristics inherent in the films themselves; they also depend on the particular culture within which they are operating. And unless there is world consensus on the subject (which is an empirical question), there is no basis for assuming that the western will be conceived in the same way in every culture. The way in which the genre term is applied can quite conceivably vary from case to case. Genre notions – except the special case of arbitrary definition – are not critics' classifications made for special purposes; they are sets of cultural conventions. Genre is what we collectively believe it to be.
>
> (Tudor, 1986: 6–7)

Thus he stresses that when critics talk of genres, they are supposed to be talking about definitions that are in operation within the broader culture, not inventions of their own. They are making claims about how films are produced and consumed. Furthermore, Tudor also argues that within the broader culture, genre categories are not necessarily about the presence or absence of essential, defining features, but are more loose and fluid sets of criteria.

For this reason, Tudor attempts to short-circuit the whole question of definition in a way that is both persuasive and appealing. Instead of seeking to identify 'factor X', Tudor claims that one should simply concentrate one's efforts on studying those films that are identified with a particular genre, and on this basis proceed to map out shapes, patterns, histories and differences. Instead of asking what a horror film is, Tudor therefore sets out to analyse what films have been understood as horror films, and the relationships between these films both within a given period and over time (Tudor, 1989).

Similar points have also been made more recently by Rick Altman, who also notes that the history of genre criticism has been dominated by the search for essences (Altman, 1999: 2). However, Altman also suggests a problem with Tudor's solution. For Altman, it is doubtful whether any sense of 'collective belief' or consensual agreement over the definition of a genre can ever actually be identified. As genre criticism itself shows, there may be very different conceptions of whether particular films are, say, horror or not. Even Tudor acknowledges this problem, but he simply argues: 'To research genre history, then, it is necessary to include as wide a range of films as possible, while trying not to misrepresent the spectrum of audience conceptions' (Tudor, 1989: 6). However, this fails to acknowledge that different audiences may hold deeply contradictory conceptions, and that these contradictions may be central to the issue of genre and genre distinctions.

For example, Altman claims that the very nature of genre makes the task of identifying collective agreement impossible. Like Tudor, he stresses that genres are not simply located in the textual features of the films themselves, and that we must 'recognise the extent to which genres appear to be initiated, stabilised and protected by a series of institutions essential to the very existence of genres' (Altman, 1999: 85). However, he argues, genre terms are used by a whole series of 'user groups', who use genre terms for different purposes and hence in different ways. Genre terms are therefore fundamentally unstable, ambiguous and resistant to any essential definition (pp. 123–4).

While this acknowledges that different users may hold deeply contradictory conceptions of a genre (and that even the same person may hold deeply contradictory conceptions at different moments), Altman only addresses these differences neutrally as if they were in some sense all equivalent. However, as Ien Ang has argued, it is not the *fact* of differences but 'the meaning of differences that matter – something that can only be grasped, interpretatively, by looking at their contexts, social and cultural bases, and impacts' (Ang, 1989: 107).

Furthermore, despite his discussion of pragmatics and of the necessary indeterminacy of genre definitions, Altman shows little interest in the consumption of genres when compared with his interest in the production and mediation of texts. For example, in his chapter 'What Role do Genres Play in the Viewing Process?', his discussion remains highly abstracted from the activities of socially concrete audiences and is mainly concerned with the activities of hypothetical spectators. In this way, his work is little different from those forms of genre criticism of which Hutchings argues:

> Clearly audiences were important . . . but did they bring anything to genres other than the particular knowledge and competence (to do with familiarity with generic conventions) which enabled them to interpret genre films 'correctly'?
>
> (Hutchings, 1995: 66)

This is not to imply that audience classifications are the only key to understanding genre – Altman brilliantly draws our attention to the importance of the generic classifications of filmmakers, publicists and critics – but it does seem that not only do audience classifications tend to get lost in his study, but Altman reduces the role of audience simply to that of 'recognizing' generic cues.

For example, Altman argues that genre films 'incorporate a series of paradigmatically designed and often repeated "crossroads"' that depend 'on a crucial opposition between two paths open to the text, each representing a different type of pleasure for the spectator'. The audience's pleasure is therefore about the potentials at these crossroads: 'we may say that one fork offers a culturally sanctioned activity or value, while the other path diverges from cultural norms in favour of generic pleasure'. However, this pleasure is dependent on the *right* audience, as these 'crossroads' are 'invisible to viewers lacking in knowledge of generic traditions', but they 'loom large in the experience of the genre fan'. In other words, generic pleasure requires 'the spectator's complicity', and their 'continued pleasure depends on the "proper" negotiation of those crossroads' (Altman, 1999: 145). In short, the audience's role in the viewing process is to identify the 'proper' codes and strategies of reading, to recognize the codes of the genre, a position that allows essential definitions in through the back door.

For example, in their use of Altman, Richard Maltby and Ian Craven are able to restabilize genres so that they seem to exist as stable and familiar entities that audiences simply and unproblematically 'recognize', rather than being constructs that are permanently indeterminate:

> Audiences recognise genres through plot structures . . . as well as through advertising, iconography, and gestural codes. Often such indicators overlap; in the practice of a genre-based criticism this is almost bound to be the case.
>
> (Maltby and Craven, 1995: 121)

This position also enables them to focus attention back onto the films themselves, rather than the discourses through which they are produced, mediated and consumed, as though it was here that genres and their meanings were really located after all. In the process, they draw on what Altman calls his 'semantic/syntactic approach to film genre', a move that allows them to re-establish essentialist definitions:

> Rick Altman has distinguished between what he calls the 'semantic' approach to genre – a cataloguing of common traits, characters, attitudes, locations, sets, or shots – and a 'syntactic' approach that defines genre in terms of the structural relationship between elements that carry its thematic and social meaning. Just as the semantic approach has been most often applied to the iconography of the Western, the structure of the Western has frequently been the subject of syntactic analysis. . . . [One] instance of the fruitful application of a structural approach to what Altman calls 'the genre's fundamental syntax' is Jim Kitses' highly suggestive tabulation of 'the shifting ideological play' between what he identifies as the genre's central opposition between civilization and the wilderness.
>
> (Maltby and Craven, 1995: 121)

By simply defining the audience's role as being to 'recognize' genres and the appropriate ways of viewing them, Maltby and Craven lose a sense of the indeterminacy of genre classifications and return once more to a presentation of genres as largely stable entities that are defined by fundamental characteristics and located within the formal features of film texts.

It is not that Altman is oblivious to questions of taste or their relationship to consumption. For example, he discusses the ways in which genres are not just 'good objects' but also 'bad objects'. In other words, he acknowledges that people form negative as well as positive identifications with genres: 'It would appear that genre's capacity for positive identification is matched by a tendency to view certain genres, and thus genre production in general, as bad objects' (Altman, 1999: 113). However, it is not simply that genres themselves are the object of criticism in these instances. As Altman himself points out, there has been a long-running assumption that the films of certain genres are not simply all the same, but that they have specific ideological functions (p. 26). As we have seen, for example, horror films have been attacked as violent and misogynist in ways that imply that a taste for horror is itself deeply problematic, and it is claims such as these that often led to the moral panics over horror as a genre (see, for example, Creed, 1986, 1993; and Neale, 1980, 1981).

As a result, genres are not just defined differently, but are bound up with struggles for distinction in which different social groups compete for authority over one another. For example, when people claim not to like horror, this is not simply a neutral claim. Often it also involves other, more implicit, claims: that horror is moronic, sick and worrying; that any person who derives pleasure from the genre is moronic, sick and potentially dangerous; that the person who is making the claim is reasonable and healthy; and that they are therefore in a position to define what, in Andrew Ross's terms, needs to be 'governed and policed as illegitimate or inadequate or even deviant' (Ross, 1989: 61). Nor do these struggles for distinction take place between those who are pro- or anti-horror, but rather, as I discuss in Part IV, they also take place between different sections of horror fandom who define the genre in different ways.

As a result, genre criticism should be about more than texts, or even the changing contexts within which they are produced. Instead, it needs to analyse the contexts of production, mediation and consumption, and to this end this collection has been divided into four parts. The first will provide a general introduction to the attempt to define the genre while the second will concentrate more specifically on claims about the sexual politics of horror. These parts will therefore provide the context for the last two, which aim to move the reader away from issues of theoretical definition and textual interpretation. For example, the third part will focus on attempts to relate horror films to the contexts of their production, but it is not intended to provide a comprehensive history of the genre. Rather it will simply provide some case studies that raise specific issues and problems. Finally, the fourth part will bring together a series of essays on the reception of horror, and it includes case studies on the marketing, critical reception, and exhibition of horror films, as well as an ethnographic study of female fans.

The selection is therefore guided by a desire both to ground the reader in the classic and even canonical articles on the horror film and to present more recent work that goes beyond textual criticism and employs approaches from film history and cultural studies.

PART ONE

THEORIZING HORROR

Introduction

As we saw in the general introduction, much work on the horror film has tried to identify the defining features of the genre. Part I looks at this particular aspect of the analysis of horror, and it contains three extracts. The first is Robin Wood's now classic essay on the horror film which was referred to in the general introduction, and, as we have seen, it develops out of both auteur theory and genre criticism. On the one hand, Wood tries to identify the central oppositions that define the genre, while on the other hand he is also concerned to establish the auteur status of a series of directors who have worked within it.

In his attempt to define the genre, like many other critics, he turns to psychoanalysis. For Wood, the clearly fantastical nature of many horror plots presents a problem: fantasy is often seen as mere escapism, a refusal to deal with 'reality', and hence as inherently unserious. The turn to psychoanalysis is therefore one way in which writers such as Wood are able to reinvest horror with seriousness. Through psychoanalysis, the fantastical nature of many horror plots can be read not as escapism, but as an attempt to deal with repressed materials. As a result, Wood draws an analogy between the horror film and dreams, in which he argues:

> Dreams—the embodiment of repressed desires, tensions, fears that our conscious mind rejects—become possible when the censor that guards our subconscious relaxes in sleep, though even then the desires can only emerge in disguise, as fantasies that are innocent or apparently meaningless.
>
> (p. 30)

Here the fantasy is therefore a symptom of something else. It is a coded expression of the tension between social norms and unconscious desires.

In other words, rather than escapism, fantasy tries to deal with the very materials that rational 'realist' discourse exists to repress, and it therefore offers a potentially subversive critique of the social world. The unconscious desires that erupt in dreams and horror films are the product of social repression, and in giving expression to these desires, horror therefore implies a critique of the social world that represses them. As Wood puts it, 'the true subject of the horror genre is the struggle for recognition of all that our civilization represses or oppresses' (p. 28).

As a result, he not only outlines the different ways in which horror monsters speak of repression and oppression, but also argues that it is due to their nature as embodiments of repressed desire that audiences have such ambivalent relationships with horror monsters. On the one hand, they are obviously monstrous – that which audiences cannot socially acknowledge and accept – but on the other they also represent our desire to flout social norms: 'Central to the effect and fascination of horror films is their fulfillment of our nightmare wish to smash the norms that oppress us and which our moral conditioning teaches us to revere' (p. 32). Audiences experience ambivalence about the monster precisely because of the contradictions between the conscious and the unconscious.

The next passage is by Noël Carroll, and while Carroll rejects psychoanalytic accounts in favour of cognitive psychology, he also presents ambivalence as being central to the horror film. The turn to cognitive psychology has become very popular within recent forms of film studies as a way of understanding how audiences make sense of films, and it is largely associated with historical poetics (see, for example, Bordwell, 1985).

In Carroll's account of horror, audiences' ambivalent responses to the figure of the monster are not primarily about the conflict between the conscious and the unconscious mind but about the way in which monsters 'violate our classifactory scheme' (p. 36). In other words, their fantastical nature is precisely about the way in which they flout our 'conceptual categories' and so produce both fascination and disgust (Carroll, 1990:185).

One of the strengths of Carroll's account is that he is therefore able to analyse how this relationship with the monster produces particular and distinctive narrative forms. For example, while he argues that horror narratives are concerned with the processes of revealing and disclosing the monster, he is also able to claim that these processes are handled differently from detective stories and disaster films.

However, there are a number of problems with Carroll's account. On the one hand, it has been argued that the preoccupation with knowledge and problem solving that is so central to cognitive psychology is ill equipped to deal with a genre so centred upon emotional affect. In other words, despite Carroll's discussion of the viewer's ambivalent responses to the monster, his analysis of the narrative concentrates on 'cognitive pleasures' associated with rational 'problem solving'. It provides little room for an understanding of the emotional processes and responses of horror audiences.

Even more problematic is Carroll's conception of the horror audience. As Wood acknowledges, it not only is the case that many people positively dislike horror films but also that the genre's 'popularity itself has a peculiar characteristic that sets it apart from other genres: it is restricted to aficionados and complemented by total rejection, people tending to go to horror films either obsessively or not at all' (Chapter 1, pp. 29–30 below). Furthermore, it is for this reason that, as Carroll observes, 'a theoretical question about horror' frequently arises that does not arise in the same way 'with respect to other popular genres' (Chapter 2, p. 33 below). According to Carroll, this question is: 'how can we explain its very existence, for why would anyone *want* to be horrified, or even art-horrified?' (p. 33). While people may not actually like specific genres, many consider the appeal of horror films a problem in itself. A taste for westerns may be strange, but a taste for horror films is often seen as somehow 'sick'.

However, if people have different responses to horror film, some deriving pleasure from the genre and others not, Wood and Carroll's discussions of it has particular problems. Their accounts purport to describe the pleasures of the genre to viewers, but it is quite clear that certain viewers do not gain pleasure from the genre, and as a result, not all viewers consume horror films in the same way.

In Chapter 3, Andrew Tudor pays particular attention to this problem and argues that the very attempt to understand how audiences gain pleasure from horror films is misconstrued. As he argues, not only do different audiences make sense of horror in different ways, but 'horror' is not a coherent entity in which all horror films work in the same way. He therefore takes issue with universal accounts of the genre that try to define it in particular ways, and he calls instead for particularistic accounts that study the consumption of specific types of horror by specific audiences within specific social settings.

The American nightmare

Horror in the 70s

1

ROBIN WOOD

[. . .]

In the previous chapter I briefly introduced the distinction between basic and surplus repression, developed out of Freud by Marcuse, and given definitive expression in a book that should be far better known than it is: *Repression*, by Gad Horowitz. The book's subtitle is "Basic and Surplus Repression in Psychoanalytic Theory: Freud, Reich, Marcuse"; it is dense, often difficult, very closely and cogently argued, and the account offered here is necessarily bald and simplified.

Basic repression is universal, necessary, and inescapable. It is what makes possible our development from an uncoordinated animal capable of little beyond screaming and convulsions into a human being; it is bound up with the ability to accept the postponement of gratification, with the development of our thought and memory processes, of our capacity for self-control, and of our recognition of and consideration for other people. Surplus repression, on the other hand, is specific to a particular culture and is the process whereby people are conditioned from earliest infancy to take on predetermined roles within that culture. In terms of our own culture, then: *basic* repression makes us distinctively human, capable of directing our own lives and co-existing with others; *surplus* represssion makes us into monogamous heterosexual bourgeois patriarchal capitalists ("bourgeois" even if we are born into the proletariat, for we are talking here of ideological norms rather than material status)—that is, *if* it works. If it doesn't, the result is either a neurotic or a revolutionary (or both), and if revolutionaries account for a very small proportion of the population, neurotics account for a very large one. Hardly surprising. All known existing societies are to some degree surplus-repressive, but the degree varies enormously, from the trivial to the overwhelming. Freud saw long ago that our own civilization had reached a point where the burden of repression was becoming all but insupportable, an insight Horowitz (following Marcuse) brilliantly relates to Marx's theory of alienated labor. The most immediately obvious characteristics of life in our culture are frustration, dissatisfaction, anxiety, greed, possessiveness, jealousy, neuroticism: no more than what psychoanalytic theory shows to be the logical product of patriarchal capitalism. What needs to be stressed is that the challenges now being made to the system—and the perceptions and recognitions that structure those challenges and give them impetus—become possible (become in the literal sense thinkable) only in the circumstances of the system's imminent disintegration. While the system retained sufficient conviction, credibility and show of coherence to suppress them, it did so. The struggle for liberation is not utopian, but a practical necessity.

Given that our culture offers an extreme example of surplus repressiveness, one can ask what, exactly, in the interests of alienated labor and the patriarchal family, is repressed. One needs here both to distinguish between the concepts of *re*pression and *op*pression and to suggest the continuity between them. In psychoanalytic terms, what is repressed is not accessible to the conscious mind (except through analysis or, if one can penetrate their disguises, in dreams). We may also not be conscious of ways in which we are oppressed, but it is much easier to become so: we are oppressed by something "out there." One might perhaps define repression as fully internalized oppression (while reminding ourselves that all the groundwork of repression is laid in infancy), thereby suggesting both the difference and the connection. A specific example may make this clearer: our social structure demands the repression of the bisexuality that psychoanalysis shows to be the natural heritage of every human individual and the oppression of homosexuals: obviously the two phenomena are not identical, but equally obviously they are closely connected. What escapes repression has to be dealt with by oppression.

What, then, is repressed in our culture? First, sexual energy itself, together with its possible successful sublimation into non-sexual creativity—sexuality being the source of creative energy in general. The "ideal" inhabitant of our culture is the individual whose sexuality is sufficiently fulfilled by the monogamous heterosexual union necessary for the reproduction of future ideal inhabitants, and whose sublimated sexuality (creativity) is sufficiently fulfilled in the totally non-creative and non-fulfilling labor (whether in factory or office) to which our society dooms the overwhelming majority of its members. The ideal, in other words, is as close as possible to an automaton in whom both sexual and intellectual energy has been reduced to a minimum. Otherwise, the ideal is a contradiction in terms and a logical impossibility—hence the necessary frustration, anxiety and neuroticism of our culture.

Second, bisexuality—which should be understood both literally (in terms of possible sexual orientation and practice) and in a more general sense. Bisexuality represents the most obvious and direct affront to the principle of monogamy and its supportive romantic myth of "the one right person"; the homosexual impulse in both men and women represents the most obvious threat to the norm of sexuality as reproductive and restricted by the ideal of family. But more generally we confront here the whole edifice of clear-cut sexual differentiation that bourgeois-capitalist ideology erects on the flimsy and dubious foundations of biological difference: the social norms of masculinity and femininity, the social definitions of manliness and womanliness, the whole vast apparatus of oppressive male/female myths, and the systematic repression from infancy ("blue for a boy") of the man's femininity and the woman's masculinity, in the interests of forming human beings for specific predetermined social roles.

Third, the particularly severe repression of female sexuality/creativity, the attribution to the female of passivity, and her preparation for her subordinate, dependent role in our culture. Clearly, a crucial aspect of the repression of bisexuality is the denial to women of drives culturally associated with masculinity: activeness, aggression, self-assertion, organizational power, creativity itself.

Fourth, and fundamentally, the repression of the sexuality of children, taking different forms from infancy, through "latency" and puberty, and into adolescence—the process moving, indeed, from repression to oppression, from the denial of the infant's nature as sexual being to the veto on the expression of sexuality before marriage.

None of these forms of repression is necessary for the existence of civilization in some form (i.e., none is "basic")—for the development of our human-ness. Indeed, they impose limitations and restrictions on that development, stunting human potential. All are the outcome of the requirements of the particular surplus-repressive civilization in which we live.

Closely linked to the concept of repression—indeed, truly inseparable from it—is another concept necessary to an understanding of ideology on which psychoanalysis throws much light, the concept of "the Other." Otherness represents that which bourgeois ideology cannot recognize or accept but must deal with (as Barthes suggests in *Mythologies*) in one of two ways: either by rejecting and if possible annihilating it, or by rendering it safe and assimilating it, converting it as far as possible into a replica of itself. The concept of Otherness can be theorized in many ways and on many levels. Its psychoanalytic significance resides in the fact that it functions not simply as something external to the culture or to the self, but also as what is repressed (though never destroyed) in the self and projected outward in order to be hated and disowned. A particularly vivid example—and one that throws light on a great many classical Westerns—is the relationship of the Puritan settlers to the Indians in the early days of America. The Puritans rejected any perception that the Indians had a culture, a civilization, of their own; they perceived them not merely as savage but, literally, as devils or the spawn of the Devil; and, since the Devil and sexuality were inextricably linked in the Puritan consciousness, they perceived them as sexually promiscuous, creatures of unbridled libido. The connection between this view of the Indian and Puritan repression is obvious: a classic and extreme case of the projection on to the Other of what is repressed within the Self in order that it can be discredited, disowned, and if possible annihilated. It is repression, in other words, that makes impossible the healthy alternative—the full recognition and acceptance of the Other's autonomy and right to exist.

Some versions follow of the figure of the Other as it operates within our culture, of its relation to repression and oppression, and of how it is characteristically dealt with:

1. *Quite simply, other people.* It is logical and probable that under capitalism all human relations will be characterized by power, dominance, possessiveness, manipulation: the extension into relationships of the property principle. Given the subordinate and dependent position of women, this is especially true of the culture's central relationship, the male/female, and explains why marriage as we have it is characteristically a kind of mutual imperialism/colonization, on exchange of different forms of possession and dependence, both economic and emotional. In theory, relations between people of the same sex stand more chance of evading this contamination, but in practice most gay and lesbian relationships tend to rely on heterosexual models. The otherness and the autonomy of the partner as well as her/his right to freedom and independence of being are perceived as a threat to the possession/dependence principle and are denied.

2. *Woman.* In a male-dominated culture, where power, money, law, and social institutions are controlled by past, present, and future patriarchs, woman as the Other assumes particular significance. The dominant images of women in our culture are entirely male created and male controlled. Woman's autonomy and independence are denied; on to women men project their own innate, repressed femininity in order to disown it as inferior (to be called "unmanly"—i.e., like a woman—is the supreme insult).

3. *The proletariat*—insofar as it still has any autonomous existence and has escaped its colonization by bourgeois ideology. It remains, at least, a conveniently available object for projection: the bourgeois obsession with cleanliness, which psychoanalysis shows to be an

outward symptom closely associated with sexual repression, and bourgeois sexual repression itself, find their inverse reflections in the myths of working-class squalor and sexuality.

4. *Other cultures*. If they are sufficiently remote, no problem arises: they can be simultaneously deprived of their true character and exoticized (e.g., Polynesian cultures as embodied by Dorothy Lamour). If they are inconveniently close, another approach predominates, of which what happened to the American Indian is a prime example. The procedure is very precisely represented in Ford's *Drums Along the Mohawk*, with its double vision of the Indians as "sons of Belial" fit only for extermination and as the Christianized, domesticated, servile, and (hopefully) comic Blueback.

5. *Ethnic groups within the culture*. Again, they function as easily available projection objects (myths of black sexuality, animality, etc.). Or they become acceptable in two ways: either they keep to their ghettos and don't trouble us with their otherness, or they behave as we do and become replicas of the good bourgeois, their Otherness reduced to the one unfortunate difference of color. We are more likely to invite a Pakistani to dinner if he dresses in a business suit.

6. *Alternative ideologies or political systems*. The exemplary case is of course Marxism, the strategy that of parody. Still almost totally repressed within our pre-university education system (despite the key importance of Marx—whatever way you look at it—in the development of twentieth-century thought), Marxism exists generally in our culture only in the form of bourgeois myth that renders it indistinguishable from Stalinism.

7. *Deviations from ideological sexual norms—notably bisexuality and homosexuality*. One of the clearest instances of the operation of the repression/projection mechanism, homophobia (the irrational hatred and fear of homosexuals) is only explicable as the product of the unsuccessful repression of bisexual tendencies: what is hated in others is what is rejected (but nonetheless continues to exist) within the self.

8. *Children*. When we have worked our way through all the other liberation movements, we may discover that children are the most oppressed section of the population (unfortunately, we cannot expect to liberate our children until we have successfully liberated ourselves). Most clearly of all, the otherness of children (see Freudian theories of infantile sexuality) is that which is repressed within ourselves, its expression therefore hated in others. What the previous generation repressed in us, we, in turn, repress in our children, seeking to mold them into replicas of ourselves, perpetuators of a discredited tradition.

All this may seem to have taken us rather far from our immediate subject. In fact, I have been laying the foundations, stone by stone, for a theory of the American horror film which (without being exhaustive) should provide us with a means of approaching the films seriously and responsibly. One could, I think, approach any of the genres from the same starting point; it is the horror film that responds in the most clear-cut and direct way, because central to it is the actual dramatization of the dual concept of the repressed/the Other, in the figure of the Monster. One might say that the true subject of the horror genre is the struggle for recognition of all that our civilization represses or oppresses, its reemergence dramatized, as in our nightmares, as an object of horror, a matter for terror, and the happy ending (when it exists) typically signifying the restoration of repression. I think my analysis of what is repressed, combined with my account of the Other as it functions within our culture, will be found to offer a comprehensive survey of horror-film monsters from German Expressionism on. It is possible to produce "monstrous" embodiments of virtually every item in the above list. Let me preface this by saying that the general sexual content of the horror film has long been recognized, and the list of monsters representing a generalized concept of Otherness offered by the first item on my list cannot be represented by specific films.

Female sexuality. Earlier examples are the panther woman of *Island of Lost Souls* and the heroine of *Cat People* (the association of women with cats runs right through and beyond the Hollywood cinema, cutting across periods and genres from *Bringing Up Baby* to *Alien*); but the definitive feminist horror film is clearly De Palma's *Sisters* (co-scripted by the director and Louisa Rose), among the most complete and rigorous analyses of the oppression of women under patriarchal culture in the whole of patriarchal cinema.

The proletariat. I would claim here Whale's *Frankenstein*, partly on the strength of its pervasive class references but more on the strength of Karloff's costume: Frankenstein could have dressed his creature in top hat, white tie and tails, but in fact chose laborer's clothes. Less disputable, in recent years we have *The Texas Chainsaw Massacre*, with its monstrous family of retired, but still practicing, slaughterhouse workers; the underprivileged devil-worshipers of *Race with the Devil*; and the revolutionary army of *Assault on Precinct 13*.

Other cultures. In the '30s the monster was almost invariably foreign; the rebellious animal-humans of *Island of Lost Souls* (though created by the white man's science) on one level clearly signify a savage, unsuccessfully colonized culture. Recently, one horror film, *The Manitou*, identified the monster with the American Indian (*Prophecy* plays tantalizingly with this possibility, also linking it to urban blacks, before opting for the altogether safer and less interesting explanation of industrial pollution).

Ethnic groups. *The Possession of Joel Delaney* links diabolic possession with Puerto Ricans; blacks (and a leader clad as an Indian) are prominent in *Assault on Precinct 13*'s monstrous army.

Alternative ideologies. The '50s science-fiction cycle of invasion movies are generally regarded as being concerned with the Communist threat.

Homosexuality and bisexuality. Both Murnau's *Nosferatu* and Whale's *Frankenstein* can be claimed as implicitly (on certain levels) identifying their monsters with repressed homosexuality. Recent, less arguable instances are Dr. Frank 'n' Furter of *The Rocky Horror Picture Show* (he, not his creation, is clearly the film's real monster) and, more impressively, the bisexual god of Larry Cohen's *Demon*.

Children. Since *Rosemary's Baby* children have figured prominently in horror films as the monster or its medium: *The Exorcist*, *The Omen*, etc. Cohen's two *It's Alive* films again offer perhaps the most interesting and impressive examples. There is also the Michael of *Halloween*'s remarkable opening.

This offers us no more than a beginning from which one might proceed to interpret specific horror films in detail as well as to explore further the genre's social significance and the insights it offers into our culture. I shall add here simply that these notions of repression and the Other afford us not merely a means of access but a rudimentary categorization of horror films in social/political terms, distinguishing the progressive from the reactionary, the criterion being the way in which the monster is presented and defined.

Return of the Repressed

I want first to offer a series of general propositions about the American horror film and then to define the particular nature of its evolution in the '60s and '70s.

1. *Popularity and Disreputability*. The horror film has consistently been one of the most popular and, at the same time, the most disreputable of Hollywood genres. The popularity

itself has a peculiar characteristic that sets it apart from other genres: it is restricted to aficionados and complemented by total rejection, people tending to go to horror films either obsessively or not at all. They are dismissed with contempt by the majority of reviewer-critics, or simply ignored. (The situation has changed somewhat since *Psycho*, which conferred on the horror film something of the dignity that *Stagecoach* conferred on the Western, but the disdain still largely continues. I have read no serious or illuminating accounts of, for example, *Raw Meat*, *It's Alive* or *The Hills Have Eyes*). The popularity, however, also continues. Most horror films make money; the ones that don't are those with overt intellectual pretensions, obviously "difficult" works like *God Told Me To* (*Demon*) and *Exorcist II*. Another psychologically interesting aspect of this popularity is that many people who go regularly to horror films profess to ridicule them and go in order to laugh, which is not true, generally speaking, of the Western or the gangster movie.

2. *Dreams and Nightmares*. The analogy frequently invoked between films and dreams is usually concerned with the experience of the audience. The spectator sits in darkness, and the sort of involvement the entertainment film invites necessitates a certain switching off of consciousness, a losing of oneself in fantasy experience. But the analogy is also useful from the point of view of the filmmakers. Dreams—the embodiment of repressed desires, tensions, fears that our conscious mind rejects—become possible when the censor that guards our subconscious relaxes in sleep, though even then the desires can only emerge in disguise, as fantasies that are innocent or apparently meaningless.

One of the functions of the concept of entertainment—by definition, that which we don't take seriously, or think about much ("It's only entertainment")—is to act as a kind of partial sleep of consciousness. For the filmmakers as well as for the audience, full awareness stops at the level of plot, action, and character, in which the most dangerous and subversive implications can disguise themselves and escape detection. This is why seemingly innocuous genre movies can be far more radical and fundamentally undermining than works of conscious social criticism, which must always concern themselves with the possibility of reforming aspects of a social system whose basic rightness must not be challenged. The old tendency to dismiss the Hollywood cinema as escapist always defined escape merely negatively as escape *from*, but escape logically must also be escape *to*. Dreams are also escapes, from the unresolved tensions of our lives into fantasies. Yet the fantasies are not meaningless; they can represent attempts to resolve those tensions in more radical ways than our consciousness can countenance.

Popular films, then, respond to interpretation as at once the personal dreams of their makers and the collective dreams of their audiences, the fusion made possible by the shared structures of a common ideology. It becomes easy, if this is granted, to offer a simple definition of horror films: they are our collective nightmares. The conditions under which a dream becomes a nightmare are that the repressed wish is, from the point of view of consciousness, so terrible that it must be repudiated as loathsome, and that it is so strong and powerful as to constitute a serious threat. The disreputability noted above—the general agreement that horror films are not to be taken seriously—works clearly *for* the genre viewed from this position. The censor (in both the common and the Freudian sense) is lulled into sleep and relaxes vigilance.

3. *The Surrealists*. It is worth noting here that one group of intellectuals did take American horror movies very seriously indeed: the writers, painters, and filmmakers of the Surrealist movement. Luis Buñuel numbers *The Beast with Five Fingers* among his favorite films and paid

homage to it in *The Exterminating Angel*; Georges Franju, an heir of the Surrealists, numbers *The Fly* among his. The association is highly significant, given the commitment of the Surrealists to Freud, the unconscious, dreams, and the overthrow of repression.

4. *Basic Formula*. At this stage it is necessary to offer a simple and obvious basic formula for the horror film: normality is threatened by the Monster. I use "normality" here in a strictly nonevaluative sense to mean simply "conformity to the dominant social norms": one must firmly resist the common tendency to treat the word as if it were more or less synonymous with "health."

The very simplicity of this formula has a number of advantages:

It covers the entire range of horror films, being applicable whether the Monster is a vampire, a giant gorilla, an extraterrestrial invader, an amorphous gooey mass, or a child possessed by the Devil, and this makes it possible to connect the most seemingly heterogeneous movies.

It suggests the possibility of extension to other genres: substitute for "Monster" the term "Indians," for example, and one has a formula for a large number of classical Westerns; substitute "transgressive woman" and the formula encompasses numerous melodramas (Vidor's *Beyond the Forest* is an especially fine example, as it links woman and Indian as "monsters").

Although so simple, the formula provides three variables: normality, the Monster, and, crucially, the relationship between the two. The definition of normality in horror films is in general boringly constant: the heterosexual monogamous couple, the family, and the social institutions (police, church, armed forces) that support and defend them. The Monster is, of course, much more protean, changing from period to period as society's basic fears clothe themselves in fashionable or immediately accessible garments—rather as dreams use material from recent memory to express conflicts or desires that may go back to early childhood.

It is the third variable, the relationship between normality and the Monster, that constitutes the essential subject of the horror film. It, too, changes and develops, the development taking the form of a long process of clarification or revelation. The relationship has one privileged form: the figure of the doppelgänger, alter ego, or double, a figure that has recurred constantly in western culture, especially during the past hundred years. The *locus classicus* is Stevenson's Dr. Jekyll and Mr. Hyde, where normality and Monster are two aspects of the same person. The figure pervades two major sources of the American horror film—German Expressionist cinema (the two Marias of *Metropolis*, the presentation of protagonist and vampire as mirror reflections in *Nosferatu*, the very title of F. W. Murnau's lost Jekyll-and-Hyde film *Der Januskopf*), and the tales of Poe. Variants can be traced in such oppositions as Ahab/the white whale in *Moby Dick* and Ethan/Scar in *The Searchers*. The Westerns of Anthony Mann are rich in doubles, often contained within families or family patterns; *Man of the West*, a film that relates very suggestively to the horror genre, represents the fullest elaboration.

I shall limit myself for the moment to one example from the horror film, choosing it partly because it is so central, partly because the motif is there partially disguised, and partly because it points forward to Larry Cohen and *It's Alive*: the relationship of Monster to creator in the *Frankenstein* films. Their identity is made explicit in *Son of Frankenstein*, the most intelligent of the Universal series, near the start of which the title figure (Basil Rathbone) complains bitterly that everyone believes "Frankenstein" to be the name of the monster. (We discover subsequently that the town has also came to be called Frankenstein, the symbiosis of Monster and creator spreading over the entire environment.) But we should be alerted to the relationship's true significance from the moment in the James Whale original where Frankenstein's decision to create his monster is juxtaposed very precisely with his decision to become engaged. The doppelgänger motif reveals the Monster as normality's shadow.

5. *Ambivalence*. The principle of ambivalence is most eloquently elaborated in A. P. Rossiter's *Angel with Horns*, among the most brilliant of all books on Shakespeare. Rossiter first expounds it with reference to Richard III. Richard, the "angel with horns," both horrifies us with his evil and delights us with his intellect, his art, his audacity; while our moral sense is appalled by his outrages, another part of us gleefully identifies with him. The application of this to the horror film is clear. Few horror films have totally unsympathetic Monsters (*The Thing* is a significant exception); in many (notably the *Frankenstein* films) the Monster is clearly the emotional center, and much more human than the cardboard representatives of normality. The Frankenstein monster suffers, weeps, responds to music, longs to relate to people; Henry and Elizabeth merely declaim histrionically. Even in *Son of Frankenstein*—the film in which the restructured monster is explicitly designated as evil and superhuman—the monster's emotional commitment to Ygor and grief over his death carries far greater weight than any of the other relationships in the film.

But the principle goes far beyond the Monster's being sympathetic. Ambivalence extends to our attitude to normality. Central to the effect and fascination of horror films is their fulfillment of our nightmare wish to smash the norms that oppress us and which our moral conditioning teaches us to revere.* The overwhelming commercial success of *The Omen* cannot possibly be explained in terms of simple, unequivocal *horror* at the devil's progress.

6. *Freudian Theses*. Finally, I restate the two elementary and closely interconnected Freudian theses that structure this article: that in a society built on monogamy and family there will be an enormous surplus of repressed sexual energy, and that what is repressed must always strive to return.

[. . .]

* A game popular in British fairgrounds actually entitled 'Breaking up the Happy Home' is of great interest in this connection: there are no prizes, the participant's gratification deriving purely from the smashing of china and domestic artifacts with the balls for which they pay.

2 Why horror?

NOËL CARROLL

There is a theoretical question about horror which, although not unique to horror, nevertheless is not one that readily arises with respect to other popular genres, such as mystery, romance, comedy, the thriller, adventure stories, and the western. The question is: why would anyone be interested in the genre to begin with? Why does the genre persist? I have written a lot about the internal elements of the genre; but many readers may feel that in doing that their attention has been deflected away from the central issue concerning horror—viz., how can we explain its very existence, for why would anyone *want* to be horrified, or even art-horrified?

This question, moreover, becomes especially pressing if my analysis of the nature of horror is accepted. For we have seen that a key element in the emotion of art-horror is repulsion or disgust. But—and this is the question of "Why horror?" in its primary form—if horror necessarily has something repulsive about it, how can audiences be attracted to it? Indeed, even if horror only caused fear, we might feel justified in demanding an explanation of what could motivate people to seek out the genre. But where fear is compounded with repulsion, the ante is, in a manner of speaking, raised.

In the ordinary course of affairs, people shun what disgusts them. Being repulsed by something that one finds to be loathsome and impure is an unpleasant experience. We do not, for example, attempt to add some pleasure to a boring afternoon by opening the lid of a steamy trash can in order to savor its unwholesome stew of broken bits of meat, moldering fruits and vegetables, and noxious, unrecognizable clumps, riven thoroughly by all manner of crawling things. And, ordinarily, checking out hospital waste bags is not our idea of a good time. But, on the other hand, many people—so many, in fact, that we must concede that they are normal, at least in the statistical sense—do seek out horror fictions for the purpose of deriving pleasure from sights and descriptions that customarily repulse them.

In short, there appears to be something paradoxical about the horror genre. It obviously attracts consumers; but it seems to do so by means of the expressly repulsive. Furthermore, the horror genre gives every evidence of being pleasurable to its audience, but it does so by means of trafficking in the very sorts of things that cause disquiet, distress, and displeasure. So different ways of clarifying the question "Why horror?" are to ask: "Why are horror audiences attracted by what, typically (in everyday life), should (and would) repell them?," or "How can horror audiences find pleasure in what by nature is distressful and unpleasant?"

In what follows, I will attempt to find a comprehensive or general answer to the question of what attracts audiences to the horror genre. That is, I shall try to frame a set of hypthoses that will supply a plausible explanation of the attracting power of horror in its many manifestations across the different centuries and decades, and across the different subgenres and media in which horror is practiced. However, in this regard it is important to emphasize that, though a general account of horror may be advanced, this does not preclude the possibility that it can be supplemented by additional accounts of why a particular horror novel or film, a particular horror subgenre, or a particular cycle within the history of horror also has some special levers of attraction over and above those that are generic to the mode of horror. That is, an explanation of basic pleasures or attractions of the horror mode is compatible with *additional* explanations of why, for example, *Rosemary's Baby* exercises its own particular fascination; of how werewolf stories, while sharing the allures of ghost stories and other horrific tales, have allures of their own; and of why horror cycles, like the Hollywood movie cycle of the thirties, gain attractive power by thematically developing concerns of especial appropriateness for the period in which they were made.

A general theory of horror will say something about the probable roots of attraction and pleasure throughout the genus of horror, but this does not deny that various of the species and specimens of the genre will have further sources of attraction and pleasure that will require, correspondingly, *added* explanations. In most cases, such (added) explanations will be developed by critics of the genre. However, I would like to address one particular case here which is especially relevant to readers of this book. In concluding, I will attempt an account of why at present horror is so compelling, that is, an account of why the horror cycle within which we find ourselves exerts such a commanding impression on its continuing, avid audiences: that is to say on us (or at least many of us).

[. . .]

I think it is fair to say that in our culture, horror thrives above all as a narrative form. Thus, in order to account for the interest we take in and the pleasure we take from horror, we may hypothesize that, in the main, the locus of our gratification is not the monster as such but the whole narrative structure in which the presentation of the monster is staged. This, of course, is not to say that the monster is in any way irrelevant to the genre, nor that the interest and pleasure in the genre could be satisfied through and/or substituted by any old narrative. For, as I have argued earlier, the monster is a functional ingredient in the type of narratives found in horror stories, and not all narratives function exactly like horror narratives.

As we saw in my analysis of horror narratives, these stories, with great frequency, revolve around proving, disclosing, discovering, and confirming the existence of something that is impossible, something that defies standing conceptual schemes. It is part of such stories—contrary to our everyday beliefs about the nature of things—that such monsters exist. And as a result, audiences' expectations revolve around whether this existence will be confirmed in the story.

Often this is achieved, as Hume says of narrative "secrets" in general, by putting off the conclusive information that the monster exists for quite a while. Sometimes this information may be deferred till the very end of the fiction. And even where this information is given to the audience right off the bat, it is still generally the case that the human characters in the tale must undergo a process of discovering that the monster exists, which, in turn, may lead to a further process of confirming that discovery in an ensuing scene or series of scenes. That is, the question of whether or not the monster exists may be transformed into the question of whether and when the human characters in the tale will establish the existence of the monster. Horror stories are often protracted series of discoveries: first the reader learns of the monster's existence, then some characters do, then some more characters do, and so on; the drama of iterated disclosure—albeit to different parties—underwrites much horror fiction.[1]

Even in overreacher plots, there is a question of whether the monsters exist—i.e., of whether they can be summoned, in the case of demons, or of whether they can be created by mad scientists and necromancers. Furthermore, even after the existence of the monster is disclosed, the audience continues to crave further information about its nature, its identity, its origin, its purposes, and its astounding powers and properties, including, ultimately, those of its weaknesses that *may* enable humanity to do it in.

Thus, to a large extent, the horror story is driven explicitly by curiosity. It engages its audience by being involved in processes of disclosure, discovery, proof, explanation, hypothesis, and confirmation. Doubt, skepticism, and the fear that belief in the existence of the monster is a form of insanity are predictable foils to the revelation (to the audience or to the characters or both) of the existence of the monster.

Horror stories, in a significant number of cases, are dramas of proving the existence of the monster and disclosing (most often gradually) the origin, identity, purposes and powers of the monster. Monsters, as well, are obviously a perfect vehicle for engendering this kind of curiosity and for supporting the drama of proof, because monsters are (physically, though generally not logically) impossible beings. They arouse interest and attention through being putatively inexplicable or highly unusual vis-à-vis our standing cultural categories, thereby instilling a desire to learn and to know about them. And since they are also outside of (justifiably) prevailing definitions of what is, they understandably prompt a need for proof (or the fiction of a proof) in the face of skepticism. Monsters are, then, natural subjects for curiosity, and they straightforwardly warrant the ratiocinative energies the plot lavishes upon them.

All narratives might be thought to involve the desire to know—the desire to know at least the outcome of the interaction of the forces made salient in the plot. However, the horror fiction is a special variation on this general narrative motivation, because it has at the center of it something which is given as in principle *unknowable*—something which, *ex hypothesi*, cannot, given the structure of our conceptual scheme, exist and that cannot have the properties it has. This is why, so often, the real drama in a horror story resides in establishing the existence of the monster and in disclosing its horrific properties. Once this is established, the monster, generally, has to be confronted, and the narrative is driven by the question of whether the creature can be destroyed. However, even at this point, the drama of ratiocination can continue as further discoveries—accompanied by arguments, explanations, and hypotheses—reveal features of the monster that will facilitate or impede the destruction of the creature. [. . .]

What is revealed and disclosed, of course, are monsters and their properties. These are appropriate objects of discovery and revelation, just because they are unknown—not only in the sense that the murderer in a detective fiction is unknown, but also because they are outside the bounds of knowledge, i.e., outside our standing conceptual schemes. This, as well, accounts for why their revelation and the disclosure of their properties is so often bound up in processes of proof, hypothesis, argument, explanation (including sci-fi flights of fancy and magical lore about mythological realms, potions, and incantations), and confirmation. That is, because horror fictions are predicated on the revelation of unknown and unknowable—unbelievable and incredible—impossible beings, they often take the form of narratives of discovery and proof. For things unknown in the way of monsters obviously are natural subjects for proof.

Applied to the paradox of horror, these observations suggest that the pleasure derived from the horror fiction and the source of our interest in it resides, first and foremost, in the processes of discovery, proof, and confirmation that horror fictions often employ. The disclosure of the existence of the horrific being and of its properties is the central source of pleasure in the genre; once that process of revelation is consummated, we remain inquisitive about whether such a creature can be successfully confronted, and that narrative question sees us through to the end of the story. Here, the pleasure involved is, broadly speaking, cognitive. Hobbes, interestingly, thought of curiosity as an appetite of the mind; with the horror fiction, that appetite is whetted by the prospect of knowing the putatively unknowable, and then satisfied through a continuous process of revelation, enhanced by imitations of (admittedly simplistic) proofs, hypotheses, counterfeits of causal reasoning, and explanations whose details and movement intrigue the mind in ways analogous to genuine ones.[2]

Moreover, it should be clear that these particular cognitive pleasures, insofar as they are set in motion by the relevant kind of unknowable beings, are especially well served by horrific monsters. Thus, there is a special functional relationship between the beings that mark off the horror genre and the pleasure and interest that many horror fictions sustain. That interest and that pleasure derive from the disclosure of unknown and impossible beings, just the sorts of things that seem to call for proof, discovery, and confirmation. Therefore, the disgust that such beings evince might be seen as part of the price to be paid for the pleasure of their disclosure. That is, the narrative expectation that the horror genre puts in place is that the being whose existence is in question be something that defies standing cultural categories; thus, disgust, so to say, is itself more or less mandated by the kind of curiosity that the horror narrative puts in place. The horror narrative could not deliver a successful, affirmative answer to its presiding question unless the disclosure of the monster indeed elicited disgust, or was of the sort that was a highly probable object of disgust.

That is, there is a strong relation of consilience between the objects of art-horror, on the one hand, and the revelatory plotting on the other. The kinds of plots and the subjects of horrific revelation are not merely compatible, but fit together or agree in a way that is highly appropriate. That the audience is naturally inquisitive about that which is unknown meshes with plotting that is concerned to render the unknown known by processes of discovery, explanation, proof, hypothesis, confirmation, and so on.

Of course, what it means to say that the horrific being is "unknown" here is that it is not accommodated by standing conceptual schemes. Moreover, if Mary Douglas's account of impurity is correct, things that violate our conceptual scheme, by (for example) being interstitial, are things that we are prone to find disturbing. Thus, that horrific beings are predictably objects of loathing and revulsion is a function of the ways they violate our classificatory scheme.

If what is of primary importance about horrific creatures is that their very impossibility vis-à-vis our conceptual categories is what makes them function so compellingly in dramas of discovery and confirmation, then their disclosure, insofar as they are categorical violations, will be attached to some sense of disturbance, distress, and disgust. Consequently, the role of the horrific creature in such narratives—where their disclosure captures our interest and delivers pleasure—will simultaneously mandate some probable revulsion. That is, in order to reward our interest by the disclosure of the putatively impossible beings of the plot, said beings ought to be disturbing, distressing, and repulsive in the way that theorists like Douglas predict phenomena that ill fit cultural classifications will be.

So, as a first approximation of resolving the paradox of horror, we may conjecture that we are attracted to the majority of horror fictions because of the way that the plots of discovery and the dramas of proof pique our curiosity, and abet our interest, ideally satisfying them in a way that is pleasurable.[3] But if narrative curiosity about impossible beings is to be satisfied through disclosure, that process must require some element of probable disgust since such impossible beings are, *ex hypothesi*, disturbing, distressful, and repulsive.

One way of making the point is to say that the monsters in such tales of disclosure have to be disturbing, distressful, and repulsive, if the process of their discovery is to be rewarding in a pleasurable way. Another way to get at this is to say that the primary pleasure that narratives of disclosure afford—i.e., the interest we take in them, and the source of their attraction—resides in the processes of discovery, the play of proof, and the dramas of ratiocination that comprise them. It is not that we crave disgust, but that disgust is a predictable concomitant of disclosing the unknown, whose disclosure is a desire the narrative instills in the audience and then goes on to gladden. Nor will that desire be satisfied unless the monster defies our conception of nature which demands that it probably engender some measure of repulsion.

In this interpretation of horror narratives, the majority of which would appear to exploit the cognitive attractions of the drama of disclosure, experiencing the emotion of art-horror is not our absolutely primary aim in consuming horror fictions, even though it is a determining feature for identifying membership in the genre. Rather, art-horror is the price we are willing to pay for the revelation of that which is impossible and unknown, of that which violates our conceptual schema. The impossible being does disgust; but that disgust is part of an overall narrative address which is not only pleasurable, but whose potential pleasure depends on the confirmation of the existence of the monster as a being that violates, defies, or problematizes standing cultural classifications. Thus, we are attracted to, and many of us seek out, horror fictions of this sort despite the fact that they provoke disgust, because that disgust is required for the pleasure involved in engaging our curiosity in the unknown and drawing it into the processes of revelation, ratiocination, etc.

One objection to this line of conjecture is to point out that many of the kinds of plot structures found in horror fiction can be found in other genres. The play of discovery and confirmation, supported by ratiocination, can be found in detective thrillers. And the plots of the disaster movies of the first half of the seventies often also look like horror plots; but instead of ghouls and vampires calling for discovery and confirmation, potential earthquakes, avalanches, floods, and simmering electrical systems are the culprits.

Of course, with detective stories and disaster films, the evil that is disclosed is not impossible nor, in principle, unknown. This not only means that these narratives do not characteristically cause disgust, but that there is a qualitative difference in the kind of curiosity they invite and reward. My point here is not that one kind of curiosity is higher or lower than another kind; but only that there can be different kinds of curiosity engaged by plot structures that at a certain level of abstract description look formally equivalent, in terms of their major movements. However, it is one thing to be curious about the unknown but natural, and another thing to be curious about the impossible. And it is the latter form of curiosity in which horror fictions typically traffic.

Two other, I think, deeper objections to the preceding hypotheses about the paradox of horror are:

1) So far the conjecture only deals with horror narratives, indeed, only with horror narratives of a certain sort—namely those involving such elements as discovery, confirmation, disclosure, revelation, explanation, hypothesis, ratiocination, etc. *But* there are instances of the horror genre, e.g., paintings, that need not involve narrative; *and* there are, according to my review of characteristic horror plots, horror narratives that don't involve these elements. There may be, for example, pure onset or pure confrontation plots. Moreover, earlier hypotheses about the paradox of horror were rejected because they were not sufficiently comprehensive. But since there are instances of horror that are not narrative and since there may be horror narratives that do not deploy the elements of disclosure so far identified as the central source of attraction to horror, this conjecture must be rejected as failing its own standards of generality.

2) This conjecture seems to make the experience of being horrified too remote from the experience of the genre. The revulsion we feel at the horrific being is too detached from the source of attraction we find in the genre. This is peculiar, since it is the emotion of art-horror that differentiates the genre. Indeed, it is very often the expectation that a given fiction is defined by this emotion that leads us to select it over candidates from other genres. So one seems justified in supposing that what makes the genre special must have some intimate connection with what draws audiences to seek it out especially. But the account, thus far, falters in this respect.

The first criticism is absolutely on target about the limitations of my hypothesis *in its present state*. My view is not yet sufficiently comprehensive. The horror genre includes examples, like photographs and paintings, that do not involve sustained narration, especially sustained narration of the particular sort I have emphasized; and, there are horror narratives of the pure onset or pure confrontation variety that do not offer audiences the refined and sometimes intricately articulated strategems of disclosure referred to above. However, I do not regard these observations as decisive counterexamples to my approach, but rather as an opportunity to deepen and expand it, indeed in ways that will also enable me to handle the second of the objections in the course of adjusting my position in order to accommodate the first objection.

I do think that the best account that can be given of the paradox of horror for the *majority* of works of horrific art will be very much like the one that I have already offered. However, it is true that it fails to cover non-narrative horror and horror fictions little concerned with the drama of disclosure. To deal with these cases more needs to be said; but the more-that-needs-to-be-said fits with what has already been said in a way that enriches while also extending the theory developed so far.

Central to my approach has been the idea that the objects of horror are fundamentally linked with cognitive interests, most notably with curiosity. The plotting gambits of disclosure/discovery narratives play with, expand, sustain, and develop this initial cognitive appetite in many directions. And as well, this is the way in which horror fictions usually go.

But it would be a mistake to think that this curiosity is *solely* a function of plotting, even if the plotting of certain types of fictions—namely those concerned with disclosure—brings it to its highest pitch. For the objects of art-horror in and of themselves engender curiosity as well. This is why they can support the kind of disclosure plots referred to above. Consequently, even if it is true that horrific curiosity is best expatiated upon within disclosure plots, and that, in its most frequent and compelling cases, it does mobilize such plots, it is also true that it can be abetted and rewarded without the narrative contextualization of disclosure/discovery plotting. Thus, it can be the case that while horror is most often, and perhaps most powerfully and most primarily, developed within narrative contexts of disclosure, it may also obtain in non-narrative and non-disclosure contexts for the same reason, viz., the power of the objects of art-horror to command curiosity.

Recall again that the objects of art-horror are, by definition, impure. This is to be understood in terms of their being anomalous. Obviously, the anomalous nature of these beings is what makes them disturbing, distressing, and disgusting. They are violations of our ways of classifying things and such frustrations of a world-picture are bound to be disturbing.

However, anomalies are also interesting. The very fact that they are anomalies fascinates us. Their deviation from the paradigms of our classificatory scheme captures our attention immediately. It holds us spellbound. It commands and retains our attention. It is an attracting force; it attracts curiosity, i.e., it makes us curious; it invites inquisitiveness about its surprising properties. One wants to gaze upon the unusual, even when it is simultaneously repelling.

Monsters, the anomalous beings who star in this book, are repelling because they violate standing categories. But for the self-same reason, they are also compelling of our attention. They are attractive, in the sense that they elicit interest, and they are the cause of, for many, irresistible attention, again, just because they violate standing categories. They are curiosities. They can rivet attention and thrill for the self-same reason that they disturb, distress, and disgust.

If these confessedly pedestrian remarks are convincing, three interesting conclusions are suggested. First, the attraction of non-narrative- and non-disclosure-type narration in horror is explicable, as is disclosure-type narrative, fundamentally by virtue of curiosity, a feature of horrific beings that follows from their anomalous status as violations of standing cultural schemes. Second, horrific creatures are able to contribute so well to sustaining interest in disclosure plots to an important degree just because in being anomalous, they can be irresistibly interesting. And lastly, with special reference to the paradox of horror, monsters, the objects of art-horror, are themselves sources of ambivalent responses, for as violations of standing cultural categories, they are disturbing and disgusting, but, at the same time, they are also objects of fascination—again, just because they transgress standing categories of thought. That is, the ambivalence that bespeaks the paradox of horror is already to be found in the very objects of art-horror which are disgusting and fascinating, repelling and attractive due to their anomalous nature.[4]

I have identified impurity as an essential feature of art-horror; specifically, the objects of art-horror are, in part, impure beings, monsters recognized as outside the natural order of things as set down by our conceptual schema. This claim may be tested by noting the truly impressive frequency with which the apparition of such monsters in horror fictions correlates explicitly in such texts with mention of revulsion, disgust, repulsion, nausea, abhorrence, and so on. The source of this attitude, moreover, seems traceable to the fact that they, as David Pole puts it, "might in a way be called messy; they defy or mess up existing categories. . . . [W]hat initially disturbs us is most often merely a jumbling [or obfuscation] of kinds."[5] But at the same time that the breakdown of our conceptual categories disturbs, it also fixes our attention. It stimulates our cognitive appetite with the prospect of something previously inconceivable.

The fascination of the horrific being comes in tandem with disturbance. And, in fact, I would submit that for those who are attracted to the genre, the fascination at least compensates for the disturbance. This may be explained to a certain extent by reference to the thought theory of fictional emotion discussed earlier in this book. According to that view, the audience knows that the object of art-horror does not exist before them. The audience is only reacting to the thought that such and such an impure being might exist. This mutes, without eliminating, the disturbing aspect of the object of art-horror and allows more opportunity for fascination with the monster to take hold.[6]

One supposes that fascination would be too great a luxury to endure, if one, against all odds, were to encounter a horrific monster in "real life." We, like the characters in horror fictions, would feel distressingly helpless; for such creatures, insofar as they defy our conceptual scheme, would leave us at a loss to think of how to deal with them—they would baffle our practical response, paralyzing us in terror (as they generally do to characters in horror fictions for the same reason). However, with art-horror, it is only the thought of the creature that is at issue; we know that it does not exist; we are not taxed literally by practical questions about what is to be done. So the fearsome and loathsome aspects of the monsters do not impinge upon us with the same practical urgency, allowing a space for fascination to take root. So, as a second approximation for resolving the paradox of horror, we can explain how it is that what would, by hypothesis, ordinarily distress, disturb, and disgust us, can also be the source of pleasure, interest, and attraction. With reference to art-horror the answer is that the monster—as a categorical violation—fascinates for the self-same reason it disgusts and, since we know the monster is but a fictional confection, our curiosity is affordable.

This position enables us to give an answer to the justified objection to our first response to the paradox of horror, which response was so wedded to disclosure-type narratives, to wit: non-narrative examples of art-horror, such as those found in the fine arts and narrative horror fictions that do not deploy disclosure devices, attract their audiences insofar as the objects of art-horror promote fascination at the same time they distress; indeed, both responses emanate from the same aspects of the horrific beings. The two responses are, as a matter of (contingent) fact, inseparable in horror. Moreover, this fascination can be savored, because the distress in question is not behaviorally pressing; it is a response to the thought of a monster, not to the actual presence of a disgusting or fearsome thing.

If it is true that fascination is the key to our attention to the art-horror in general, then it is also the case that the curiosity and fascination that is basic to the genre also receive especial amplification in what I have referred to as narratives of disclosure and discovery. There curiosity, fascination, and our cognitive inquisitiveness are engaged, addressed, and sustained in a highly articulated way through what I have called the drama of proof and such processes of continuous revelation as ratiocination, discovery, hypothesis formation, confirmation, and so on.

At this point, then, I am in a position to summarize my approach to the paradox of horror. It is a twofold theory, whose elements I refer to respectively as the universal theory and the general theory. The universal theory of our attraction to art-horror—which covers non-narrative horror, non-disclosure horror narratives, *and* disclosure narratives—is that what leads people to seek out horror is fascination as characterized in the analyses above. This is the basic, generic calling card of the form.

At the same time, I should also like to advance what I call a general—rather than a universal—theory of the appeal of art-horror. The most commonly recurring—that is to say the most generally found—exercises in the horror genre appear to be horror narratives of the disclosure sort. The attraction of these instances, like all other examples of the genre, are to be explained in terms of curiosity and fascination. However, with these cases, the initial curiosity and fascination found in the genre are developed to an especially high degree through devices that enhance and sustain curiosity. If the genre begins, so to speak, in curiosity, it is enhanced by the consilient structures of disclosure plotting. In such cases, then, what attracts us to this sort of horror—which seems to me the most pervasive[7]—is the whole structure and staging of curiosity in the narrative, in virtue of the experience of the extended play of fascination it affords. That is, as Hume noted of tragedy, the source of our aesthetic pleasure in such examples of horror is primarily the whole structure of the narrative in which, of course, the apparition of the horrific being is an essential, and, as the universal theory shows, a facilitating part.

[. . .]

One advantage of this theoretical approach over some of the rival theories, like psychoanalysis, is that it can accommodate our interest in horrific beings whose imagery does not seem straightforwardly, or even circuitously, rooted in such things as repression. That is, the religious awe explanation and psychoanalytic explanations of horror confront counterexamples in those cases of horror where the monsters seem to be produced by what might be thought of as virtually formal processes of "categorical-jamming." Wells's cephalopods engender neither cosmic awe nor are they worked up pointedly enough in the text to be linked with some identifiably repressed material. Thus, these attempted explanations are not sufficiently comprehensive, because they cannot assimilate that which we can call formalistically (or formulaically) constructed horrific beings.

My approach, on the other hand, has no such problems with horrific beings generated solely by classificatory obfuscation, since I trace their fascination (as well as their distressfulness) to their category-jamming. Thus, the comprehensiveness of my theory in the face of such counterexamples counts as a strong consideration in favor of my theory.

At this point, it may be helpful to remind the reader that I have been concerned to find a comprehensive account of the appeal of horror—that is, an account of horror that pertains to its attraction across periods of time, across subgenres and across particular works of horror, whether they be masterpieces or not. In this respect, I am, in part, regarding horror as what Fredric Jameson has called a mode. He writes:

> when we speak of a mode, what can we mean but that this particular type of literary discourse is not bound to the conventions of a given age, nor indissolubly linked to a given type of verbal artifact, but rather persists as a temptation and a mode of expression across a whole range of historical periods, seeming to offer itself, if only intermittently, as a formal possibility which can be revived and renewed?[8]

To ask what is compelling about horror as a mode is to ask for the most basic, recurring "temptations" afforded by the genre for what one supposes to be the average audience. My answer is the detailed account of fascination and curiosity found above. This answer seems more comprehensive than psychoanalytic and religious explanations of horror as a mode—more encompassing of the widest number of recurring cases.[9]

However, having said this, I do not necessarily preclude that psychoanalytic and religious explanations may not offer supplemental insight into why particular works of horror, particular periodic cycles, or why specified subgenres may exert their own special attractions over and above the generic attraction of the mode. Whether and to what extent such explanations are convincing depends on the critical and interpretive analysis of individual subgenres, cycles, and works. I have no theoretical reason to announce ahead of time that such critical work may not inform us about the levers of attraction that certain cycles, subgenres, and individual works deploy over and above the generic attractions of the mode. The persuasiveness of such critical work will have to be judged on a case-by-case basis. I have only been concerned to advance a view of the generic power of the horror mode and I will not here and now express any principled reservation to the possibility of the application of religious criticism, myth criticism, psychoanalytic criticism, cosmic-awe criticism, etc. to isolated cycles, subgenres and works in the horror mode.

It is my impression that the curiosity/fascination resolution that I have offered to the paradox of horror—despite its reliance on somewhat technical notions like categorical violations, and co-existentialism—is pretty obvious. It is certainly not as jazzy as many reductivist psychoanalytic theories. In fact, it may strike many as not being theoretical at all, but as nothing but a long-winded exercise in common sense.

I do think that the approach—especially in the way it works out the interplay of the forces of attraction and repulsion—is elucidating; though I can see why when stated in abbreviated form—horror attracts because anomalies command attention and elicit curiosity—it may sound platitudinous. Three remarks seem appropriate here: first, the very comprehensiveness of the explanation of the phenomena that we are seeking might tend to make the solution appear truistic and trivially broad, even if it is not; second, that the theory seems common-sensical need not count against it—there is no reason to think that common sense cannot contribute insight; and last, as perhaps a corollary to the latter observation, that competing explanations resort to arcane sources is not of necessity a virtue in their favor.

[. . .]

Notes

1 The special fermata over the discovery/disclosure of the monster in horror narratives is also in evidence in some of the most standardly employed expositional strategies in movies. For example, with respect to point-of-view editing in horror films, J. P. Telotte writes: "one of the most frequent and compelling images in the horror film repertoire is that of the wide, staring eyes of some victim, expressing stark terror or disbelief and attesting to an ultimate threat to the human proposition. To maximize the effect of this image, though, the movie most often reverses what is a standard film technique and, in fact, the natural sequence of events. Normally an action is presented and then commented upon with reaction shots; the cause is shown and then its effect. The horror film, however, tends to reverse the process, offering the reaction shot first and thus fostering a chilling suspense by holding the terrors in abeyance for a moment; furthermore, such an arrangement upsets our ordinary cause–effect orientation. What is eventually betrayed is the onset of some unbelievable terror, something which stubbornly refuses to be accounted for by our normal perceptual patterns." Though I do not agree with the analysis—in terms of identification—that Telotte appends to this description, the

description itself is an apt one of a recurring cinematic strategy in horror films, and it suggests the way in which this editing figure reflects, in the form of a "mini-narrative," the larger rhythms of discovery and disclosure in horror plotting. See J. P. Telotte, "Faith and Idolatry in the Horror Film," in *Planks of Reason*, ed. Barry Keith Grant (Metuchen, New Jersey: The Scarecrow Press, 1984), pp. 25–26.

2 In claiming that the pleasures derived from horror are cognitive in the broad sense—of engaging curiosity—I am attempting to explain why the genre often engages us. I am not attempting to justify the genre as worthy of our attention because its appeal is cognitive. Nor by saying that it is cognitive, in the special sense of engaging curiosity, am I even implicitly signaling that I think it superior to some other genres whose appeal might be said to be exclusively emotive.

3 "Ideally" here is meant to take note of the fact that not all such horror fictions are successful.

4 This is not said to retract my earlier claim that with disclosure-type narration our fascination fastens primarily on the way in which our curiosity is orchestrated. However, in order to be orchestrated and so have that orchestration rewarded, the monster will ideally be capable of some independent source of fascination. And that source of fascination, I conjecture, is its anomalous nature.

5 David Pole, *Aesthetics, Form and Emotion* (New York: St. Martin's Press, 1983), pp. 228–29.

In composing the last stages of this book I was pleasantly surprised to learn that the late David Pole had reached a number of the same conclusions about disgust and horror that I advanced in the opening part of this book in his essay "Disgust and Other Forms of Aversion" (in *Aesthetics, Form and Emotion*). Much of this correspondence in approach is explicable by the fact that both Pole and I rely very heavily on the researches of Mary Douglas. Pole explicitly cites Mary Douglas's book *Implicit Meanings*, a text that I also independently consulted in the construction of my theory. (See Mary Douglas, *Implicit Meanings* [London: Routledge & Kegan Paul, 1975].)

There are, however, some differences between Pole's view and my own. He considers horror in the actual contexts as well as aesthetic ones, whereas my focus is narrowly on art-horror. Also, whereas I am only concerned with the way in which entities, specifically beings, are horrifying, Pole is interested in horrifying events as well as entities. Nevertheless, both of us take disgust to be a central element in horror, and both see the disgust and fascination of horrific things to be grounded in their categorically anomalous nature.

But there is one point of strong disagreement between Pole and myself. Pole thinks that every instance of horror involves self-identification of the audience with the object of horror. When the horrific is manifested we incorporate it through some process of identification such that it becomes part of us (p. 225). The gesture of being horrified, then, is seen as an extrusion or expulsion of that which is disgusting, which has been incorporated. The model of being horrified here is that of vomiting.

I find this hypothesis dubious. In previous sections I have argued against the notion of identification. Also, I have maintained that if identification amounts to admiring or being seduced by horrific creatures like Dracula, then, even in this loose sense, identification is not definitory of all our encounters with horrific beings. That is, identification in this psychologically inoffensive sense is not a comprehensive feature of art-horror.

Undoubtedly, an advocate of Pole's position would respond to this objection by noting that Pole includes under the rubric of *self-identification* being interested in or fascinated by the object of horror. But to view identification (even "self-identification"), interest, and fascination in the same light distorts all of the concepts in this cluster beyond recognition. I do not have to identify with everything that interests me; nor need I be fascinated by everything with which I identify (for I might not be fascinated by myself). In any case, the extension of the concept of identification to subsume interest is clearly strained. Therefore, I question the viability of the identification/fascination/interest characterization of horror, which, of course, also challenges the extrusion/vomiting model of the horrific response as an adequate, general theory.

Moreover, Pole appears to me to want us to think of disgust exclusively as a process in which we imaginatively swallow the object of our loathing and then spit it out. But with regard to horror, it is hard to imagine swallowing something as big as Mothra or even something the size of the Creature from the Black Lagoon. And in any case, not all disgust, it seems to me, is connected with oral incorporation, e.g., the aversion to funestation (something that comes into play with many monsters, such as zombies).

6 In her article, "A Strange Kind of Sadness," Marcia Eaton postulates that in order to appreciate distressing fictional events we must somehow be in control. As Gary Iseminger points out—in his "How Strange A Sadness?"—the idea of control here is a bit ambiguous. However, if the control that Eaton has in mind is self-control (rather than control over the events in the story), then adoption of the thought theory of fictional response with respect to horror could explain how we have this control, by virtue of the fact that we are knowingly only responding to the thought that some impure creature is devouring human flesh. Indeed, perhaps the very notion that I am merely *entertaining* this thought implies the requisite self-control. See Marcia Eaton, "A Strange Kind of Sadness," in *The Journal of Aesthetics and Art Criticism*, vol. 41, no. 1 (Fall 1982); and Gary Iseminger, "How Strange A Sadness?" in *The Journal of Aesthetics and Art Criticism*, vol. 42, no. 1 (Fall 1983).

In his "Enjoying Negative Emotions in Fictions," John Moreall also cites the importance of control in enjoying fictions. He seems to suggest that such control enables us to vicariously feel the pleasure of the characters when they are angry or sad (p. 102). But I am not convinced that it is correct to say of the victims in horror fictions that they can feel pleasure in the state they are in. Perhaps some examples of anger and sadness have pleasurable dimensions. But surely not all the emotional states of fictional characters have such a dimension—surely, for example, horror does not. See John Moreall, "Enjoying Negative Emotions in Fiction," in *Philosophy and Literature*, vol. 9, no. 1 (April 1985).

7 If I am statistically wrong about the pervasiveness of disclosure narration in the genre, then I would probably want to rename the second part of my view *the special theory* of the appeal of horror. For I think the account of the appeal of disclosure narration offered above is right for that "special" group of horror narratives even if that group does not represent the most common formation in the genre. Needless to say, however, at present, I still am of the opinion that the drama of disclosure—in the ways discussed earlier in the book—is the most commonly practiced form in the genre.

8 Fredric Jameson, "Magical Narratives: Romance as Genre," *New Literary History*, 7, 1 (Autumn 1975), pp. 133–63.

9 Some readers may be surprised that I have not reviewed the possibility of some sort of catharsis explanation—after the fashion often attributed to Aristotle's analysis of

tragedy—of the pleasures of horror. Such an approach sees the aesthetic pleasure of distressful representations to be a matter of having our negative emotions relieved. Stated one way, this kind of theory is quite absurd. The pleasure in a given genre is located in getting rid of certain negative feelings that we have. But we only have these feelings because a given instance of the genre has engendered the relevant displeasure in us in the first place. And this hardly makes the interest we have in the works in the genre plausible. For it would make no sense for me to put my hand in a vise simply for the pleasure of having my pain relieved when the vise is loosened.

Of course, a catharsis theorist might avoid this attempted refutation by analogy by claiming that the negative emotions relieved are not those engendered by the fiction itself but rather are negative emotions that have built up over the course of everyday life. The cathartic effect, then, would be the evacuation of these pent-up emotions. But if this is the way that catharsis is thought of, then it will clearly have no application to art-horror. For horror of the sort found in horror fictions has no correlate in ordinary life and, therefore, cannot be pent-up in the course of everyday events. This is entailed by the fact that we don't encounter monsters in everyday life; so we are not accumulating the requisite sort of negative emotion to be relieved upon attending to horror fictions. This indicates that catharsis cannot possibly be the correct model for art-horror; whether it is relevant to the discussion of other negative, aesthetic emotions is an issue beyond the scope of this book.

Why horror?

3

The peculiar pleasures of a popular genre

ANDREW TUDOR

[. . .]

Horror, especially on film or video, provokes strong responses. Self-appointed moral guardians are apt to condemn the genre sight unseen, while media coverage routinely scapegoats 'video nasties' in much publicized cases of violence and murder. Critics otherwise benevolently disposed towards popular culture often view horror as the lowest of the low, and even liberal gentlefolk are suspicious about the motives and character failings of its consumers. Are they sick? Are they disturbed people indulging nasty, perverse desires? Or have they merely become so jaded as to be addicted to ever-increasing doses of violent excess? What such responses reflect, of course, is the bewilderment and affront that non-consumers feel when faced with such a singular taste. For, as Brophy (1986: 5) suggests in an illuminating if sweeping generalization, the

> gratification of the contemporary Horror film is based upon tension, fear, anxiety, sadism and masochism – a disposition that is overall both tasteless and morbid. The pleasure of the text is, in fact, getting the shit scared out of you – and loving it; an exchange mediated by adrenalin.

What 'normal' person is going to indulge in preoccupations like that?

The fascination and the puzzle is precisely that so many apparently quite normal people do appear to relish such experiences. Though we lack reliable data on the audiences for different forms of horror, no observer would deny that horror, literary and audio-visual, has proved attractive throughout the modern era and has been particularly prominent in the popular culture of the past two decades. So what *is* its appeal? Although scholars of different disciplinary persuasions have recently researched the genre at some length (see, for example, Carroll, 1990; Clover, 1992; Crane, 1994; Creed, 1993; Dika, 1990; Grixti, 1989; Jancovich, 1992; Tudor, 1989; Twitchell, 1985) none of them, however instructive in other respects, provides an entirely satisfactory answer to that question. In part the problem is empirical. These studies are unable to marshal any more than anecdotal evidence as to the composition and preferences of horror audiences and so are forced to build their arguments on what may be ill-founded speculations. However, this is by no means the only source of difficulty. A satisfactory answer is also hard to come by because we lack clarity and agreement on a satisfactory way of posing the explanatory question in the first place. When we ask 'why horror?', precisely what we are asking is far from clear.

Even at its simplest the question has two distinct aspects, involving either or both of 'what is it about people who like horror?' and 'what is it about horror that people like?'. In the former, the main focus is on the distinctive characteristics of people (who like horror) and, though it often carries overtones to the effect that liking horror is a bit peculiar, it is in principle no different to asking what kind of people like musicals, thrillers or weepies. In effect, it leaves the question of what actually constitutes horror (or musicals or thrillers or weepies) to consumers themselves. They are seen as a self-selected group by virtue of their conjoint taste, and analysts seeking explanations suppose, therefore, that this group must share some distinguishable characteristic which underlies their singular predisposition.

In practice, however, many explanations of this kind crucially fail to discriminate consumers from non-consumers. Take, for example, the familiar 'beast within' approaches that Grixti (1989) has so cogently documented. He traces their expression in the views of such popular horror writers as James Herbert and Stephen King as well as in those academic perspectives which invoke catharsis as a key mechanism or claim that horror appeals to deep-seated, psychoanalytically intelligible repressed desires. Underlying such arguments, he says, is the belief 'that human beings are rotten at the core' (Grixti, 1989: 86), whether by nature or nurture, and that horror resonates with this feature of the human condition. The genre serves as a channel releasing the bestiality concealed within its users. If the model is that of catharsis, then the process is deemed to be beneficial: a safety valve. If the model is one of articulation and legitimation, then the genre is conceived to encourage consumers in their own horrific behaviour. Either way, the attraction of horror derives from its appeal to the 'beast' concealed within the superficially civilized human.

Whatever virtues and failings may be apparent in the detail of such arguments, they face an obvious problem as answers to the 'why horror?' question. 'Beast within' diagnoses are generally claims applicable to all human beings – to be human, they suggest, is to contain the beast, whatever its specific causation. So it still remains to explain why in some cases this leads to a liking for horror, yet in others it does not. If human beings have evolved in such a way as to control and constrain their animal nature, or if their infant experience leads to the repression of, say, incestuous desires, such characteristics cannot be used to explain the appeal of horror without supplementary hypotheses enabling us to distinguish consumers of horror from non-consumers. We may indeed like horror because it appeals to our unreconstructed animal nature – but if so, some of us must be more unreconstructed than others. And that simply reposes the question, though now in terms of the differential characteristics of the horror audience. Thus, even if 'beast within' arguments are *prima facie* plausible, they do not really answer 'what is it about people who like horror?' That requires a different kind of explanation.

Those addressing the second version of 'why horror?' – 'what is it about horror that people like?' – also seek general explanations. They suppose that there is something quite distinctive about the appeal of horror, that this appeal requires special explanation, and that an adequate explanation will encompass the full range of horror forms. They ask, in effect, what is it that people-in-general like about horror-in-general. Of course, they fully recognize that, popular though it may be, horror is not popular with everybody. The universality of their approach lies in the attempt to distinguish what it is about horror, as opposed to other forms of fiction, which appeals to those who consume it, supposing in the process that horror-in-general presents special problems of explanation over and above our customary accounts of the appeal of this or that fictional form. In a way, that is, they accept the common-sense view with which I began this discussion, that there is something rather peculiar about enjoying horror, and it is this peculiarity which requires special explanations distinguishing horror's appeal from that of other forms of fiction.

In practice, of course, most commentators interweave claims based upon interpretations of what is distinctive about horror texts with claims about key features of the horror audience, even if, as we shall see, they weight the two elements differently. Quite how they do so depends on the substance of the theoretical perspectives that they bring to bear, and in this context there is an important difference of emphasis between those approaches which take their inspiration from the psychoanalytic tradition and those which do not.

[. . .]

One source of confusion here is that those seeking explanations of horror's appeal routinely adopt a nominalist approach to defining the genre, identifying by fiat its allegedly universal distinguishing characteristics. In so doing, they commit what might be termed the fallacy of generic concreteness. But genres are not fixed nor are they only bodies of textual material. They are composed as much of the beliefs, commitments and social practices of their audiences as by texts, better understood as particular 'sub-cultures of taste' than as autonomous assemblies of cultural artefacts. Accordingly, it is only possible to speak of the appeal of a genre in a particular socio-temporal context. Genres change over time and sustain differently constructed audiences. And in as much as audiences are composed of active agents they can and do conceive genres variably, taking divergent pleasures from them. In such circumstances pursuit of a truly universal explanation is misguided. We can only seek to explore the *particular* patterns of causation of a genre's popularity, encompassing thereby the network of interacting factors which mould genre activity. Non-psychoanalytic attempts at general explanation such as Carroll's, therefore, are likely to dissolve into a series of particular explanations relating to specific textual features, mutable audiences, different historical periods and distinctive social contexts. And psychoanalytic models, arguably already excessively reductive, will be particularly misleading, conceptually inclined to neglect the variability of audience responses in the name of spurious generality.

Why horror?

What, then, would count as a satisfactory way of posing the 'why horror' question? To confront this topic it is first necessary to question the presumed homogeneity of horror. After all, if horror fans are asked about the nature of their enjoyment of the genre, their answers vary in scope and character. Many such responses relate to narrative devices, to the fascination of not knowing what is going to happen next and to the ambivalently pleasurable tension which attends that uncertainty. Such features, of course, are not specific to horror, though the genre may invest them with particular significance and convey them with its own distinctive stylistic flourishes. The tension promoted by horror movies, for instance, is more likely to produce physically manifest responses. Hiding one's eyes, jumping at moments of shock, holding one's breath, giving vent to nervous laughter, all are apparent in the behaviour of horror audiences and are invoked by them as significant indicators of a good movie. Indeed, collective display of such 'symptoms' is part of the process through which a pleasurable horror movie experience is *socially* constructed, an essential aspect of the occasion's generic character. Youthful audiences learn to comport themselves thus, to take pleasure in witnessing and exhibiting appropriate responses. But sources of pleasure are also much broader, and general narrative qualities – a 'good story', characters for whom one can feel concern, verisimilitude, striking settings, and so on – can be as important to audiences here as anywhere else.

Along with narrative tension, which is an expectation audiences have of every kind of horror movie, horror fans also clearly expect monstrosity, though in quite what form is open to question. The genre encompasses everything from monsters present only by suggestion or inference through to graphic portrayals of monstrous creatures and the excesses of their depredations, while audience responses run the gamut from repulsion through ambivalent fascination and on to self-conscious, knowing humour. This variation is why, *pace* Carroll, the fascination of monsters cannot be taken in and of itself as the defining feature of the genre's appeal since – as audiences themselves are eminently aware – monstrosity can be made pleasurable in diverse ways. Indeed, precisely the same representation of a monster might be found frightening, repulsive, ludicrous, pitiful or laughable by audiences in different social circumstances and at different times. Who now is terrified by Bela Lugosi? Who has not witnessed the fragile verisimilitude of a horror movie undermined by a volubly sceptical audience? Expectation of monstrosity, then, is a very general expectation: it is its specific form which needs examination as an aspect of the diverse pleasures that the genre affords. What kind of monstrous threat appeals to whom, when and where does it do so, and why?

There are a number of such particularistic accounts in the literature. However, since by their very nature they neither advance general explanations of the appeal of horror nor insist on the explanatory homogeneity of horror fans, they are not easily amenable to brief summary. It is true that they often coincide in resisting prevailing inclinations to analyse horror in terms of its psychological or psychoanalytic significance, attending instead to the shared social experience of horror consumers. But quite which aspect of that social context provides their major focus varies from case to case. Perhaps the easiest way to convey the character of such approaches is to describe some of the different levels of analysis at which their explanations may be posed. Here I shall consider three such 'levels', though it should be borne in mind that these distinctions are made for analytical and expository convenience only and that particular studies can and do range up and down the scale. Given that qualification, then, first there are those accounts operating at a relatively low level of abstraction which lay claim to a direct thematic link between specific features of the genre and aspects of agents' everyday social experience. Second, there are those which focus upon genre developments apparent only in the longer term (an increase in explicit violence, say, or a growing emphasis on sexuality), seeking to demonstrate their congruence with more macroscopic currents of social change. And lastly there are arguments about the relation between whole horror discourses and the typical structures of social interaction which they presuppose and to which they contribute. Let me expand a little on each of these with a view to identifying their common features.

The simplest and most frequent claims (though by no means the least important) are those which focus on clearly apparent thematic features of the horror films of particular periods, treating them as articulations of the felt social concerns of the time. Thus, for example, it is common to examine 1950s sf-horror in terms of an interlinked cluster of themes, including the threat of alien invasion, the risks of nuclear power, and the roles of science and scientists. Typically, it is argued that such films articulate distinctive American fears (xenophobia, anti-communism, anxiety about technocracy and mass society, etc.) apparent in both the public discourse and private lives of the period. Biskind (1983: 4), for example, offers a portrait of 'an era of conflict and contradiction, an era in which a complex set of ideologies contended for public allegiance', examining horror movies, therefore, in the context of the wider range of film output of the 1950s in which these 'warring ideologies' find expression. Jancovich (1992: 62) is rather more specific, identifying the implementation of 'corporate or "Fordist" modes of social organization' in the post-war period as central to growing fears about a system so profoundly dependent upon scientific-technical rationality. For him, then, alien invasion movies are not simply reflections of anti-communist fears; they are also responses to a growing anxiety about technocratic regulation of American social life. What these and similar approaches share, however, is an assumption that texts appeal to their audiences in part because they express in accessible and entertaining popular cultural terms the characteristic fears of their time. Such an ideographic strategy can, of course, be applied to any widely recognized thematic emphasis in genre history, only provided that appropriate detailed links can be made.

The connection between text and context need not be limited to discrete themes, of course, and affinities may be proposed at higher levels of abstraction and in relation to more macroscopic social change. This moves us into the realm of the second 'level' distinguished above. Here, for example, both Carroll (1990: 206–14) and Tudor (1995) have focused on categorial transgression in horror. The idea that horror texts trade centrally in categorial transgressions is both familiar and instructive, often playing a role in putative general explanations of horror's appeal (cf. Kristeva (1982) for a psychoanalytic version and Carroll (1990) for an alternative). However, it is also possible to focus more specifically upon the *changing* character of transgression in horror, relating such shifts to larger social and cultural currents. Hence the argument that the distinctive boundary-breaching characteristics of modern, post-1970s horror – especially those found in so-called 'body horror' – are intimately related to aspects of 'postmodern' social experience. Carroll (1990: 210) even goes so far as to claim that 'the contemporary horror genre is the exoteric expression of the same feelings that are expressed in the esoteric discussions of the intelligentsia with respect to post-modernism', capturing in popular cultural terms the latter's distinctive conceptual and moral relativism. In effect, the characteristic ambiguity and fluidity of bodily boundaries in modern horror is seen to be substantially different to the typical boundary-breaching of earlier periods, because it gives expression to postmodern 'experience[s] of social fragmentation and to the constantly threatening confrontation between embattled "selves" and the risky and unreliable world that they inhabit' (Tudor, 1995: 40). In a somewhat different way, such an association is also to be found in Dika's (1990) attempt to relate the 'deep structure' of the stalker film to recent political and cultural change, and in Jancovich's (1992: 112–17) discussion of 'the crisis of identity' in the context of body horror.

Such work begins to spill over onto a yet more general level, that at which whole systems of horror discourse form the focus for analysis. As with all genres, the systems of codes and conventions that constitute horror change over time in major as well as minor ways, changing also the terms in which horror appeals to its users. At this level, then, the analytic task is to identify the patterns of such discursive change and relate them to their socio-cultural environments. Elsewhere (Tudor, 1989; 1995) I have made one such attempt, arguing that the macroscopic dynamics of change in horror can best be understood in relation to two distinctive horror discourses (the 'secure' and the 'paranoid'), each of which is deeply embedded in and dependent upon the typical structures of social interaction of their respective periods of genre dominance. There is no need to repeat the detail of that argument here (for a brief summary see Tudor, 1995: 34–7). Methodologically, however, my strategy is to use the headings 'secure' and 'paranoid' to summarize key oppositions in a wide range of horror codes (expressed in such contrasts as effective expertise vs ineffective expertise, sustainable order vs escalating disorder, external threats vs internal threats, and so on) with a view to asking in what kind of social world would such discourses make sense. Thus, the discourse of paranoid horror, very much a product of the last twenty-five years, presupposes a thoroughly unreliable world. In this respect it is popular and pleasurable because its basic codes correlate with our distinctive experience of fear, risk and instability in modern societies.

In all these cases, whatever their variation in other ways and however little they are directly concerned with horror's attraction, the appeal of particular features of the genre is understood in relation to specified aspects of their socio-historical context. Accordingly, the model that such analyses presuppose about the satisfactions that horror affords its consumers is in some contrast to that proposed in psychoanalytic theories, where emphasis is often on releasing repressed affect or indulging deep-seated sadomasochistic desires. The mechanism of pleasure found here is more active, proposing that social agents recognize in texts features of the everyday world of social experience, transmuted perhaps, but none the less pleasurable in their sense of familiarity and relevance. Thus, the fearfulness inspired by 1950s space-invader movies articulates widespread cold-war fears in fictional form. Or, more elaborately, if late-twentieth-century horror is distinctively 'paranoid', its appeal lies in the fact that such paranoia is perceived by spectators to gel with particular features of modern life. Furthermore, the act of genre-recognition itself is part of the process of making sense of the social world, a source of shared frameworks through which we come to understand, among other things, what is fearful and what it is to be frightened. Hence Grixti's (1989: 164) observation that horror stories are:

> exercises in the discovery and exploration of map-territory relations, in that they provide a safely distanced and stylised means of making sense of and coming to terms with phenomena and potentialities of experience which under normal (i.e. functional) conditions would be found too threatening and disturbing.

Such processes take place at the level of 'practical consciousness' (Giddens, 1984); they are part of the knowledgability of social agents about and within their everyday world. And although this approach does not necessarily exclude the unconscious and repression as a point of departure for at least some of the pleasures of horror, it has the virtue of insisting on the active involvement of people in the consumption and comprehension of their favoured texts.

Broadly, then, two kinds of models have dominated attempts to understand the appeal of horror. On the one hand – and much the more prominent – there are those accounts which seek universal explanations, identifying particular features of horror texts and/or audiences which are said to uniquely capture the genre's appeal. Such approaches are reductive in as much as they 'explain' horror by reference to seemingly immutable characteristics of the genre or its consumers, while the mechanism of appeal that they propose is one predicated upon gratification of pre-established needs. They assume, that is, a social ontology wherein human agents are pre-constituted in key respects: they harbour basic repressions; they are driven by fundamental, bestial needs; their given nature is routinely to take pleasure in transgressive representations. On the other hand, there are those accounts which focus upon particular explanations, refusing the universalizing challenge of 'why horror?' Here the appeal of horror is understood to be a product of the interaction between specific textual features and distinct social circumstances. Their tacit social ontology is one centred on active social agents who, in sustaining practical consciousness of their social and cultural environments, use cultural artefacts as resources in rendering coherent their everyday lives. In this approach the appeal of horror is not seen as need-gratifying in the sense of unconsciously tapping into deep-seated desires; it is more cognitive and constructivist in emphasis. Elements of the fiction resonate, as it were, with features of the social experience of its consumers.

It might be argued, of course, that such particularistic accounts do not offer an explanation at all, that they fail to address the 'why horror?' question in the form with which I began this discussion. And in a sense that is true, for they do assume that, like all popular genres, horror appeals to people for as many reasons as its consumers can find ways of making use of genre products. For some, no doubt, horror may be a source of titillation. For others, a fount of salutary warnings, and for yet others, an occasion for collective hilarity. Some horror fans relish and rely upon the stigma that attaches to such officially undervalued culture. Some experience going to horror movies as an essential element in sustaining individual identity within a distinctive peer-group context. And across cultures, variations multiply and deepen in the context of radically different cultural practices. In these circumstances it is a mistake to seek an explanation of horror's appeal which aspires to universality and which has no recourse to information about the diversity of horror audiences both within and across cultures. Horror fans, after all, are no less active agents than are any other cultural consumers, even if routine prejudice may wish to suggest otherwise. As Crane (1994: 47) observes: 'For a horror film to work, the audience must not only suspend disbelief, they have to *manufacture* particular kinds of belief' (my italics). It is that productive activity which now insistently demands the attention of any student of horror.

Of course, such a concern with active agency confronts us with acute methodological problems. Where, as so often, our focus is historical we have at best only indirect access to agents' conceptions, and much of the time not even that. In such circumstances it is essential to begin genre analysis at the most prosaic of levels, contextualizing genre activity in such a way that we can explore the diverse possibilities that texts make available to differently structured, heterogeneous audiences. Lacking direct evidence of the use that agents made of particular historical forms, we must resort to disciplined speculation, asking in what sorts of social circumstances this material could be made to make sense by its consumers. This kind of 'thought experiment', combined with a full account of the social and cultural contexts in which the genre operates, would generate a potential repertoire of the pleasures and practices available to genre consumers who make their choices from that range. As we have seen in the cases that I have considered, there is a good deal of evidence available to underwrite such analysis, whatever the difficulties of inference and method. But such difficulties are anyway not limited to historical work. Even contemporary material is hardly unproblematic in these respects, where the task of documenting reading practices and assessing diverse cultural competencies would call for a formidable range of cultural, ethnographic and sociological skills on the part of the researcher.

But these are problems which must be confronted. If we really are to understand horror's appeal, and hence its social and cultural significance, we need to set aside the traditionally loaded ways in which 'why horror?' has been asked. For the question should not be 'why horror?' at all. It should be, rather, why do *these* people like *this* horror in *this* place at *this* particular time? And what exactly are the consequences of their constructing their everyday sense of fearfulness and anxiety, their 'landscapes of fear' (Tuan, 1979), out of such distinctive cultural materials?

Acknowledgements

I am grateful to Davey Butler, John Hill, Barry Sandywell and to an anonymous *Cultural Studies* reviewer for their comments on an earlier draft of this paper.

References

Biskind, Peter (1983) *Seeing is Believing: How Hollywood Taught Us to Stop Worrying and Love the Fifties*, London: Pluto Press.

Britton, Andrew, Lippe, Richard, Williams, Tony and Wood, Robin (1979) *American Nightmare: Essays on the Horror Film*, Toronto: Festival of Festivals.

Brophy, Philip (1986) 'Horrality – the textuality of contemporary horror films', *Screen*, 27 (1): 2–13.

Carroll, Noël (1990) *The Philosophy of Horror: or Paradoxes of the Heart*, New York and London: Routledge.

—— (1992a) 'A paradox of the heart: a response to Alex Neill', *Philosophical Studies*, 65: 67–74.

—— (1992b) 'Disgust or fascination: a response to Susan Feagin', *Philosophical Studies*, 65: 85–90.

Clover, Carol (1987) 'Her body, himself: gender in the slasher film', *Representations*, 20: 187–228.

—— (1992) *Men, Women, and Chain Saws: Gender in the Modern Horror Film*, London: BFI Publishing.

Crane, Jonathan Lake (1994) *Terror and Everyday Life: Singular Moments in the History of the Horror Film*, London: Sage.

Creed, Barbara (1986) 'Horror and the monstrous-feminine: an imaginary abjection', *Screen*, 27 (1): 44–70.

—— (1990) 'Review article: Andrew Tudor, *Monsters and Mad Scientists: A Cultural History of the Horror Movie*', *Screen*, 31 (2): 236–42.

—— (1993) *The Monstrous-Feminine: Film, Feminism, Psychoanalysis*, London, New York: Routledge.

Dika, Vera (1990) *Games of Terror:* Halloween, Friday the 13th, *and the Films of the Stalker Cycle*, London and Toronto: Associated University Presses.

Douglas, Mary (1966) *Purity and Danger: An Analysis of Concepts of Pollution and Taboo*, Harmondsworth: Penguin.

Feagin, Susan (1992) 'Monsters, disgust and fascination', *Philosophical Studies*, 65: 75–84.

Freud, Sigmund (1955) [1919] 'The "Uncanny"', in J. Strachey (ed.) *The Standard Edition of the Complete Psychological Works of Sigmund Freud*, London: The Hogarth Press.

Giddens, Anthony (1984) *The Constitution of Society: Outline of the Theory of Structuration*, Cambridge: Polity Press.

Grixti, Joseph (1989) *Terrors of Uncertainty: The Cultural Contexts of Horror Fiction*, London and New York: Routledge.

Jancovich, Mark (1992) *Horror*, London: B. T. Batsford.

Kristeva, Julia (1982) *Powers of Horror: An Essay on Abjection*, New York: Columbia University Press.

Metz, Christian (1982) *Psychoanalysis and Cinema: The Imaginary Signifier*, London: Macmillan.

Mulvey, Laura (1975) 'Visual pleasure and narrative cinema', *Screen*, 10(3): 6–18.

Neill, Alex (1992) 'On a paradox of the heart', *Philosophical Studies*, 65: 53–65.

Tuan, Yi-fu (1979) *Landscapes of Fear*, Oxford: Basil Blackwell.

Tudor, Andrew (1989) *Monsters and Mad Scientists: A Cultural History of the Horror Movie*, Oxford and Cambridge, Mass.: Basil Blackwell.

—— (1995) 'Unruly bodies, unquiet minds', *Body and Society*, 1 (1): 25–41.

Twitchell, James (1985) *Dreadful Pleasures: An Anatomy of Modern Horror*, New York and Oxford: Oxford University Press.

PART TWO

GENDER, SEXUALITY AND THE HORROR FILM

Introduction

If, as we saw in Part I, many people turned to psychoanalysis in order to deal with the fantastical aspects of the horror genre, but the use of psychoanalysis also had other motivations and effects. On the one hand, as we saw with Wood, it encouraged critics to concentrate on issues of gender and sexuality in their analysis of horror but, on the other, it was also legitimated by a long-running association between horror and these issues, an association that dates back as least as far as the Gothic novels of the late eighteenth and early nineteenth centuries. For example, it has been repeatedly claimed that horror involves not only violence against women, but violence that is itself highly sexualized (Jancovich, 1992).

Although such claims were in no way exclusively feminist in nature, these concerns received particular attention in the 1970s and 1980s, which saw not only a particularly prominent resurgence of the horror genre, but also the emergence of a psychoanalytically informed feminist film theory.

Chapter 4 is a particularly important example of this moment, and here Linda Williams draws on feminist theories of the gaze to claim not only that horror addresses a male spectator but that it is founded on the subjugation of women. In patriarchal culture (or a culture defined by male domination), women are defined not only as inferior to men, but as Other, as different, deviant and even monstrous. These relations have effects on the visual organization of film in general so that the act of looking is defined as both masculine and desiring. The gaze is associated with activity and control, and women are therefore either refused the active gaze or punished for exercising it.

In the specific case of the horror film, Williams argues not only that the woman is effectively denied the gaze but that the images with which she is presented (both as character within the film and as viewer in the audience) provide her with a distorted image of herself. In other words, she is made to bear strong associations with the monster, who, like her, is defined by its difference from the masculine norm. As Williams claims, when the woman looks at the monster, she 'recognizes their similar status within patriarchal structures of seeing' (p. 62).

In this way, it is argued, woman's difference from the masculine norm is not only defined as monstrous, but is also punished. For Williams, the problem is not simply that her difference implies her inferiority, but rather that it may actually imply the opposite. Both the woman and the monster therefore prove deeply 'threatening to male power' and must be 'violently punished' (p. 65). If women avert their eyes from horror films, it is because there is no position from which they can look that is not 'simultaneous with [their] own victimization' (Doane quoted in Williams, p. 61).

A similar position is offered in Chapter 5, in which Barbara Creed also claims that the horror movie associates the woman with the monster through their difference from the male norm, but, like Carroll, she also associated the monster with category violation. It is associated with all that is marginal, that is both of the self and not of the self, all that must be excluded and expelled from the self to provide a clear sense of identity and independence. As Creed puts it:

> The ultimate in abjection is the corpse. The body protects itself from bodily wastes such as shit, blood, urine and pus by ejecting these substances just as it expels food that, for whatever reason, the subject finds loathsome. The body extricates itself from them and from the place where they fall, so that it might continue to live.
>
> (p. 70)

However, the fear of the abject is not just human, but specifically tied to masculinity within the horror film.

In horror, Creed claims, the abject is coded as feminine and the narrative is a ritual through which the male subject reproduces itself through the renunciation and expulsion of the feminine. For Creed, the male subject is formed through its separation from, and rejection of, the initially close and powerful relationship with the mother and, in the horror film, this process of separation and rejection is repeated in symbolic form through the violent eradication of the abject monster.

Both Williams and Creed, however, rely on fairly fixed notions of gendered identity and particularly on the viewing positions of the male spectator. Indeed, both writers assume, as did most of their contemporaries, that cross-gender identification was not simply unusual but virtually impossible, at least for male viewers. The assumption was that males could really identify only with the male hero and affirm their superiority to women through their objectification.

Clover, however, demonstrates that not only is cross-gender identification possible but it is central to the slasher movie, which featured a female rather than a male hero. Thus, while other accounts have seen horror films as clear stories of violence against women, Clover argues that 'the relation between the sexes in slasher films' (Chapter 6, p. 77) is nowhere near as clear these accounts would have us believe.

Indeed, while Williams claimed that 'the woman is punished for looking in both the classic horror film and in the more recent "psychopathic" forms of the genre' (Chapter 4, p. 62), Clover argues that 'the female exercise of scopic control results not in her annihilation, in the manner of classic cinema, but in her triumph; indeed, her triumph *depends* on her assumption of the gaze' (p. 84).

Unfortunately, while this could be seen as radically revising our understanding of the sexual politics of both the slasher movie and of cinema more generally, Clover's argument ends up reaffirming many of the established assumptions about the sexual politics of the genre and of its audience. Once again, the audience is presumed to be male, and the genre is seen to have little to offer the female spectator, despite Clover's admission that she is an avid consumer of these films. Furthermore, while the genre is now seen to appeal to primarily masochistic rather than sadistic pleasures, these are still seen basically to affirm masculinity.

In short, the presence of the female hero is seen as a way of providing the male with a point of masochistic identification, while also allowing its disavowal. Male viewers can take pleasure in a masochistic identification while still telling themselves that victimhood is synonymous with femininity. Furthermore, as the narrative progresses, the female hero becomes masculinized while the monster is effectively feminized and, in this way, male viewers are able to engage in masochistic fantasy while also reaffirming their own sense of superiority and power.

One of the problems with all these accounts, however, is that their discussions of gender are remorselessly heterosexual in their configuration. While they criticize the system for its 'compulsory heterosexuality', they equate gender and sexuality too directly. As a result, they give little sense of either the ways in which homosexuality is dealt with in these films or how they might operate in relation to gay and lesbian viewers.

However, from the outset horror has had a long history of being produced and consumed by gays and lesbians (see Dyer, 1988). Rather than straightforwardly affirming heterosexual relations, horror has been obsessed with 'perverse' desires that threaten 'normal' sexual relations. Chapter 7, by Harry M. Benshoff, which is taken from the introduction to his book *Monsters in the Closet*, presents a queer take on the genre. Here 'queer' does not imply simply gay or lesbian but rather suggests that all such sexual identities are in fact social constructions that are used to order and regulate desires that are far more fluid and perverse than the identities 'straight', 'gay' or 'lesbian'. Nonetheless, he does show the ways in which the horror film can be seen as articulating concerns about homosexuality. In other words, while some films might overtly identify specific characters as gay or lesbian, it is more usual for these issues to be dealt with covertly through allusion and connotation. Nor is the handling of these issues straightforward; it has a long and contradictory history.

When the woman looks

4

LINDA WILLIAMS

Whenever the movie screen holds a particularly effective image of terror, little boys and grown men make it a point of honor to look, while little girls and grown women cover their eyes or hide behind the shoulders of their dates. There are excellent reasons for this refusal of the woman to look, not the least of which is that she is often asked to bear witness to her own powerlessness in the face of rape, mutilation and murder. Another excellent reason for the refusal to look is the fact that women are given so little to identify with on the screen. Laura Mulvey's extremely influential article on visual pleasure in narrative cinema has best defined this problem in terms of a dominant male look at the woman that leaves no place for the woman's own pleasure in seeing: she exists only to be looked at.[1]

Like the female spectator, the female protagonist often fails to look, to return the gaze of the male who desires her. In the classical narrative cinema, to see is to desire. It comes as no surprise, then, that many of the "good girl" heroines of the silent screen were often figuratively, or even literally, blind.[2] Blindness in this context signifies a perfect absence of desire, allowing the look of the male protagonist to regard the woman at the requisite safe distance necessary to the voyeur's pleasure, with no danger that she will return that look and in so doing express desires of her own. The relay of looks within the film thus duplicates the voyeuristic pleasure of the cinematic apparatus itself—a pleasure that Christian Metz and Laura Mulvey have suggested to be one of the primary pleasures of film viewing: the impression of looking in on a private world unaware of the spectator's own existence.[3]

[. . .]

The bold, smoldering dark eyes of the silent screen vamp offer an obvious example of a powerful female look.[4] But the dubious moral status of such heroines, and the fact that they must be punished in the end, undermine the legitimacy and authentic subjectivity of this look, frequently turning it into a mere parody of the male look.[5] More instructive are those moments when the "good girl" heroines are granted the power of the look, whether in the woman's film, as discussed by Mary Ann Doane in this volume,[6] or in the horror film as discussed below. In both cases, as Doane suggests, "the woman's exercise of an active investigating gaze can only be simultaneous with her own victimization."[7] The woman's gaze is punished, in other words, by narrative processes that transform curiosity and desire into masochistic fantasy.

The horror film offers a particularly interesting example of this punishment in the woman's terrified look at the horrible body of the monster. In what follows I will examine the various ways the woman is punished for looking in both the classic horror film and in the more recent "psychopathic" forms of the genre. I hope to reveal not only the process of punishment but a surprising (and at times subversive) affinity between monster and woman, the sense in which her look at the monster recognizes their similar status within patriarchal structures of seeing.

In F. W. Murnau's *Nosferatu* (1922), for example, Nina's ambiguous vigil by the sea is finally rewarded, not by the sight of her returning husband who arrives by land in a carriage, but by the vampire's ship towards which a wide-eyed Nina in a trance-like state reaches out her arms.[8] Later, from the windows of facing houses, Nina and the vampire stare at one another until she finally opens the window. When the vampire's shadow approaches, she again stares at him in wide-eyed terror until he attacks.

There are several initial distinctions to be made between what I have characterized above as the desiring look of the male-voyeur-subject and the woman's look of horror typified by Nina's trance-like fascination. First, Nina's look at the vampire fails to maintain the distance between observer and observed so essential to the "pleasure" of the voyeur. For where the (male) voyeur's properly distanced look safely masters the potential threat of the (female) body it views, the woman's look of horror paralyzes her in such a way that distance is overcome; the monster or the freak's own spectacular appearance holds her originally active, curious look in a trance-like passivity that allows him to master her through *her* look. At the same time, this look momentarily shifts the iconic center of the spectacle away from the woman to the monster.

Rupert Julian's 1925 version of *The Phantom of the Opera*, starring Lon Chaney and Mary Philbin, offers another classic example of the woman's look in the horror film. Christine, an aspiring young opera singer, is seduced by the voice of the Phantom speaking to her through the walls of her dressing room at the Paris Opera. She follows "her master's voice" by stepping through the mirror of her dressing room. Her first glimpse of the masked Phantom occurs as she turns to respond to the touch of his hand on her shoulder. Thus her look occurs *after* the film audience has had its own chance to see him—they are framed in a two-shot that has him standing slightly behind her; only when she turns does she see his masked face.

Similarly, in the famous unmasking scene, Christine first thrills to the sound of the organ music the Phantom plays ("Don Juan Triumphant"), then sneaks up behind him and hesitates several times before finally pulling the string that will drop his mask. Since both he and Christine face the camera in a two-shot (with Christine situated behind him) we again see the Phantom's face, this time unmasked, before Christine does. The audience thus receives the first shock of the horror even while it can still see the curiosity and desire *to see* on Christine's face.[9]

Everything conspires here to condemn the desire and curiosity of the woman's look. Our prior knowledge of what she will see encourages us to judge her look as a violation of the Phantom's privacy. Her unmasking of his face reveals the very wounds, the very lack, that the Phantom had hoped her blind love would heal. It is as if she has become responsible for the horror that her look reveals, and is punished by not being allowed the safe distance that ensures the voyeur's pleasure of looking. "Feast your eyes, glut your soul, on my accursed ugliness!" cries the Phantom as he holds her face up close to his.

When the men in this film look at the Phantom, the audience first sees the man looking, then adopts his point of view to see what he sees. The audience's belated adoption of the woman's point of view undermines the usual audience identification and sympathy with the look of the cinematic character. But it may also permit a different form of identification and sympathy to take place, not between the audience and the character who looks, but between the two objects of the cinematic spectacle who encounter one another in this look—the woman and the monster.

In *The Phantom of the Opera* Christine walks through her mirror to encounter a monster whose face lacks the flesh to cover its features. Lon Chaney's incarnation of the Phantom's nose, for example, gives the effect of two large holes; the lips fail to cover a gaping mouth. Early in the film women dancers from the corps de ballet argue excitedly about his nose: "He had no nose!" "Yes he did, it was enormous!" The terms of the argument suggest that the monster's body is perceived as freakish in its possession of too much or too little. Either the monster is symbolically castrated, pathetically lacking what Christine's handsome lover Raoul possesses ("He had no nose!"), or he is overly endowed and potent ("Yes he did, it was enormous!"). Yet it is a truism of the horror genre that sexual interest resides most often in the monster and not the bland ostensible heroes like Raoul who often prove powerless at the crucial moment. (*The Phantom of the Opera* is no exception. Raoul passes out when most needed and Christine's rescue is accomplished by her accidental fall from the Phantom's racing carriage.)

Clearly the monster's power is one of sexual difference from the normal male. In this difference he is remarkably like the woman in the eyes of the traumatized male: a biological freak with impossible and threatening appetites that suggest a frightening potency precisely where the normal male would perceive a lack. In fact, the Phantom's last act of the film is to restage the drama of the lack he represents to others. Cornered by a crowd more bestial than he has ever been, a crowd that wants to tear him apart, the Phantom pulls back his hand as if threatening to detonate an explosive device. The crowd freezes, the Phantom laughs and opens his hand to reveal that it contains . . . nothing at all.

It is this absence, this nothing at all so dramatically brandished by the Phantom, that haunts a great many horror films and often seems the most effective element of their horror. It may very well be, then, that the power and potency of the monster body in many classic horror films—*Nosferatu*, *The Phantom of the Opera*, *Vampyr*, *Dracula*, *Freaks*, *Dr. Jekyll and Mr. Hyde*, *King Kong*, *Beauty and the Beast*—should not be interpreted as an eruption of the normally repressed animal sexuality of the civilized male (the monster as double for the male viewer and characters in the film), but as the feared power and potency of a different kind of sexuality (the monster as double for the women).

As we have seen, one result of this equation seems to be the difference between the look of horror of the man and of the woman. The male look expresses conventional fear at that which differs from itself. The female look—a look given preeminent position in the horror film—shares the male fear of the monster's freakishness, but also recognizes the sense in which this freakishness is similar to her own difference. For she too has been constituted as an exhibitionist-object by the desiring look of the male. There is not that much difference between an object of desire and an object of horror as far as the male look is concerned. (In one brand of horror film this difference may simply lie in the age of its female stars. The Bette Davises and the Joan Crawfords considered too old to continue as spectacle-objects nevertheless persevere as horror objects in films like *Whatever Happened to Baby Jane?* and *Hush . . . Hush, Sweet Charlotte*.) The strange sympathy and affinity that often develops between the monster and the girl may thus be less an expression of sexual desire (as in *King Kong*, *Beauty and the Beast*) and more a flash of sympathetic identification.

In Carson McCullers' *The Member of the Wedding*, Frankie fears that the carnival freaks look at her differently, secretly connecting their eyes with hers, saying with their look "We know you. We are you!"[10] Similarly, in *The Phantom of the Opera*, when Christine walks through a mirror that ceases to reflect her, it could very well be that she does so because she knows she will encounter a truer mirror in the freak of the Phantom on the other side. In other words, in the rare instance when the cinema permits the woman's look, she not only sees a monster, she sees a monster that offers a distorted reflection of her own image. The monster is thus a particularly insidious form of the many mirrors patriarchal structures of seeing hold up to the woman. But there are many kinds of mirrors; and in this case it may be useful to make a distinction between beauty and the beast in the horror film.

Laura Mulvey has shown that the male look at the woman in the cinema involves two forms of mastery over the threat of castration posed by her "lack" of a penis: a sadistic voyeurism which punishes or endangers the woman through the agency of an active and powerful male character; and fetishistic over-valuation, which masters the threat of castration by investing the woman's body with an excess of aesthetic perfection.[11]

Stephen Heath, summarizing the unspoken other side of Mulvey's formulation, suggests that the woman's look can only function to entrap her further within these patriarchal structures of seeing:

> If the woman looks, the spectacle provokes, castration is in the air, the Medusa's head is not far off; thus, she must not look, is absorbed herself on the side of the seen, seeing herself seeing herself, Lacan's femininity.[12]

In other words, her look even here becomes a form of not seeing anything more than the castration she so exclusively represents for the male.

If this were so, then what the woman "sees" would only be the mutilation of her own body displaced onto that of the monster. The destruction of the monster that concludes so many horror films could therefore be interpreted as yet another way of disavowing and mastering the castration her body represents. But here I think it may be helpful to introduce a distinction into Mulvey's, Heath's, and ultimately Freud's, notion of the supposed "mutilation" of the "castrated" woman that may clarify the precise meaning of the woman's encounter with a horror version of her own body.

A key moment in many horror films occurs when the monster displaces the woman as site of the spectacle. In *King Kong*, Kong is literally placed on stage to "perform" before awed and fearful audiences. In *The Phantom of the Opera*, the Phantom makes a dramatic, show-stopping entrance at the Masked Ball as the Masque of the Red Death, wearing a mask modeled on the absences of his own face beneath. Count Dracula, in both the Murnau and the Browning versions, makes similarly show-stopping performances. Tod Browning's *Freaks* begins and ends with the side-show display of the woman who has been transformed by the freaks into part bird, part woman. These spectacular moments displaying the freakish difference of the monster's body elicit reactions of fear and awe in audiences that can be compared to the Freudian hypothesis of the reaction of the male child in his first encounter with the "mutilated" body of his mother.

In her essay, "Pornography and the Dread of Women," Susan Lurie offers a significant challenge to the traditional Freudian notion that the sight of the mother's body suggests to the male child that she has herself undergone castration. According to Lurie, the real trauma for the young boy is not that the mother is castrated but that she *isn't*: she is obviously *not* mutilated the way he would be if his penis were taken from him. The notion of the woman as a castrated version of a man is, according to Lurie, a comforting, wishful fantasy intended to combat the child's imagined dread of what his mother's very real power could do to him. This protective fantasy is aimed at convincing himself that "women are what men would be if they had no penises—bereft of sexuality, helpless, incapable."[13]

I suggest that the monster in the horror film is feared by the "normal" males of such films in ways very similar to Lurie's notion of the male child's fear of this mother's power-in-difference. For, looked at from the woman's perspective, the monster is not so much lacking as he is powerful in a different way. The vampire film offers a clear example of the threat this different form of sexuality represents to the male. The vampiric act of sucking blood, sapping the life fluid of a victim so that the victim in turn becomes a vampire, is similar to the female role of milking the sperm of the male during intercourse.[14] What the vampire seems to represent then is a sexual power whose threat lies in its difference from a phallic "norm." The vampire's power to make its victim resemble itself is a very real mutilation of the once human victim (teeth marks, blood loss), but the vampire itself, like the mother in Lurie's formulation, is not perceived as mutilated, just different.

Thus what is feared in the monster (whether vampire or simply a creature whose difference gives him power over others) is similar to what Lurie says is feared in the mother: not her own mutilation, but the power to mutilate and transform the vulnerable male. The vampire's insatiable need for blood seems a particularly apt analogue for what must seem to the man to be an insatiable sexual appetite—yet another threat to his potency. So there is a sense in which the woman's look at the monster is more than simply a punishment for looking, or a narcissistic fascination with the distortion of her own image in the mirror that patriarchy holds up to her; it is also a recognition of their similar status as potent threats to a vulnerable male power. This would help explain the often vindictive destruction of the monster in the horror film and the fact that this destruction generates the frequent sympathy of the women characters, who seem to sense the extent to which the monster's death is an exorcism of the power of their own sexuality. It also helps to explain the conventional weakness of the male heroes of so many horror films (e.g., David Manners in *Dracula*, Colin Clive in *Frankenstein*) and the extreme excitement and surplus danger when the monster and the woman get together.

Thus I suggest that, in the classic horror film, the woman's look at the monster offers at least a potentially subversive recognition of the power and potency of a non-phallic sexuality. Precisely because this look is so threatening to male power, it is violently punished.

[. . .]

Notes

1 Laura Mulvey, "Visual Pleasure and Narrative Cinema," *Screen*, vol. 16, no. 3 (Autumn 1975), pp. 6–18. See also John Berger's description of the different "social presence" of the woman in western painting and advertisement, in *Ways of Seeing* (London: Penguin Books, 1978), pp. 46–47. Berger argues that where the man in such works simply "surveys" the woman before acting towards her, the woman is split into a "surveyor" and a "surveyed." In other words, she is constantly aware of being looked at, even as she herself looks. Mary Ann

Doane similarly notes the woman's status as spectacle rather than spectator and goes on to make a useful distinction between primary and secondary identifications within these structures of seeing in "Misrecognition and Identity," *Ciné-Tracts*, vol. 3, no. 3 (Fall 1980), pp. 25–31.

2 The pathetic blind heroine is a cliché of melodrama from D. W. Griffith's *Orphans of the Storm* to Chaplin's *City Lights* to Guy Green's *A Patch of Blue*.

3 Mulvey, "Visual Pleasure." Also Christian Metz, "The Imaginary Signifier," *Screen*, vol. 16, no. 2 (Summer 1975), pp. 14–76.

4 It could very well be that the tradition of the fair-haired virgin and the dark-haired vamp rests more upon this difference in the lightness or darkness of the eyes than in hair color. The uncanny light eyes of many of Griffith's most affecting heroines—Mae Marsh, Lillian Gish and even his wife Linda Arvidson, who plays Annie Lee—contribute to an effect of innocent blindness in many of his films. Light eyes seem transparent, unfocused, easy to penetrate, incapable of penetration themselves, while dark eyes are quite the reverse.

5 Mae West is, of course, one "master" of such reversals.

6 Mary Ann Doane, "The 'Woman's Film': Possession and Address" see *Re-Vision: Essays in Feminist Film Criticism*, eds Mary Ann Doane, Patricia Mellencamp and Linda Williams, Los Angeles, American Film Institute.

7 Ibid.

8 Miriam White points out that the film's visuals suggest that Nina is really awaiting the Count, not her husband, even though the film's intertitles construe Nina's behavior only in relation to her husband: "Narrative Semantic Deviation: Duck-Rabbit Texts of Weimar Cinema." (Paper delivered at the University of Wisconsin-Milwaukee, Center for Twentieth Century Studies conference on Cinema and Language, March 1979.)

9 I am indebted to Bruce Kawin for pointing out to me the way in which the audience receives the first shock of this look at the Phantom.

10 Leslie Fiedler refers to this passage in *Freaks: Myths and Images of the Secret Self* (New York: Simon and Schuster, 1978), p. 17.

11 Mulvey, pp. 10–16.

12 Stephen Heath, "Difference," *Screen*, vol. 19, no. 3 (Autumn 1978), p. 92.

13 Susan Lurie, "Pornography and the Dread of Woman," in *Take Back the Night*, ed. Laura Lederer (New York: William Morrow, 1980), pp. 159–173. Melanie Klein, in *Psycho-Analysis of Children* (London: Hogarth Press, 1932), has written extensively of the child's terror of being devoured, torn up, and destroyed by the mother, although for Klein these fears derive from a pre-oedipal stage and apply to both male and female infants.

14 According to Stan Brakhage the word "nosferatu" itself means "splashed with milk" in Transylvanian. A Romanian legend tells how a servant woman frightened by Count Dracula spilled a pitcher of milk on him. Brakhage thus suggests that the word connotes a homosexual allusion of "sucking for milk." (*Film Biographies* [Berkeley, CA: Turtle Island, 1977], p. 256.)

Horror and the monstrous-feminine

An imaginary abjection

5

BARBARA CREED

I

Mother's not herself today. – Norman Bates, *Psycho*

All human societies have a conception of the monstrous-feminine, of what it is about woman that is shocking, terrifying, horrific, abject. 'Probably no male human being is spared the terrifying shock of threatened castration at the sight of the female genitals', Freud wrote in his paper, 'Fetishism' in 1927.[1] Joseph Campbell, in his book, *Primitive Mythology*, noted that:

> . . . there is a motif occurring in certain primitive mythologies, as well as in modern surrealist painting and neurotic dream, which is known to folklore as 'the toothed vagina' – the vagina that castrates. And a counterpart, the other way, is the so-called 'phallic mother', a motif perfectly illustrated in the long fingers and nose of the witch.[2]

Classical mythology also was populated with gendered monsters, many of which were female. The Medusa, with her 'evil eye', head of writhing serpents and lolling tongue, was queen of the pantheon of female monsters; men unfortunate enough to look at her were turned immediately to stone.

It is not by accident that Freud linked the sight of the Medusa to the equally horrifying sight of the mother's genitals, for the concept of the monstrous-feminine, as constructed within/by a patriarchal and phallocentric ideology, is related intimately to the problem of sexual difference and castration. In 1922 he argued that the 'Medusa's head takes the place of a representation of the female genitals';[3] if we accept Freud's interpretation, we can see that the Perseus myth is mediated by a narrative about the *difference* of female sexuality as a difference which is grounded in monstrousness and which invokes castration anxiety in the male spectator. 'The sight of the Medusa's head makes the spectator stiff with terror, turns him to stone.'[4] The irony of this was not lost on Freud, who pointed out that becoming stiff also means having an erection. 'Thus in the original situation it offers consolation to the spectator: he is still in possession of a penis, and the stiffening reassures him of the fact.'[5] One wonders if the experience of horror – of viewing the horror film – causes similar alterations in the body of the male spectator. And what of other phrases that apply to both male and female viewers – phrases such as: 'It scared the shit out of me'; 'It made me feel sick'; 'It gave me the creeps'? What is the relationship between physical states, bodily wastes (even if metaphoric ones) and the horrific – in particular, the monstrous-feminine?

II

Julia Kristeva's *Powers of Horror*[6] provides us with a preliminary hypothesis for an analysis of these questions. Although this study is concerned with literature, it nevertheless suggests a way of situating the monstrous-feminine in the horror film in relation to the maternal figure and what Kristeva terms 'abjection', that which does not 'respect borders, positions, rules' . . . that which 'disturbs identity, system, order' (p. 4). In general terms, Kristeva is attempting to explore the different ways in which abjection, as a source of horror, works within patriarchal societies, as a means of separating the human from the non-human and the fully constituted subject from the partially formed subject. Ritual becomes a means by which societies both renew their initial contact with the abject element and then exclude that element.

Through ritual, the demarcation lines between human and non-human are drawn up anew and presumably made all the stronger for that process. One of the key figures of abjection is the mother who becomes an abject at that moment when the child rejects her for the father who represents the symbolic order. The problem with Kristeva's theory, particularly for feminists, is that she never makes clear her position on the oppression of women. Her theory moves uneasily between explanation of, and justification for, the formation of human societies based on the subordination of women.

Kristeva grounds her theory of the maternal in the abject, tracing its changing definitions from the period of the pagan or mother-goddess religions through to the time of Judaic monotheism and to its culmination in Christianity. She deals with abjection in the following forms: as a rite of defilement in paganism; as a biblical abomination, a taboo, in Judaism; and as self-defilement, an interiorisation, in Christianity. Kristeva, however, does not situate abjection solely within a ritual or religious context. She argues that it is 'rooted historically (in the history of religions) and subjectively (in the structuration of the subject's identity), in the cathexis of maternal function – mother, woman, reproduction' (p. 91). Kristeva's central interest, however, lies with the structuring of subjectivity within and by the processes of abjectivity in which the subject is spoken by the abject through both religious and cultural discourses, that is, through the subject's position within the practices of the rite as well as within language.

> But the question for the analyst-semiologist is to know how far one can analyze ritual impurity. The historian of religion stops soon: the critically impure is that which is based on a natural 'loathing.' The anthropologist goes further: there is nothing 'loathsome' in itself; the loathsome is that which disobeys classification rules peculiar to the given symbolic system. But as far as I am concerned, I keep asking questions. . . . Are there no subjective structurations that, within the organization of each speaking being, correspond to this or that symbolic-social system and represent, if not stages, at least *types* of subjectivity and society? Types that would be defined, in the last analysis, according to the subject's position in language . . .?
>
> (p. 92)

A full examination of this theory is outside the scope of this article; I propose to draw mainly on Kristeva's discussion of abjection in its construction in the human subject in relation to her notions of (a) the 'border' and (b) the mother–child relationship. At crucial points, I shall also refer to her writing on the abject in relation to religious discourses. This area cannot be ignored, for what becomes apparent in reading her work is that definitions of the monstrous as constructed in the modern horror text are grounded in ancient religious and historical notions of abjection – particularly in relation to the following religious 'abominations': sexual immorality and perversion; corporeal alteration, decay and death; human sacrifice; murder; the corpse; bodily wastes; the feminine body and incest.

The place of the abject is 'the place where meaning collapses' (p. 2), the place where 'I' am not. The abject threatens life; it must be 'radically excluded' (p. 2) from the place of the living subject, propelled away from the body and deposited on the other side of an imaginary border which separates the self from that which threatens the self. Kristeva quotes Bataille:

> Abjection (. . .) is merely the inability to assume with sufficient strength the imperative act of excluding abject things (and that act establishes the foundations of collective existence).
>
> (p. 56)

Although the subject must exclude the abject, it must, nevertheless, be tolerated, for that which threatens to destroy life also helps to define life. Further, the activity of exclusion is necessary to guarantee that the subject take up his/her proper place in relation to the symbolic.

> To each ego its object, to each superego its abject. It is not the white expanse or slack boredom of repression, not the translations and transformations of desire that wrench bodies, nights and discourse; rather it is a brutish suffering that 'I' puts up with, sublime and devastated, for 'I' deposits it to the father's account (*versé au père – père-version*): I endure it, for I imagine such is the desire of the other. . . . On the edge of non-existence and hallucination, of a reality that, if I acknowledge it, annihilates me. There, abject and abjection are my safeguards. The primers of my culture.
>
> (p. 2)

The abject can be experienced in various ways – one of which relates to biological bodily functions, the other of which has been inscribed in a symbolic (religious) economy. For instance, Kristeva claims that food loathing is 'perhaps the most elementary and archaic form of abjection' (p. 2). Food, however, only becomes abject if it signifies a border 'between two distinct entities or territories' (p. 75). Kristeva describes how, for her, the skin on the top of milk, which is offered to her by her father and mother, is a 'sign of their desire', a sign separating her world from their world, a sign which she does not want. 'But since the food is not an "other" for "me", who am only in their desire, I expel *myself*, I spit *myself* out, I abject *myself* within the same motion through which "I" claim to establish *myself*' (p. 3). Dietary prohibitions are, of course, central to Judaism. Kristeva argues that these are directly related to the prohibition of incest; she argues this not just because this position is supported by psychoanalytic discourse and structural anthropology but also because 'the biblical text, as it proceeds, comes back, at the intensive moments of its demonstration and expansion, to that mytheme of the archaic relation to the mother' (p. 106).

The ultimate in abjection is the corpse. The body protects itself from bodily wastes such as shit, blood, urine and pus by ejecting these substances just as it expels food that, for whatever reason, the subject finds loathsome. The body extricates itself from them and from the place where they fall, so that it might continue to live.

> Such wastes drop so that I might live, until, from loss to loss, nothing remains in me and my entire body falls beyond the limit – *cadere*, cadaver. If dung signifies the other side of the border, the place where I am not and which permits me to be, the corpse, the most sickening of wastes, is a border that has encroached upon everything. It is no longer I who expel. 'I' is expelled.
>
> (pp. 3–4)

Within the biblical context, the corpse is also utterly abject. It signifies one of the most basic forms of pollution – the body without a soul. As a form of waste it represents the opposite of the spiritual, the religious symbolic.

> Corpse fanciers, unconscious worshippers of a soulless body, are thus preeminent representatives of inimical religions, identified by their murderous cults. The priceless debt to great mother nature, from which the prohibitions of Yahwistic speech separates us, is concealed in such pagan cults.
>
> (p. 109)

In relation to the horror film, it is relevant to note that several of the most popular horrific figures are 'bodies without souls' (the vampire), the 'living corpse' (the zombie) and corpse-eater (the ghoul). Here, the horror film constructs and confronts us with the fascinating, seductive aspect of abjection. What is also interesting is that such ancient figures of abjection as the vampire, the ghoul, the zombie and the witch (one of whose many crimes was that she used corpses for her rites of magic) continue to provide some of the most compelling images of horror in the modern cinema. The werewolf, whose body signifies a collapse of the boundaries between human and animal, also belongs to this category.

Abjection also occurs where the individual fails to respect the law and where the individual is a hypocrite, a liar, a traitor.

> Any crime, because it draws attention to the fragility of the law, is abject, but premeditated crime, cunning murder, hypocritical revenge are even more so because they heighten the display of such fragility. He who denies morality is not abject, there can be grandeur in amorality. . . . Abjection, on the other hand, is immoral, sinister, scheming, and shady. . . .
>
> (p. 4)

Thus, abject things are those which highlight the 'fragility of the law' and which exist on the other side of the border which separates out the living subject from that which threatens its extinction. But abjection is not something of which the subject can ever feel free – it is always there, beckoning the self to take up its place, the place where meaning collapses. The subject, constructed in/through language, through a desire for meaning, is also spoken by the abject, the place of meaninglessness – thus, the subject is constantly beset by abjection which fascinates desire but which must be repelled for fear of self-annihilation. The crucial point is that abjection is always ambiguous. Like Bataille, Kristeva emphasises the attraction, as well as the horror, of the undifferentiated.

> We may call it a border; abjection is above all ambiguity. Because, while releasing a hold, it does not radically cut off the subject from what threatens it – on the contrary, abjection acknowledges it to be in perpetual danger. But also because abjection itself is a composite of judgement and affect, of condemnation and yearning, of signs and drives. Abjection preserves what existed in the archaism of pre-objectal relationship. . . .
>
> (pp. 9–10)

To the extent that abjection works on the socio-cultural arena, the horror film would appear to be, in at least three ways, an illustration of the work of abjection. Firstly, the horror film abounds in images of abjection, foremost of which is the corpse, whole and mutilated, followed by an array of bodily wastes such as blood, vomit, saliva, sweat, tears and putrifying flesh. In terms of Kristeva's notion of the border, when we say such-and-such a horror film 'made me sick' or 'scared the shit out of me'[7] we are actually foregrounding that specific horror film as a 'work of abjection' or 'abjection at work' – in both a literal and metaphoric sense. Viewing the horror film signifies a desire not only for perverse pleasure (confronting sickening, horrific images, being filled with terror/desire for the undifferentiated) but also a desire, having taken pleasure in perversity, to throw up, throw out, eject the abject (from the safety of the spectator's seat).

Secondly, there is, of course, a sense in which the concept of a border is central to the construction of the monstrous in the horror film; that which crosses or threatens to cross the 'border' is abject. Although the specific nature of the border changes from film to film, the function of the monstrous remains the same – to bring about an encounter between the symbolic order and that which threatens its stability. In some horror films the monstrous is produced at the border between human and inhuman, man and beast (*Dr. Jekyll and Mr Hyde*, *Creature from the Black Lagoon*, *King Kong*); in others the border is between the normal and the supernatural, good and evil (*Carrie*, *The Exorcist*, *The Omen*, *Rosemary's Baby*); or the monstrous is produced at the border which separates those who take up their proper gender roles from those who do not (*Psycho*, *Dressed to Kill*, *Reflection of Fear*); or the border is between normal and abnormal sexual desire (*Cruising*, *The Hunger*, *Cat People*).

In relation to the construction of the abject within religious discourses, it is interesting to note that various sub-genres of the horror film seem to correspond to religious categories of abjection. For instance, blood as a religious abomination becomes a form of abjection in the 'splatter' movie (*The Texas Chainsaw Massacre*); cannibalism, another religious abomination, is central to the 'meat' movie (*Night of the Living Dead*, *The Hills Have Eyes*); the corpse as abomination becomes the abject of ghoul and zombie movies (*The Evil Dead*; *Zombie Flesheaters*); blood as a taboo object within religion is central to the vampire film (*The Hunger*) as well as the horror film in general (*Bloodsucking Freaks*); human sacrifice as a religious abomination is constructed as the abject of virtually all horror films; and bodily disfigurement as a religious abomination is also central to the slash movie, particularly those in which woman is slashed, the mark a sign of her 'difference', her impurity (*Dressed to Kill*, *Psycho*).

III

The third way in which the horror film illustrates the work of abjection refers to the construction of the maternal figure as abject. Kristeva argues that all individuals experience abjection at the time of their earliest attempts to break away from the mother. She sees the mother–child relation as one marked by conflict: the child struggles to break free but the mother is reluctant to release it. Because of the 'instability of the symbolic function' in relation to this most crucial area – 'the prohibition placed on the maternal body (as a defense against autoeroticism and incest taboo)' (p. 14) – Kristeva argues that the maternal body becomes a site of conflicting desires. 'Here, drives hold sway and constitute a strange space that I shall name, after Plato (*Timaeus*, 48–53), a *chora*, a receptacle' (p. 14). The position of the child is rendered even more unstable because, while the mother retains a close hold over the child, it can serve to authenticate her existence – an existence which needs validation because of her problematic relation to the symbolic realm.

> It is a violent, clumsy breaking away, with the constant risk of falling back under the sway of a power as securing as it is stifling. The difficulty the mother has in acknowledging (or being acknowledged by) the symbolic realm – in other words, the problem she has with the phallus that her father or husband stands for – is not such as to help the future subject leave the natural mansion.
>
> (p. 13)

In the child's attempts to break away, the mother becomes an abject; thus, in this context, where the child struggles to become a separate subject, abjection becomes *'a precondition of narcissism'* (p. 13). Once again we can see abjection at work in the horror text where the child struggles to break away from the mother, representative of the archaic maternal figure, in a context in which the father is invariably absent (*Psycho*, *Carrie*, *The Birds*). In these films, the maternal figure is constructed as the monstrous-feminine. By refusing to relinquish her hold on her child, she prevents it from taking up its proper place in relation to the Symbolic. Partly consumed by the desire to remain locked in a blissful relationship with the mother and partly terrified of separation, the child finds it easy to succumb to the comforting pleasure of the dyadic relationship. Kristeva argues that a whole area of religion has assumed the function of tackling this danger:

> This is precisely where we encounter the rituals of defilement and their derivatives, which, based on the feeling of abjection and all converging on the maternal, attempt to symbolize the other threat to the subject: that of being swamped by the dual relationship, thereby risking the loss not of a part (castration) but of the totality of his living being. The function of these religious rituals is to ward off the subject's fear of his very own identity sinking irretrievably into the mother.
>
> (p. 64)

How, then, are prohibitions against contact with the mother enacted and enforced? In answering this question, Kristeva links the universal practices of rituals of defilement to the mother. She argues that within the practices of all rituals of defilement, polluting objects fall into two categories: excremental, which threatens identity from the outside, and menstrual, which threatens from within.

> Excrement and its equivalents (decay, infection, disease, corpse, etc.) stand for the danger to identity that comes from without: the ego threatened by the non-ego, society threatened by its outside, life by death. Menstrual blood, on the contrary, stands for the danger issuing from within identity (social or sexual); it threatens the relationship between the sexes within a social aggregate and, through internalization, the identity of each sex in the face of sexual difference.
>
> (p. 71)

Both categories of polluting objects relate to the mother; the relation of menstrual blood is self-evident, the association of excremental objects with the maternal figure is brought about because of the mother's role in sphincteral training. Here, Kristeva argues that the subject's first contact with 'authority' is with the maternal authority when the child learns, through interaction with the mother, about its body: the shape of the body, the clean and unclean, the proper and improper areas of the body. Kristeva refers to this process as a 'primal mapping of the body' which she calls 'semiotic'. She distinguishes between maternal 'authority' and 'paternal laws':

> Maternal authority is the trustee of that mapping of the self's clean and proper body; it is distinguished from paternal laws within which, with the phallic phase and acquisition of language, the destiny of man will take shape.
>
> (p. 72)

In her discussion of rituals of defilement in relation to the Indian caste system, Kristeva draws a distinction between the maternal authority and paternal law. She argues that the period of the 'mapping of the self's clean and proper body' is characterised by the exercise of 'authority without guilt', a time when there is a 'fusion between mother and nature'. However, the symbolic ushers in a 'totally different universe of socially signifying performances where embarrassment, shame, guilt, desire etc. come into play – the order of the phallus'. In the Indian context, these two worlds exist harmoniously side by side because of the working of defilement rites. Here, Kristeva is referring to the practice of public defecation in India. She quotes V. S. Naipaul who says that no one ever mentions 'in speech or in books, those squatting figures, because, quite simply, no one sees them'. Kristeva argues that this split between the world of the mother (a universe without shame) and the world of the father (a universe of shame), would in other social contexts produce psychosis; in India it finds a 'perfect socialization':

> This may be because the setting up of the rite of defilement takes on the function of the hyphen, the virgule, allowing the two universes of *filth* and *prohibition* to brush lightly against each other without necessarily being identified as such, as *object* and as *law*.
>
> (p. 74)

Images of blood, vomit, pus, shit, etc, are central to our culturally/socially constructed notions of the horrific. They signify a split between two orders: the maternal authority and the law of the father. On the one hand, these images of bodily wastes threaten a subject that is already constituted, in relation to the symbolic, as 'whole and proper'. Consequently, they fill the subject – both the protagonist in the text and the spectator in the cinema – with disgust and loathing. On the other hand, they also point back to a time when a 'fusion between mother and nature' existed; when bodily wastes, while set apart from the body, were not seen as objects of embarrassment and shame. Their presence in the horror film may invoke a response of disgust from the audience situated as it is within the symbolic but at a more archaic level the representation of bodily wastes may invoke pleasure in breaking the taboo on filth – sometimes described as a pleasure in perversity – and a pleasure in returning to that time when the mother–child relationship was marked by an untrammelled pleasure in 'playing' with the body and its wastes.

The modern horror film often 'plays' with its audience, saturating it with scenes of blood and gore, deliberately pointing to the fragility of the symbolic order in the domain of the body which never ceases to signal the repressed world of the mother. This is particularly evident in *The Exorcist*, where the world of the symbolic, represented by the priest-as-father, and the world of the pre-symbolic, represented by woman aligned with the devil, clashes head-on in scenes where the foulness of woman is signified by her putrid, filthy body covered in blood, urine, excrement and bile. Significantly, a pubescent girl about to menstruate played the woman who is possessed – in one scene blood from her wounded genitals mingles with menstrual blood to provide one of the film's key images of horror. In *Carrie*, the film's most monstrous act occurs when the couple are drenched in pig's blood which symbolises menstrual blood – women are referred to in the film as 'pigs', women 'bleed like pigs', and the pig's blood runs down Carrie's body at a moment of intense pleasure, just as her own menstrual blood runs down her legs during a similar pleasurable moment when she enjoys her body in the shower. Here, women's blood and pig's blood flow together, signifying horror, shame and humiliation. In this film, however, the mother speaks for the symbolic, identifying with an order which has defined women's sexuality as the source of all evil and menstruation as the sign of sin. The horror film's obsession with blood, particularly the bleeding body of woman, where her body is transformed into the 'gaping wound', suggests that castration anxiety is a central concern of the horror film – particularly the slasher sub-genre. Woman's body is slashed and mutilated, not only to signify her own castrated state, but also the possibility of castration for the male. In the guise of a 'madman' he enacts on her body the one act he most fears for himself, transforming her entire body into a bleeding wound.

Kristeva's semiotic posits a pre-verbal dimension of language which relates to sounds and tone and to direct expression of the drives and physical contact with the maternal figure; 'it is dependent upon meaning, but in a way that is not that of *linguistic* signs nor of the *symbolic* order they found' (p. 72). With the subject's entry into the symbolic, which separates the child from the mother, the maternal figure and the authority she signifies are repressed. Kristeva argues that it is the function of defilement rites, particularly those relating to menstrual and excremental objects, to point to the 'boundary' between the maternal semiotic authority and the paternal symbolic law.

> Through language and within highly hierarchical religious institutions, man hallucinates partial 'objects' – witnesses to an archaic differentiation of the body on its way toward ego identity which is also sexual identity. The *defilement* from which ritual protects us is neither sign nor matter. Within the rite that extracts it from repression and depraved desire, defilement is the translinguistic spoor of the most archaic boundaries of the self's clean and proper body. In that sense, if it is a jettisoned object, it is so from the mother. . . . By means of the symbolic institution of ritual, that is to say, by means of a system of

> ritual exclusions, the partial-object consequently becomes *scription* – an inscription of limits, an emphasis placed not on the (paternal) Law but on (maternal) Authority through the very signifying order.
>
> (p. 73)

Kristeva argues that, historically, it has been the function of religion to purify the abject but with the disintegration of these 'historical forms' of religion, the work of purification now rests solely with 'that catharsis par excellence called art' (p. 17).

> In a world in which the Other has collapsed, the aesthetic task – a descent into the foundations of the symbolic construct – amounts to retracing the fragile limits of the speaking being, closest to its dawn, to the bottomless 'primacy' constituted by primal repression. Through that experience, which is nevertheless managed by the Other, 'subject' and 'object' push each other away, confront each other, collapse, and start again – inseparable, contaminated, condemned, at the boundary of what is assimilable, thinkable: abject.
>
> (p. 18)

This, I would argue, is also the central ideological project of the popular horror film – purification of the abject through a 'descent into the foundations of the symbolic construct'. In this way, the horror film brings about a confrontation with the abject (the corpse, bodily wastes, the monstrous-feminine) in order, finally, to eject the abject and re-draw the boundaries between the human and non-human. As a form of modern defilement rite, the horror film works to separate out the symbolic order from all that threatens its stability, particularly the mother and all that her universe signifies. In Kristeva's terms, this means separating out the maternal authority from paternal law.

As mentioned earlier, the central problem with Kristeva's theory is that it can be read in a prescriptive rather than a descriptive sense. This problem is rendered more acute by the fact that, although Kristeva distinguishes between the maternal and paternal figures, when she speaks of the subject who is being constituted, she never distinguishes between the child as male or female. Obviously, the female child's experience of the semiotic chora must be different from that of the male's experience in relation to the way it is spoken to, handled, etc. For the mother is already constituted as a gendered subject living within a patriarchal order and thus aware of the differences between the 'masculine' and the 'feminine' in relation to questions of desire. Thus, the mother might relate to a male child with a more acute sense of pride and pleasure. It is also possible that the child, depending on its gender, might find it more or less difficult to reject the mother for the father. Kristeva does not consider any of these issues. Nor does she distinguish between the relation of the adult male and female subject to rituals of defilement – for instance, menstruation taboos, where one imagines notions of the gendered subject would be of crucial importance. How, for instance, do women relate to rites of defilement, such as menstruation rites which reflect so negatively on them? How do women within a specific cultural group see themselves in relation to taboos which construct their procreative functions as abject? Is it possible to intervene in the social construction of woman as abject? Or is the subject's relationship to the processes of abjectivity, as they are constructed within subjectivity and language, completely unchangeable? Is the abjection of women a precondition for the continuation of sociality? Kristeva never asks questions of this order. Consequently her theory of abjection could be interpreted as an apology for the establishment of sociality at the cost of women's equality. If, however, we read it as descriptive, as one which is attempting to explain the origins of patriarchal culture, then it provides us with an extremely useful hypothesis for an investigation of the representation of women in the horror film.[8]

[. . .]

Notes

1 Sigmund Freud, 'Fetishism', *On Sexuality*, Harmondsworth, Penguin, Pelican Freud Library, vol. 7, 1981, p. 354.
2 Joseph Campbell, *The Masks of God*: Primitive Mythology, New York, Penguin, 1969, p. 73.
3 Sigmund Freud, 'Medusa's Head', in James Strachey (ed.), *The Standard Edition of the Complete Psychological Works of Sigmund Freud*, vol. 18, London, Hogarth Press, 1964, pp. 273–274.
4 ibid, p. 273.
5 ibid.
6 Julia Kristeva, *Powers of Horror: An Essay on Abjection*, New York, Columbia University Press, 1982. All page citations will be included in the text.
7 For a discussion of the way in which the modern horror film works upon its audience see Philip Brophy, 'Horrality', reprinted in *Screen* 27(1), January–February, 1986.
8 For a critique of *Powers of Horror* see Jennifer Stone, 'The Horrors of Power: A Critique of "Kristeva"', in F. Barker, P. Hulme, M. Iversen, D. Loxley (eds), *The Politics of Theory*, Colchester, University of Essex, 1983, pp. 38–48.

Her body, himself

Gender in the slasher film

6

CAROL J. CLOVER

[. . .]

The Body

On the face of it, the relation between the sexes in slasher films could hardly be clearer. The killer is with few exceptions recognizably human and distinctly male; his fury is unmistakably sexual in both roots and expression; his victims are mostly women, often sexually free and always young and beautiful ones. Just how essential this victim is to horror is suggested by her historical durability. If the killer has over time been variously figured as shark, fog, gorilla, birds, and slime, the victim is eternally and prototypically the damsel. Cinema hardly invented the pattern. It has simply given visual expression to the abiding proposition that, in Poe's famous formulation, the death of a beautiful woman is the "most poetical topic in the world."[1] As slasher director Dario Argento puts it, "I like women, especially beautiful ones. If they have a good face and figure, I would much prefer to watch them being murdered than an ugly girl or a man."[2] Brian De Palma elaborates: 'Women in peril work better in the suspense genre. It all goes back to the *Perils of Pauline*. . . . If you have a haunted house and you have a woman walking around with a candelabrum, you fear more for her than you would for a husky man."[3] Or Hitchcock, during the filming of *The Birds*: "I always believe in following the advice of the playwright Sardou. He said 'Torture the women!' The trouble today is that we don't torture women enough."[4] What the directors do not say, but show, is that "Pauline" is at her very most effective in a state of undress, borne down upon by a blatantly phallic murderer, even gurgling orgasmically as she dies. The case could be made that the slasher films available at a given neighborhood video rental outlet recommend themselves to censorship under the Dworkin-MacKinnon guidelines at least as readily as the hard-core films the next section over, at which that legislation is aimed; for if some victims are men, the argument goes, most are women, and the women are brutalized in ways that come too close to real life for comfort. But what this line of reasoning does not take into account is the figure of the Final Girl. Because slashers lie for all practical purposes beyond the purview of legitimate criticism, and to the extent that they have been reviewed at all have been reviewed on an individual basis, the phenomenon of the female victim-hero has scarcely been acknowledged.

It is, of course, "on the face of it" that most of the public discussion of film takes place—from the Dworkin-MacKinnon legislation to Siskel's and Ebert's reviews to our own talks with friends on leaving the movie house. Underlying that discussion is the assumption that the sexes are what they seem; that screen males represent the Male and screen females the Female; that this identification along gender lines authorizes impulses toward sexual violence in males and encourages impulses toward victimization in females. In part because of the massive authority cinema by nature accords the image, even academic film criticism has been slow—slower than literary criticism—to get beyond appearances. Film may not appropriate the mind's eye, but it certainly encroaches on it; the gender characteristics of a screen figure are a visible and audible given for the duration of the film. To the extent that the possibility of cross-gender identification has been entertained, it has been in the direction female-with-male. Thus some critics have wondered whether the female viewer, faced with the screen image of a masochistic/narcissistic female, might not rather elect to "betray her sex and identify with the masculine point of view."[5] The reverse question—whether men might not also, on occasion, elect to betray their sex and identify with screen females—has scarcely been asked, presumably on the assumption that men's interests are well served by the traditional patterns of cinematic representation. Then too there is the matter of the "male gaze." As E. Ann Kaplan sums it up: "Within the film text itself, men gaze at women, who become objects of the gaze; the spectator, in turn, is made to identify with this male gaze, and to objectify the women on the screen; and the camera's original 'gaze' comes into play in the very act of filming."[6] But if it is so that all of us, male and female alike, are by these processes "made to" identify with men and "against" women, how are we then to explain the appeal to a largely male audience of a film genre that features a female victim-hero? The slasher film brings us squarely up against a fundamental question of film analysis: where does the literal end and the figurative begin; how do the two levels interact and what is the significance of the particular interaction; and to which, in arriving at a political judgment (as we are inclined to do in the case of low horror and pornography), do we assign priority?

A figurative or functional analysis of the slasher begins with the processes of point of view and identification. The male viewer seeking a male character, even a vicious one, with whom to identify in a sustained way has little to hang on to in the standard example. On the good side, the only viable candidates are the schoolmates or friends of the girls. They are for the most part marginal, underdeveloped characters; more to the point, they tend to die early in the film. If the traditional horror film gave the male spectator a last-minute hero with whom to identify, thereby "indulging his vanity as protector of the helpless female,"[7] the slasher eliminates or attenuates that role beyond any such function; indeed, would-be rescuers are not infrequently blown away for their efforts, leaving the girl to fight her own fight. Policemen, fathers, and sheriffs appear only long enough to demonstrate risible incomprehension and incompetence. On the bad side, there is the killer. The killer is often unseen, or barely glimpsed, during the first part of the film, and what we do see, when we finally get a good look, hardly invites immediate or conscious empathy. He is commonly masked, fat, deformed, or dressed as a woman. Or "he" *is* a woman: woe to the viewer of *Friday the Thirteenth* I who identifies with the male killer only to discover, in the film's final sequences, that he was not a man at all but a middle-aged woman. In either case, the killer is himself eventually killed or otherwise evacuated from the narrative. No male character of any stature lives to tell the tale.

The one character of stature who does live to tell the tale is of course female. The Final Girl is introduced at the beginning and is the only character to be developed in any psychological detail. We understand immediately from the attention paid it that hers is the main story line. She is intelligent, watchful, level-headed; the first character to sense something amiss and the only one to deduce from the accumulating evidence the patterns and extent of the threat; the only one, in other words, whose perspective approaches our own privileged understanding of the situation. We register her horror as she stumbles on the corpses of her friends; her paralysis in the face of death duplicates those moments of the universal nightmare experience on which horror frankly trades. When she downs the killer, we are triumphant. She is by any measure the slasher film's hero. This is not to say that our attachment to her is exclusive and unremitting, only that it adds up, and that in the closing sequence it is very close to absolute.

An analysis of the camerawork bears this out. Much is made of the use of the I-camera to represent the killer's point of view. In these passages—they are usually few and brief, but powerful—we see through his eyes and (on the sound track) hear his breathing and heartbeat. His and our vision is partly obscured by bushes or windowblinds in the foreground. By such means we are forced, the argument goes, to identify with the killer. In fact, however, the relation between camera point of view and the processes of viewer identification are poorly understood; the fact that Steven Spielberg can stage an attack in *Jaws* from the shark's point of view (underwater, rushing upward toward the swimmer's flailing legs) or Hitchcock an attack in *The Birds* from the birds'-eye perspective (from the sky, as they gather to swoop down on the streets of Bodega Bay) would seem to suggest either that the viewer's identificatory powers are unbelievably elastic or that point-of-view shots can sometimes be pro forma.[8] But let us for the moment accept the equation point of view = identification. We are linked, in this way, with the killer in the early part of the film, usually before we have seen him directly and before we have come to know the Final Girl in any detail. Our closeness to him wanes as our closeness to the Final Girl waxes—a shift underwritten by story line as well as camera position. By the end, point of view is hers: we are in the closet with her, watching with her eyes the knife blade stab through the door; in the room with her as the killer breaks through the window and grabs at her; in the car with her as the killer stabs through the convertible top, and so on. With her, we become if not the killer of the killer then the agent of his expulsion from the narrative vision. If, during the film's course, we shifted our sympathies back and forth, and dealt them out to other characters along the way, we belong in the end to the Final Girl; there is no alternative. When Stretch eviscerates Chop Top at the end of *Texas Chain Saw II*, she is literally the only character left alive, on either side.

Audience response ratifies this design. Observers unanimously stress the readiness of the "live" audience to switch sympathies in midstream, siding now with the killer and now, and finally, with the Final Girl. As Schoell, whose book on shocker films wrestles with its own monster, "the feminists," puts it:

> Social critics make much of the fact that male audience members cheer on the misogynous misfits in these movies as they rape, plunder, and murder their screaming, writhing female victims. Since these same critics walk out of the moviehouse in disgust long before the movie is over, they don't realize that these same men cheer on (with renewed enthusiasm, in fact) the heroines, who are often as strong, sexy, and independent as the [earlier] victims, as they blow away the killer with a shotgun or get him

> between the eyes with a machete. All of these men are said to be identifying with the maniac, but they enjoy *his* death throes the most of all, and applaud the heroine with admiration.[9]

What filmmakers seem to know better than film critics is that gender is less a wall than a permeable membrane.[10]

No one who has read "Red Riding Hood" to a small boy or participated in a viewing of, say, *Deliverance* (an all-male story that women find as gripping as men) or, more recently, *Alien* and *Aliens*, with whose space-age female Rambo, herself a Final Girl, male viewers seem to engage with ease, can doubt the phenomenon of cross-gender identification.[11] This fluidity of engaged perspective is in keeping with the universal claims of the psychoanalytic model: the threat function and the victim function coexist in the same unconscious, regardless of anatomical sex. But why, if viewers can identify across gender lines and if the root experience of horror is sex blind, are the screen sexes not interchangeable? Why not more and better female killers, and why (in light of the maleness of the majority audience) not Pauls as well as Paulines? The fact that horror film so stubbornly genders the killer male and the principal victim female would seem to suggest that representation itself is at issue—that the sensation of bodily fright derives not exclusively from repressed content, as Freud insisted, but also from the bodily manifestations of that content.

Nor is the gender of the principals as straightforward as it first seems. The killer's phallic purpose, as he thrusts his drill or knife into the trembling bodies of young women, is unmistakable. At the same time, however, his masculinity is severely qualified: he ranges from the virginal or sexually inert to the transvestite or transsexual, is spiritually divided ("the mother half of his mind") or even equipped with vulva and vagina. Although the killer of *God Told Me To* is represented and taken as a male in the film text, he is revealed, by the doctor who delivered him, to have been sexually ambiguous from birth: "I truly could not tell whether that child was male or female; it was as if the sexual gender had not been determined . . . as if it were being developed."[12] In this respect, slasher killers have much in common with the monsters of classic horror—monsters who, in Linda Williams's formulation, represent not just "an eruption of the normally repressed animal sexual energy of the civilized male" but also the "power and potency of a *non-phallic* sexuality." To the extent that the monster is constructed as feminine, the horror film thus expresses female desire only to show how monstrous it is.[13] The intention is manifest in *Aliens*, in which the Final Girl, Ripley, is pitted in the climactic scene against the most terrifying "alien" of all: an egg-laying Mother. [. . .]

The gender of the Final Girl is likewise compromised from the outset by her masculine interests, her inevitable sexual reluctance (penetration, it seems, constructs the female), her apartness from other girls, sometimes her name. At the level of the cinematic apparatus, her unfemininity is signaled clearly by her exercise of the "active investigating gaze" normally reserved for males and hideously punished in females when they assume it themselves; tentatively at first and then aggressively; the Final Girl looks *for* the killer, even tracking him to his forest hut or his underground labyrinth, and then *at* him, therewith bringing him, often for the first time, into our vision as well.[14] When, in the final scene, she stops screaming, looks at the killer, and reaches for the knife (sledge hammer, scalpel, gun, machete, hanger, knitting needle, chainsaw), she addresses the killer on his own terms. To the critics' objection that *Halloween* in effect punished female sexuality, director John Carpenter responded:

> They [the critics] completely missed the boat there, I think. Because if you turn it around, the one girl who is the most sexually uptight just keeps stabbing this guy with a long knife. She's the most sexually frustrated. She's the one that killed him. Not because she's a virgin, but because all that repressed energy starts coming out. She uses all those phallic symbols on the guy. . . . She and the killer have a certain link: sexual repression.[15]

For all its perversity, Carpenter's remark does underscore the sense of affinity, even recognition, that attends the final encounter. But the "certain link" that puts killer and Final Girl on terms, at least briefly, is more than "sexual repression." It is also a shared masculinity, materialized in "all those phallic symbols"—and it is also a shared femininity, materialized in what comes next (and what Carpenter, perhaps significantly, fails to mention): the castration, literal or symbolic, of the killer at her hands. His eyes may be put out, his hand severed, his body impaled or shot, his belly gashed, or his genitals sliced away or bitten off. The Final Girl has not just manned herself; she specifically unmans an oppressor whose masculinity was in question to begin with. By the time the drama has played itself out, darkness yields to light (often as day breaks) and the close quarters of the barn (closet, elevator, attic, basement) give way to the open expanse of the yard (field, road, lakescape, cliff). With the Final Girl's appropriation of "all those phallic symbols" comes the quelling, the dispelling, of the "uterine" threat as well. Consider again the paradigmatic ending of *Texas Chain Saw* II. From the underground labyrinth, murky and bloody, in which she faced saw, knife, and hammer, Stretch escapes through a culvert into the open air. She clambers up the jutting rock and with a chainsaw takes her stand. When her last assailant comes at her, she slashes open his lower abdomen—the sexual symbolism is all too clear—and flings him off the cliff. Again, the final scene shows her in extreme long shot, standing on the pinnacle, drenched in sunlight, buzzing chainsaw held overhead.

The tale would indeed seem to be one of sex and parents. The patently erotic threat is easily seen as the materialized projection of the dreamer's (viewer's) own incestuous fears and desires. It is this disabling cathexis to one's parents that must be killed and rekilled in the service of sexual autonomy. When the Final Girl stands at last in the light of day with the knife in her hand, she has delivered herself into the adult world. Carpenter's equation of the Final Girl with the killer has more than a grain of truth. The killers of *Psycho*, *The Eyes of Laura Mars*, *Friday the Thirteenth* II–VI, and *Cruising*, among others, are explicitly figured as sons in the psychosexual grip of their mothers (or fathers, in the case of *Cruising*). The difference is between past and present and between failure and success. The Final Girl enacts in the present, and successfully, the parenticidal struggle that the killer himself enacted unsuccessfully in his own past—a past that constitutes the film's backstory. She is what the killer once was; he is what she could become should she fail in her battle for sexual selfhood. "You got a choice, boy," says the tyrannical father of Leatherface in *Texas Chain Saw* II, "sex or the saw; you never know about sex, but the saw—the saw is the family."

But the tale is no less one of maleness. If the early experience of the oedipal drama can be—is perhaps ideally—enacted in female form, the achievement of full adulthood requires the assumption and, apparently, brutal employment of the phallus. The helpless child is gendered feminine; the autonomous adult or subject is gendered masculine; the passage from childhood to adulthood entails a shift from feminine to masculine. It is the male killer's tragedy that his incipient femininity is not reversed but completed (castration) and the Final Girl's victory that her incipient masculinity is not thwarted but realized (phallicization). When

De Palma says that female frailty is a predicate of the suspense genre, he proposes, in effect, that the lack of the phallus, for Lacan the privileged signifier of the symbolic order of culture, is itself simply horrifying, at least in the mind of the male observer. Where pornography (the argument goes) resolves that lack through a process of fetishization that allows a breast or leg or whole body to stand in for the missing member, the slasher film resolves it either through eliminating the woman (earlier victims) or reconstituting her as masculine (Final Girl). The moment at which the Final Girl is effectively phallicized is the moment that the plot halts and horror ceases. Day breaks, and the community returns to its normal order.

Casting psychoanalytic verities in female form has a venerable cinematic history. Ingmar Bergman has made a career of it, and Woody Allen shows signs of following his lead. One immediate and practical advantage, by now presumably unconscious on the part of makers as well as viewers, has to do with a preestablished cinematic "language" for capturing the moves and moods of the female body and face. The cinematic gaze, we are told, is male, and just as that gaze "knows" how to fetishize the female form in pornography (in a way that it does not "know" how to fetishize the male form),[16] so it "knows," in horror, how to track a woman ascending a staircase in a scary house and how to study her face from an angle above as she first hears the killer's footfall. A set of conventions we now take for granted simply "sees" males and females differently.

To this cinematic habit may be added the broader range of emotional expression traditionally allowed women. Angry displays of force may belong to the male, but crying, cowering, screaming, fainting, trembling, begging for mercy belong to the female. Abject terror, in short, is gendered feminine, and the more concerned a given film with that condition—and it is the essence of modern horror—the more likely the femaleness of the victim. It is no accident that male victims in slasher films are killed swiftly or offscreen, and that prolonged struggles, in which the victim has time to contemplate her imminent destruction, inevitably figure females. Only when one encounters the rare expression of abject terror on the part of a male (as in *I Spit on Your Grave*) does one apprehend the full extent of the cinematic double standard in such matters.[17]

It is also the case that gender displacement can provide a kind of identificatory buffer, an emotional remove, that permits the majority audience to explore taboo subjects in the relative safety of vicariousness. Just as Bergman came to realize that he could explore castration anxiety more freely via depictions of hurt female bodies (witness the genital mutilation of Karin in *Cries and Whispers*), so the makers of slasher films seem to know that sadomasochistic incest fantasies sit more easily with the male viewer when the visible player is female. It is one thing for that viewer to hear the psychiatrist intone at the end of *Psycho* that Norman as a boy (in the backstory) was abnormally attached to his mother; it would be quite another to see that attachment dramatized in the present, to experience in nightmare form the elaboration of Norman's (the viewer's own) fears and desires. If the former is playable in male form, the latter, it seems, is not.

The Final Girl is, on reflection, a congenial double for the adolescent male. She is feminine enough to act out in a gratifying way, a way unapproved for adult males, the terrors and masochistic pleasures of the underlying fantasy, but not so feminine as to disturb the structures of male competence and sexuality. Her sexual inactivity, in this reading, becomes all but inevitable; the male viewer may be willing to enter into the vicarious experience of defending himself from the possibility of symbolic penetration on the part of the killer, but real vaginal penetration on the diegetic level is evidently more femaleness than he can bear.

[. . .] It may be through the female body that the body of the audience is sensationalized, but the sensation is an entirely male affair. [. . .]

If the slasher film is "on the face of it" a genre with at least a strong female presence, it is in these figurative readings a thoroughly strong male exercise, one that finally has very little to do with femaleness and very much to do with phallocentrism. Figuratively seen, the Final Girl is a male surrogate in things oedipal, a homoerotic stand-in, the audience incorporate; to the extent she "means" girl at all, it is only for purposes of signifying phallic lack, and even that meaning is nullified in the final scenes. Our initial question—how to square a female victim-hero with a largely male audience—is not so much answered as it is obviated in these readings. The Final Girl is (apparently) female not despite the maleness of the audience, but precisely because of it. The discourse is wholly masculine, and females figure in it only insofar as they "read" some aspect of male experience. To applaud the Final Girl as a feminist development, as some reviews of *Aliens* have done with Ripley, is, in light of her figurative meaning, a particularly grotesque expression of wishful thinking.[18] She is simply an agreed-upon fiction, and the male viewer's use of her as a vehicle for his own sadomasochistic fantasies an act of perhaps timeless dishonesty.

For all their immediate appeal, these figurative readings loosen as many ends as they tie together. The audience, we have said, is predominantly male; but what about the women in it? Do we dismiss them as male-identified and account for their experience as an "immasculated" act of collusion with the oppressor?[19] This is a strong judgment to apply to large numbers of women; for while it may be that the audience for slasher films is mainly male, that does not mean that there are not also many female viewers who actively like such films, and of course there are also women, however few, who script, direct, and produce them. These facts alone oblige us at least to consider the possibility that female fans find a meaning in the text and image of these films that is less inimical to their own interests than the figurative analysis would have us believe. Or should we conclude that males and females read these films differently in some fundamental sense? Do females respond to the text (the literal) and males the subtext (the figurative)?[20]

Some such notion of differential understanding underlies the homoerotic reading. The silent presupposition of that reading is that male identification with the female as female cannot be, and that the male viewer/reader who adjoins feminine experience does so only by homosexual conversion. But does female identification with male experience then similarly indicate a lesbian conversion? Or are the processes of patriarchy so one-way that the female can identify with the male directly, but the male can identify with the female only by transsexualizing her? Does the Final Girl mean "girl" to her female viewers and "boy" to her male viewers? If her masculine features qualify her as a transformed boy, do not the feminine features of the killer qualify him as a transformed woman (in which case the homoerotic reading can be maintained only by defining that "woman" as phallic and retransforming her into a male)? [. . .] Further: is it simple coincidence that this combination tale—trials, then triumph—bears such a striking resemblance to the classic (male) hero story? Does the standard hero story featuring an anatomical female "mean" differently from one featuring an anatomical male?

[. . .]

The last point is the crucial one: the same *female* body does for both. The Final Girl 1) undergoes agonizing trials, and 2) virtually or actually destroys the antagonist and saves herself. By the lights of folk tradition, she is not a heroine, for whom phase 1 consists in being saved by someone else, but a hero, who rises to the occasion and defeats the adversary with his own wit and hands. Part 1 of the story sits well on the female; it is the heart of heroine stories in general (Red Riding Hood, Pauline), and in some figurative sense, in ways we have elaborated in some detail, it is gendered feminine even when played by a male. Odysseus' position, trapped in the cave of the Cyclops, is after all not so different from Pauline's position tied to the tracks or Sally's trapped in the dining room of the slaughterhouse family. The decisive moment, as far as the fixing of gender is concerned, lies in what happens next: those who save themselves are male, and those who are saved by others are female. No matter how "feminine" his experience in phase 1, the traditional hero, if he rises against his adversary and saves himself in phase 2, will be male.

What is remarkable about the slasher film is that it comes close to reversing the priorities. Presumably for the various functional or figurative reasons we have considered in this essay, phase 1 wants a female: on that point all slashers from *Psycho* on are agreed. Abject fear is still gendered feminine, and the taboo anxieties in which slashers trade are still explored more easily via Pauline than Paul. The slippage comes in phase 2. As if in mute deference to a cultural imperative, slasher films from the seventies bring in a last-minute male, even when he is rendered supernumerary by the Final Girl's sturdy defense. By 1980, however, the male rescuer is either dismissably marginal or dispensed with altogether; not a few films have him rush to the rescue only to be hacked to bits, leaving the Final Girl to save herself after all. At the moment that the Final Girl becomes her own savior, she becomes a hero; and the moment that she becomes a hero is the moment that the male viewer gives up the last pretense of male identification. Abject terror may still be gendered feminine, but the willingness of one immensely popular current genre to re-represent the hero as an anatomical female would seem to suggest that at least one of the traditional marks of heroism, triumphant self-rescue, is no longer strictly gendered masculine.

So too the cinematic apparatus. The classic split between "spectacle and narrative," which "supposes the man's role as the active one of forwarding the story, making things happen," is at least unsettled in the slasher film.[21] When the Final Girl (in films like *Hell Night*, *Texas Chain Saw* II, and even *Splatter University*) assumes the "active investigating gaze," she exactly reverses the look, making a spectacle of the killer and a spectator of herself. Again, it is through the killer's eyes (I-camera) that we saw the Final Girl at the beginning of the film, and through the Final Girl's eyes that we see the killer, often for the first time with any clarity, toward the end. The gaze becomes, at least for a while, female. More to the point, the female exercise of scopic control results not in her annihilation, in the manner of classic cinema, but in her triumph; indeed, her triumph *depends* on her assumption of the gaze. It is no surprise, in light of these developments, that the Final Girl should show signs of boyishness. Her symbolic phallicization, in the last scenes, may or may not proceed at root from the horror of lack on the part of audience and maker. But it certainly proceeds from the need to bring her in line with the epic laws of Western narrative tradition—the very unanimity of which bears witness to the historical importance, in popular culture, of the literal representation of heroism in male form—and it proceeds no less from the need to render the reallocated gaze intelligible to an audience conditioned by the dominant cinematic apparatus.

It is worth noting that the higher genres of horror have for the most part resisted such developments. The idea of a female who outsmarts, much less outfights—or outgazes—her assailant is unthinkable in the films of De Palma and Hitchcock. Although the slasher film's victims may be sexual teases, they are not in addition simple-minded, scheming, physically incompetent, and morally deficient in the manner of these filmmakers' female victims. And however revolting their special effects and sexualized their violence, few slasher murders approach the level of voluptuous sadism that attends the destruction of women in De Palma's films. For reasons on which we can only speculate, femininity is more conventionally elaborated and inexorably punished, and in an emphatically masculine environment, in the higher forms—the forms that *are* written up, and not by Joe Bob Briggs.

That the slasher film speaks deeply and obsessively to male anxieties and desires seems clear—if nothing else from the maleness of the majority audience. And yet these are texts in which the categories masculine and feminine, traditionally embodied in male and female, are collapsed into one and the same character—a character who is anatomically female and one whose point of view the spectator is unambiguously invited, by the usual set of literary–structural and cinematic conventions, to share. The willingness and even eagerness (so we judge from these films' enormous popularity) of the male viewer to throw in his emotional lot, if only temporarily, with not only a woman but a woman in fear and pain, at least in the first instance, would seem to suggest that he has a vicarious stake in that fear and pain. If it is also the case that the act of horror spectatorship is itself registered as a "feminine" experience—that the shock effects induce bodily sensations in the viewer answering the fear and pain of the screen victim—the charge of masochism is underlined. This is not to say that the male viewer does not also have a stake in the sadistic side; narrative structure, cinematic procedures, and audience response all indicate that he shifts back and forth with ease. It is only to suggest that in the Final Girl sequence his empathy with what the films define as the female posture is fully engaged, and further, because this sequence is inevitably the central one in any given film, that the viewing experience hinges on the emotional assumption of the feminine posture. Kaja Silverman takes it a step further: "I will hazard the generalization that it is always the victim—the figure who occupies the passive position—who is really the focus of attention, and whose subjugation the subject (whether male or female) experiences as a pleasurable repetition from his/her own story," she writes. "Indeed, I would go so far as to say that the fascination of the sadistic point of view is merely that it provides the best vantage point from which to watch the masochistic story unfold."[22]

The slasher is hardly the first genre in the literary and visual arts to invite identification with the female; one cannot help wondering more generally whether the historical maintenance of images of women in fear and pain does not have more to do with male vicarism than is commonly acknowledged. What distinguishes the slasher, however, is the absence or untenability of alternative perspectives and hence the exposed quality of the invitation. As a survey of the tradition shows, this has not always been the case. The stages of the Final Girl's evolution—her piecemeal absorption of functions previously represented in males—can be located in the years following 1978. The fact that the typical patrons of these films are the sons of marriages contracted in the 1960s or even early 1970s leads us to speculate that the dire claims of that era—that the women's movement, the entry of women into the workplace, and the rise of divorce and woman-headed families would yield massive gender confusion in the next generation—were not entirely wrong. We may prefer, in the eighties, to speak of the cult of androgyny, but the point is roughly the same. The fact that we have in the killer a feminine male and in the main character a masculine female—parent and Everyteen, respectively—would seem, especially in the latter case, to suggest a loosening of the categories, or at least of the equation sex = gender. It is not that these films show us gender and sex in free variation; it is that they fix on the irregular combinations, of which the combination masculine female repeatedly prevails over the combination feminine male. The fact that masculine males (boyfriends, fathers, would-be rescuers) are regularly dismissed through ridicule or death or both would seem to suggest that it is not masculinity per se that is being privileged, but masculinity in conjunction with a female body—indeed, as the term victim-hero contemplates, masculinity in conjunction with femininity. For if "masculine" describes the Final Girl some of the time, and in some of her more theatrical moments, it does not do justice to the sense of her character as a whole. She alternates between registers from the outset; before her final struggle she endures the deepest throes of "femininity"; and even during that final struggle she is now weak and now strong, now flees the killer and now charges him, now stabs and is stabbed, now cries out in fear and now shouts in anger. She is a physical female and a characterological androgyne: like her name, not masculine but either/or, both, ambiguous.[23]

Robin Wood speaks of the sense that horror, for him the by-product of cultural crisis and disintegration, is "currently the most important of all American [film] genres and perhaps the most progressive, even in its overt nihilism."[24] Likewise Vale and Juno say of the "incredibly strange films," mostly low-budget horror, that their volume surveys: "They often present unpopular—even radical—views addressing the social, political, racial, or sexual inequities, hypocrisy in religion or government."[25] And Tania Modleski rests her case against the standard critique of mass culture (stemming from the Frankfurt School) squarely on the evidence of the slasher, which does *not* propose a spurious harmony; does *not* promote the "specious good" (but indeed often exposes and attacks it); does *not* ply the mechanisms of identification, narrative continuity, and closure to provide the sort of narrative pleasure constitutive of the dominant ideology.[26] One is deeply reluctant to make progressive claims for a body of cinema as spectacularly nasty toward women as the slasher film is, but the fact is that the slasher does, in its own perverse way and for better or worse, constitute a visible adjustment in the terms of gender representation. That it is an adjustment largely on the male side, appearing at the furthest possible remove from the quarters of theory and showing signs of trickling upwards, is of no small interest.

Notes

I owe a special debt of gratitude to James Cunniff and Lynn Hunt for criticism and encouragement. Particular thanks to James (not Lynn) for sitting with me through not a few of these movies.

1 "The Philosophy of Composition," in *Great Short Works of Edgar Allan Poe*, ed. G. R. Thompson (New York, 1970), 55.
2 As quoted in William Schoell, *Stay Out of the Shower* (New York, 1985), 56.
3 As quoted in ibid., 41.
4 Donald Spoto, *The Dark Side of Genius: The Life of Alfred Hitchcock* (New York, 1983), 483.
5 Silvia Bovenschen, "Is There a Feminine Aesthetic?" *New German Critique* 10 (1977): 114. See also Mary Ann Doane, "Misrecognition and Identity," *Cine-Tracts* 11 (1980): 25–32.

6 E. Ann Kaplan, *Women and Film: Both Sides of the Camera* (London, 1983), 15. The discussion of the gendered "gaze" is lively and extensive. See above all Laura Mulvey, "Visual Pleasure and Narrative Cinema," *Screen* 16 (1975): 6–18; reprinted in *Film Theory and Criticism: Introductory Readings*, ed. Gerald Mast and Marshall Cohen, 3rd edn. (New York, 1985), 803–16; also Christine Gledhill, "Recent Developments in Feminist Criticism," *Quarterly Review of Film Studies* (1978); reprinted in Mast and Cohen, *Film Theory and Criticism*, 817–45.

7 Robin Wood, "Beauty Bests the Beast," *American Film* 8 (1983): 64.

8 The locus classicus in this connection is the view-from-the-coffin shot in Carl Dreyer's *Vampyr*, in which the I-camera sees through the eyes of a dead man. See Nash, "*Vampyr* and the Fantastic," esp. 32–33. The 1987 remake of *The Little Shop of Horrors* (itself originally a low-budget horror film, made the same year as *Psycho* in two days) lets us see the dentist from the proximate point of view of the patient's tonsils.

9 Two points in this paragraph deserve emending. One is the suggestion that rape is common in these films; it is in fact virtually absent, by definition. The other is the characterization of the Final Girl as "sexy." She may be attractive (though typically less so than her friends), but she is with few exceptions sexually inactive. For a detailed analysis of point-of-view manipulation, together with a psychoanalytic interpretation of the dynamic, see Steve Neale, "*Halloween*: Suspense, Aggression, and the Look," *Framework* 14 (1981).

10 Robin Wood is struck by the willingness of the teenaged audience to identify "against" itself, with the forces of the enemy of youth. "Watching it [*Texas Chain Saw Massacre I*] recently with a large, half-stoned youth audience, who cheered and applauded every one of Leatherface's outrages against their representatives on the screen, was a terrifying experience"; "Return of the Repressed," *Film Comment* 14 (1978): 32.

11 "I really appreciate the way audiences respond," Gail Anne Hurd, producer of *Aliens*, is reported to have said. "They buy it. We don't get people, even rednecks, leaving the theater saying, 'That was stupid. No woman would do that.' You don't have to be a liberal ERA supporter to root for Ripley": as reported in the *San Francisco Examiner Datebook*, 10 August 1986, 19. *Time*, 28 July 1986, 56, suggests that Ripley's maternal impulses (she squares off against the worst aliens of all in her quest to save a little girl) give the audience "a much stronger rooting interest in Ripley, and that gives the picture resonances unusual in a popcorn epic."

12 Further: "When she [the mother] referred to the infant as a male, I just went along with it. Wonder how that child turned out—male, female, or something else entirely?" The birth is understood to be parthenogenetic, and the bisexual child, literally equipped with both sets of genitals, is figured as the reborn Christ.

13 Linda Williams, "When the Woman Looks," in *Re-Vision: Essays in Feminist Film Criticism*, ed. Mary Ann Doane, Patricia Mellencamp, and Linda Williams, American Film Institute monograph series (Los Angeles, 1984), 90. Williams's emphasis on the phallic leads her to dismiss slasher killers as a "non-specific male killing force" and hence a degeneration in the tradition. "In these films the recognition and affinity between woman and monster of classic horror film gives way to pure identity: she *is* the monster, her mutilated body is the only visible horror" (96). This analysis does not do justice to the obvious bisexuality of slasher killers, nor does it take into account the new strength of the female victim. The slasher film may not, in balance, be more subversive than traditional horror, but it is certainly not less so.

14 "The woman's exercise of an active investigating gaze can only be simultaneous with her own victimization. The place of her specularization is transformed into the locus of a process of seeing designed to unveil an aggression against itself"; Mary Ann Doane, "The 'Woman's Film,'" in *Re-Vision*, 72.
15 John Carpenter interviewed by Todd McCarthy, "Trick and Treat," *Film Comment* 16 (1980): 23–24.
16 This is not so in traditional film, nor in heterosexual pornography, in any case. Gay male pornography however, films some male bodies in much the same way that heterosexual pornography films female bodies.
17 Compare the visual treatment of the (male) rape in *Deliverance* with the (female) rapes in Hitchcock's *Frenzy* or Wes Craven's *Last House on the Left* or Ingmar Bergman's *The Virgin Spring*. The latter films study the victims' faces at length and in closeup during the act; the first looks at the act intermittently and in long shot, focusing less on the actual victim than on the victim's friend who must look on.
18 This would seem to be the point of the final sequence of Brian De Palma's *Blow Out*, in which we see the boyfriend of the victim-hero stab the killer to death but later hear the television announce that the woman herself vanquished the killer. The frame plot of the film has to do with the making of a slasher film ("Co-Ed Frenzy"), and it seems clear that De Palma means his ending to stand as a comment on the Final Girl formula of the genre. De Palma's (and indirectly Hitchcock's) insistence that only men can kill men, or protect women from men, deserves a separate essay.
19 The term is Judith Fetterly's. See her *The Resisting Reader: A Feminist Approach to American Fiction* (Bloomington, Ind., 1978).
20 On the possible variety of responses to a single film, see Norman N. Holland, "I-ing Film," *Critical Inquiry* 12 (1986): 654–71.
21 Mulvey, "Visual Pleasure and Narrative Cinema," 12.
22 Kaja Silverman, "Masochism and Subjectivity," *Framework* 12 (1979): 5. Needless to say, this is not the explanation for the girl-hero offered by the industry. *Time* magazine on *Aliens*: "As Director Cameron says, the endless 'remulching' of the masculine hero by the 'male-dominated industry' is, if nothing else, commercially shortsighted. 'They choose to ignore that 50% of the audience is female. And I've been told that it has been proved demographically that 80% of the time it's women who decide which film to see'"; 28 July 1986. It is of course not Cameron who established the female hero of the series but Ridley Scott (in *Alien*), and it is fair to assume, from his careful manipulation of the formula, that Scott got her from the slasher film, where she has flourished for some time with audiences that are heavily male. Cameron's analysis is thus both self-serving and beside the point.
23 If this analysis is correct, we may expect horror films of the future to feature Final Boys as well as Final Girls. Two recent figures may be incipient examples: Jesse, the pretty boy in *A Nightmare on Elm Street II*, and Ashley, the character who dies last in *The Evil Dead* (1983). Neither quite plays the role, but their names, and in the case of Jesse the characterization, seem to play on the tradition.
24 For the opposite view (based on classic horror in both literary and cinematic manifestations), see Franco Moretti, "The Dialectic of Fear," *New Left Review* 136 (1982): 67–85.
25 Vale and Juno, *Incredibly Strange Films*, 5.

26 Tania Modleski, "The Terror of Pleasure: The Contemporary Horror Film and Postmodern Theory," in *Studies in Entertainment: Critical Approaches to Mass Culture*, ed. Tania Modleski (Bloomington, Ind., 1986), 155–66. (Like Modleski, I stress that my comments are based on many slashers, not all of them.) This important essay (and volume) appeared too late for me to take it into full account in the text.

The monster and the homosexual

7

HARRY M. BENSHOFF

In a 1984 study of anti-homosexual attitudes, the investigators broke heterosexuals' fears of gay and lesbian sexuality into three topic areas:

(1) Homosexuality as a threat to the individual – that someone you know (or you yourself) might be homosexual.
(2) Homosexuality as a threat to others – homosexuals have been frequently linked in the media to child molestation, rape, and violence.
(3) Homosexuality as a threat to the community and other components of culture – homosexuals supposedly represent the destruction of the procreative nuclear family, traditional gender roles, and (to use a buzz phrase) "family values."[1]

In short, for many people in our shared English-language culture, homosexuality is a monstrous condition. Like an evil Mr. Hyde, or the Wolfman, a gay or lesbian self inside of you might be striving to get out. Like Frankenstein's monster, homosexuals might run rampant across the countryside, claiming "innocent" victims. Or worst of all, like mad scientists or vampires, who dream of revolutionizing the world through some startling scientific discovery or preternatural power, homosexual activists strike at the very foundations of society, seeking to infect or destroy not only those around them but the very concepts of Western Judeo-Christian thought upon which civil society is built. For the better part of the twentieth century, homosexuals, like vampires, have rarely cast a reflection in the social looking-glass of popular culture. When they are seen, they are often filtered through the iconography of the horror film: ominous sound cues, shocked reaction shots, or even thunder and lightning. Both movie monsters and homosexuals have existed chiefly in shadowy closets, and when they do emerge from these proscribed places into the sunlit world, they cause panic and fear. Their closets uphold and reinforce culturally constructed binaries of gender and sexuality that structure Western thought. To create a broad analogy, monster is to "normality" as homosexual is to heterosexual.

Ostensibly based upon these melodramatic fears, as well as a host of others, the conservative right-wing and Fundamentalist Christian sectors of American society have sought to demonize homosexuals within all aspects of civil(ian) life, as well as more specialized sectors such as the military and institutionalized pedagogy. They do so primarily by painting the gay and lesbian community in shocking, horrifying colors. *The Gay Agenda* (1993), a recent anti-gay propaganda videotape (which was produced in Antelope Valley, California by a Christian group calling itself the Springs of Life Ministry), uses discredited "experts" purportedly to tell the truth about what depraved creatures homosexuals actually are: carefully selected footage from gay and lesbian pride festivals "document" their claims. The point comes across loudly and clearly: homosexuals are violent, degraded monsters and their evil agenda is to destroy the very fabric of American society. Many members of Congress, who received this tape *gratis* from the helpful Springs of Life Ministry, seemed to find its argument compelling and reasonable, especially during the recent national hysteria surrounding the question of whether or not homosexuals should be legally discriminated against within the Armed Services. A similar use of horror movie iconography has recently been employed by other Fundamentalist Christian groups in seasonal Halloween "Hell Houses." In an attempt to frighten teenage patrons into conforming to heterosexual norms, the traditional Halloween haunted house tour is reappropriated for anti-gay propaganda. Instead of showcasing vampires and werewolves, these "Hell Houses" now use monstrous effects to delineate the horrors of homosexuality and AIDS.[2]

The AIDS crisis, which has spurred Christian compassion from some quarters, has also significantly fueled this "homosexual as monster" rhetoric: now more than ever, gay men are contagions – vampires – who, with a single mingling of blood, can infect a pure and innocent victim, transforming him or her into the living dead. Some people have always considered *anything* that opposes or lies outside the ideological status quo intrinsically monstrous and unnatural. Perhaps expectedly, an ideological approach to fictional monsters frequently bleeds into an accounting of real-life horrors such as AIDS: recent critical essays on the mass media have demonstrated how the representational codes and narrative tropes of the monster movie (plague, contagion, victimization, panic) have been grafted onto much television and newspaper coverage of AIDS.[3] Yet, in his book on how the media in Great Britain have covered the AIDS crisis, Simon Watney warns us that "Aids commentary does not 'make' gay men into monsters, for homosexuality is, and always has been, constructed as intrinsically monstrous within the heavily over-determined images inside which notions of 'decency,' 'human nature,' and so on are mobilized and relayed throughout the internal circuitry of the mass media marketplace."[4] The multiple social meanings of the words "monster" and "homosexual" are seen to overlap to varying but often high degrees. Certain sectors of the population still relate homosexuality to bestiality, incest, necrophilia, sadomasochism, etc. – the very stuff of classical Hollywood monster movies. The concepts "monster" and "homosexual" share many of the same semantic charges and arouse many of the same fears about sex and death.

True to the postmodern condition, it seems clear from the preceding examples that the melodramatic formulas and patterns of representation to be found in the horror film have slipped into the realm of "real-life" politics. And while horror films and monster movies are frequently dismissed as children's fare or vacuous, meaningless escapism, the demonization (or "monsterization") of homosexuals in American society is a very serious life and death issue. One might well wish that American society could dismiss anti-gay propaganda like *The Gay Agenda* as easily as it does the latest B horror film. To do so would require the unmasking of another institutionalized power hierarchy, one embedded in the form of media texts themselves: documentaries (no matter how propagandistically they are produced) are usually perceived as somehow inherently true, while fictional film and television shows, in an attempt perhaps to bolster their own significance, maintain their own hierarchies of meaningfulness.

Thus, "political significance" in fictional film and television is reserved for realist "social problem" formats, while horror movies, like soap operas and comic books, lie at the bottom of those particular media hierarchies. What these denigrated artifacts might have to say about the culture they encode and provoke is frequently ignored and/or discounted. In what follows, however, I will be insisting that there is much to learn from looking at such texts, and arguing that the figure of the monster throughout the history of the English-language horror film can in some way be understood as a metaphoric construct standing in for the figure of the homosexual. However, while this work will argue that the figure of the monster can frequently be equated (with greater or lesser degrees of ease) with that of the homosexual, what this means from decade to decade and from film to film can be shown to change dramatically, according to the forces behind their production as well as the societal awareness and understanding of human sexuality as it is constructed in various historical periods.

Theorizing the monster queer

In the 1970s, in a series of essays exploring the horror film, critic Robin Wood suggested that the thematic core of the genre might be reduced to three interrelated variables: normality (as defined chiefly by a heterosexual patriarchal capitalism), the Other (embodied in the figure of the monster), and the relationship between the two.[5] According to Wood's formulation, these monsters can often be understood as racial, ethnic, and/or political/ideological Others, while more frequently they are constructed primarily as sexual Others (women, bisexuals, and homosexuals). Since the demands of the classical Hollywood narrative system usually insist on a heterosexual romance within the stories they construct, the monster is traditionally figured as a force that attempts to block that romance. As such, many monster movies (and the source material they draw upon) might be understood as being "about" the eruption of some form of queer sexuality into the midst of a resolutely heterosexual milieu. By "queer," I mean to use the word both in its everyday connotations ("questionable . . . suspicious . . . strange . . .") and also as how it has been theorized in recent years within academia and social politics. This latter "queer" is not only what differs "in some odd way from what is usual or normal," but ultimately is what opposes the binary definitions and proscriptions of a patriarchal heterosexism. Queer can be a narrative moment, or a performance or stance which negates the oppressive binarisms of the dominant hegemony (what Wood and other critics have identified as the variable of "normality") both within culture at large, and within texts of horror and fantasy. It is somewhat analogous to the moment of hesitation that demarcates Todorov's Fantastic, or Freud's theorization of the Uncanny: queerness disrupts narrative equilibrium and sets in motion a questioning of the status quo, and in many cases within fantastic literature, the nature of reality itself.[6]

Sociologically, the term queer has been used to describe an "oxymoronic community of difference,"[7] which includes people who might also self-identify as gay and/or lesbian, bisexual, transsexual, transvestite, drag queen, leather daddy, lipstick lesbian, pansy, fairy, dyke, butch, femme, feminist, asexual, and so on – any people not explicitly defining themselves in "traditional" heterosexual terms. Queer seeks to go beyond these and all such categories based on the concepts of normative heterosexuality and traditional gender roles to encompass a more inclusive, amorphous, and ambiguous contra-heterosexuality (thus there are those individuals who self-identify as "straight queers"). Queer is also insistent that issues of race, gender, disability, and class be addressed within its politics, making interracial sex and sex between physically challenged people dimensions of queer sex also, and further linking the queer corpus with the figure of the Other as it has been theorized by Wood in the horror film. Queer activism itself has been seen as unruly, defiant, and angry: like the mad scientists of horror films, queer proponents do want to restructure society by calling attention to and eventually dismantling the oppressive assumptions of heterocentrist discourse. As one theorist has noted,

> the queer, unlike the rather polite categories of gay and lesbian, revels in the discourse of the loathsome, the outcast, the idiomatically proscribed position of same-sex desire. Unlike petitions for civil rights, queer revels constitute a kind of activism that attacks the dominant notion of the natural. The queer is the taboo-breaker, the monstrous, the uncanny. Like the Phantom of the Opera, the queer dwells underground, below the operatic overtones of the dominant; frightening to look at, desiring, as it plays its own organ, producing its own music.[8]

Queer even challenges "the Platonic parameters of Being – the borders of life and death."[9] Queer suggests death over life by focusing on non-procreative sexual behaviors, making it especially suited to a genre which takes sex and death as central thematic concerns.

Other film genres – the melodrama, the musical – also lend themselves to such queer theorization, yet few do so as readily as the fantastic genres. While each of these genres are very different in many ways, they are similar in that they create a ready-made (non-realist) hyperspace for their spectators, diegetic worlds in which heterocentrist assumptions may be as "real" or as "make-believe" as magic and monsters. As Alexander Doty has noted, "*everyone's* pleasure in these genres is 'perverse,' is queer, as much of it takes place within the space of the contra-heterosexual and the contra-straight."[10] In the case of monster movies and science fiction films, the narrative elements themselves demand the depiction of alien "Otherness," which is often coded (at the site of production and/or reception) as lesbian, gay, or otherwise queer. As one bibliographic review of the genre notes,

> Fantastic literature has always contained depictions of homosexuality, both female and male. It has also contained portraits of androgynes, transsexuals, gender-switching people, and alien sexuality that is clearly not heterosexual. In the centuries before writers could deal explicitly with homosexuality, they used fantastic literature's various forms to disguise homoerotic passions.[11]

In this respect, horror stories and monster movies, perhaps more than any other genre, actively invoke queer readings, because of their obvious metaphorical (non-realist) forms and narrative formats which disrupt the heterosexual status quo.

Yet, as products of a patriarchal culture, these artifacts also tend to narrow the scope of the word queer by reflecting the dominant culture's masculinist bias, wherein all of queer's multifarious plurality is most frequently signified in terms of (white) men and male homosexuality. The female here serves as the source of the monstrous taint: the male homosexual or queer is monstrous precisely because he embodies characteristics of the feminine, either in outward displays or in the selection of a sexual object choice traditionally reserved for women. (Julia Kristeva reached this conclusion with her study of the "abject" – "that which does not 'respect borders, positions, rules' . . . that which 'disturbs identity, system, order.'"[12] Kristeva centrally locates the abject in patriarchal culture's fear of and revulsion towards the specifically maternal body with its fluid boundary-crossing potential; it destroys rigid territoriality and undermines binary oppositions, just as queer theory insists.)

Furthermore, in accordance with the masculine/feminine model in which Hollywood homosexuality is/was usually depicted, gay or quasi-gay couples in film are often made to mimic heterosexual role-models. This stereotype has broad implications, as Richard Dyer points out:

> Where gayness occurs in films it does so as *part of* dominant ideology. It is not there to express itself, but rather to express something about sexuality in general *as understood by heterosexuals* . . . how homosexuality is thought and felt by heterosexuals is part and parcel of the way the culture teaches them (and us) to think and feel about their heterosexuality. Anti-gayness is not a discrete ideological system, but part of the overall sexual ideology of our culture.[13]

The stereotype of the butch and femme halves of the homosexual couple (or the monster queer couple) reflects the inherent sexism in the heterosexual model: the sexist ideology enforces the belief that men and women cannot be equal by disallowing the possibility of a relationship between two (same-sex) equals. This coded inequality of the sexes becomes one of the bases for the dominant ideology's fear and loathing of male homosexuals. According to this model, one man "must" feminize himself (give up the phallus) and act as the "woman" to another man. Reflecting this, as well as other cultural and formal sexist imperatives, the majority of homosexual figures in the American cinema (especially during the classical period) have been and still are coded as masculine with some type of feminine and/or monstrous taint.[14] In horror films, monsters which might be understood as displaced lesbian figures occur far less frequently (although perhaps they are more readily acknowledged, as in the construct of the overtly lesbian vampire). Also rarer in Hollywood cinema, though certainly present, are those monsters which might be understood as reflecting the fears of androgyny or transsexualism. Yet, because American culture has generally constructed its ideas about and fears of homosexuality within a framework of male homosexuality, the majority of the monsters investigated in the following pages reflects this bias. As such, what this work will be chiefly investigating might be considered a "subset" of queer: (primarily male) homosexuality, even as it draws from the expanding body of queer theory and historiography of twentieth-century gay and lesbian experience.[15]

Earlier critical thinking on the monster movie frequently drew upon metaphysical or psychoanalytic concepts relating to the genre's twin obsessions, sex and death. Some earlier writing on the links between cinematic horror and (homo)sexuality used a Freudian model of repression as a theoretical rubric. In Margaret Tarratt's groundbreaking essay of the early 1970s, "Monsters from the Id," the author examined Hollywood monster movies of the 1950s and persuasively postulated that the monster represented an eruption of repressed sexual desire.[16] Thus, 1951's *The Thing (from Another World)* develops explicit parallels between the monster in question and the libidinous nature of the film's male lead, Captain Hendry. The monster serves as a metaphoric expression of Hendry's lusts; it is a displaced and concretized figure of phallic desire. Even a cursory glance at the monster movies of this era will repeatedly reveal this trope: *The Creature from the Black Lagoon* (1954), *The Giant Gila Monster* (1959), and most of their scaly brethren seem to "pop up" like clockwork whenever the hero and heroine move into a romantic clinch. The ideas put forth by Tarratt became common and useful tools to understanding the functioning of the genre, but what is perhaps less well known was that her essay was initially published in the British journal *Films and Filming*, which was produced and marketed primarily for and to a gay male readership.[17]

During the 1970s and 1980s, in a series of articles and books, Canadian film scholar Robin Wood further developed Tarratt's ideas, expanding them generally to all horror films, and specifically to the films of 1970s-horror auteurs such as Larry Cohen, Wes Craven, and Tobe Hooker. (Robin Wood is himself a gay man who makes certain distinctions between his pre- and post- "coming out" work in film criticism).[18] Drawing on Herbert Marcuse's and Gad Horowitz's readings of Marx and Freud (in *Eros and Civilization* and *Repression*, respectively),[19] Wood invokes concepts of basic and surplus repression to sketch a model of life under patriarchal capitalism. According to this model, society cannot be formed or continue to exist without a certain amount of basic repression. Surplus repression, on the other hand, is used by those in control to keep all "Others" subjugated to the dominant order. The Other reciprocally bolsters the image of "normality": as Simon Watney has observed, "Straight society needs us [homosexuals]. We are its necessary 'Other.' Without gays, straights are not straight."[20] According to Wood's readings of the American horror film, it is easy to see these Others cast in the role of the monster: repressed by society, these sociopolitical and psychosexual Others are displaced (as in a nightmare) onto monstrous signifiers, in which form they return to wreak havoc in the cinema. While some have critiqued this model as essentialist, Wood did note the importance of historical parameters in understanding the relationship between normality and monsters, asserting that "[t]he monster is, of course, much more protean, changing from period to period as society's basic fears clothe themselves in fashionable or immediately accessible garments."[21]

For many, the repressive hypothesis explicit in Tarratt's and Wood's readings of the genre was overturned by the work of the French theorist Michel Foucault, who, in *The History of Sexuality* (1978) argued that sexuality is in fact not repressed by society, but rather explicitly constructed and regulated via a series of discourses which include those of the medical, legal, religious, and media establishments. While many of these discourses have the same effect on certain sectors of society as might be argued under the repressive hypothesis (the exclusion from the public sphere, dehumanization, and monsterization of certain forms of sexuality), Foucault argues that "it is a ruse to make prohibition into the basic and constitutive element from which one would be able to write the history of what has been said concerning sex starting from the modern epoch."[22] In a by now famous turn of phrase, Foucault noted of "repression" that "[t]here is not one but many silences."[23] (This does not mean that basic psychoanalytic concepts such as sexual repression and ego-dystonic homosexuality will not be discussed within the following pages. Indeed, homosexual repression – as it might exist within an individual psyche rather within society at large – is still a potent formulation in how one might understand the homosexual and/or homophobic dynamics of many horror films.)

Like Wood, Foucault was a homosexual cultural critic who drew upon (and eventually expanded) a Marxist understanding of how society regulates human sexuality, developing a more precisely historicized formulation which examines how power and knowledge are embedded in the practice of social discourse. Shifting the debate from the repression of sex to the production of sexuality, Foucault noted that ours is now a culture wherein "the politics of the body does not require the elision of sex or its restriction solely to the reproductive function; it relies instead on a multiple channeling into the controlled circuits of the economy – on what has been called [by Marcuse] a hyper-repressive desublimation."[24] As sex and sexuality become more ever-present in the public sphere, they are nonetheless regulated into certain cultural constructions through powerful social discourses. Yet, as Foucault further asserts,

> we must conceive discourse as a series of discontinuous segments whose tactical function is neither uniform nor stable. To be more precise, we must not imagine a world of discourse divided between accepted discourse and excluded discourse, or between the dominant discourse and the dominated one; but as a multiplicity of discursive elements that can come into play in various strategies.[25]

As British cultural theorists such as Stuart Hall have pointed out, the multiplicity of these discourses and their multiple sites of reception also allow for the active negotiation of these issues. Thus, when talking about a cultural product or "discursive object" such as a filmic genre system, one would be wise to take into consideration the historical discourses not only of production (where meanings are encoded) but also those of reception (where meanings are decoded according to a multiplicity of different reading positions).[26]

[. . .]

How actual practices of spectatorship interact with the narrative patterns of a genre system must then be considered when discussing the queer pleasures of a horror film text itself. Where does the viewer of monster movies position him/herself in relation to the text? The overtly heterosexualized couple of the classical horror film of the 1930s might be said to represent the most common (or intended?) site of spectatorial identification for these particular films, yet as many theorists have pointed out, it is more likely that specific shot mechanisms within the film's formal construction will link the spectator's gaze to that of the gothic villain or monster.[27] Furthermore, there is more to the processes of spectatorial identification than patterns of subjective shots and cinematic suture.[28] For example, the heterosexualized couple in these films is invariably banal and underdeveloped in relation to the sadomasochistic villain(s), whose outrageous exploits are, after all, the *raison d'être* of the genre. To phrase it in Richard Dyer's terms, in the horror film, it is usually the heterosexualized hero and heroine who are stereotyped – painted with broad brush strokes – while the villains and monsters are given more complex, "novelistic" characterizations.[29] As the titular stars of their own filmic stories, perhaps it is the monsters that the audience comes to enjoy, experience, and identify with; in many films, normative heterosexuality is reduced to a trifling narrative convention, one which becomes increasingly unnecessary and outmoded as the genre evolves across the years.

[. . .]

The focus of this work – for a hopefully welcome change – presupposes a queer spectator who attends these genre films for pleasure and entertainment. What does it mean if lesbians identify with the beautiful female vampires of *The Hunger* (1983), or if gay men go to see Tom Cruise bite Brad Pitt in *Interview with the Vampire* (1994)? In what ways does this happen and what is the "price paid" in culture-at-large for yet another depiction of monstrous predatory homosexuals? Identification with the monster can mean many different things to many different people, and is not necessarily always a negative thing for the individual spectators in question, even as some depictions of queer monsters undoubtedly conflate and reinforce certain sexist or homophobic fears within the public sphere. For spectators of all types, the experience of watching a horror film or monster movie might be understood as similar to that of the Carnival as it has been theorized by Bakhtin, wherein the conventions of normality are ritualistically overturned within a prescribed period of time in order to celebrate the lure of the deviant.[30] Halloween functions similarly, allowing otherwise "normal" people the pleasures of drag, or monstrosity, for a brief but exhilarating experience. However, while straight participants in such experiences usually return to their daylight worlds, both the monster and the homosexual are permanent residents of shadowy spaces: at worst caves, castles, and closets, and at best a marginalized and oppressed position within the cultural hegemony. Queer viewers are thus more likely than straight ones to experience the monster's plight in more personal, individualized terms.

What then exactly makes the experience of a horror film or monster movie gay, lesbian, or queer? There are at least four different ways in which homosexuality might intersect with the horror film. The first and most obvious of these occurs when a horror film includes identifiably gay and/or lesbian characters. These characters might be victims, passers-by, or the monsters themselves, although gay and lesbian people (to this point in time) have never been placed in the role of the normative hero or heroine.[31] Broadly speaking, the appearance of overtly homosexual film characters doesn't occur until the late 1960s and early 1970s, following the demise of the Production Code and its restrictions against the depiction of "sex perversion." Films such as *Blacula* (1972), *Theatre of Blood* (1973), or *The Sentinel* (1977) fall into this category. In these films, gay or lesbian characters fall victim to the monster just as straight characters do, although somewhat disturbingly their fates are frequently deemed "deserved" by the films they inhabit, often solely on the basis of their characters' homosexuality. Other films such as *The Fearless Vampire Killers* (1967), *The Vampire Lovers* (1971), or *The Hunger* (1983), characterize their vampires as specifically homosexual or bisexual. These films have perhaps done much to cement into place the current social construction of homosexuals as unnatural, predatory, plague-carrying killers, even as they also might provide a pleasurable power-wish fulfillment fantasy for some queer viewers.

The second type of homo-horror film is one written, produced, and/or directed by a gay man or lesbian, even if it does not contain visibly homosexual characters. Reading these films as gay or lesbian is predicated upon (what some might call a debased) concept of the cinematic auteur, which would argue that gay or lesbian creators of film products infuse some sort of "gay sensibility" into their films either consciously or otherwise. Yet such questions of authorship, which are certainly important and hold bearing on this particular study (for example the films of James Whale or Ed Wood) will herein be of lesser importance, since it is not necessary to be a self-identified homosexual or queer in order to produce a text which has something to say about homosexuality, heterosexuality, and the queerness that those two terms proscribe and enforce.[32] A variation on the homo-horror auteur approach is that in which a gay or lesbian film star (whether "actually" homosexual or culturally perceived as such) brings his/her persona to a horror film. Classical Hollywood cinema is full of such performers, who, regardless of their off-screen lives, bring an unmistakable homosexual air to the characters they create: Eric Blore, Franklin Pangborn, Robert Walker, George Sanders, Judith Anderson, Eve Arden, Greta Garbo, and Marlene Dietrich, to name just a few. The characters created in 1930s horror films by Charles Laughton or by Vincent Price in the 1960s and early 1970s best typify this type of homo-horror film.

The third and perhaps most important way that homosexuality enters the genre is through subtextual or connotative avenues. For the better part of cinema's history, homosexuality on screen has been more or less allusive: it lurks around the edges of texts and characters rather than announcing itself forthrightly. In films such as *White Zombie* (1932), *The Seventh Victim* (1943), or *How To Make a Monster* (1958), homosexuality becomes a subtle but undoubtedly present signifier which usually serves to characterize the villain or monster. This particular trope is not exclusive to the horror film. It has been pointed out in films *noir*, action films, and in other films wherever homosexuality is used to further delineate the depravity of the villain.[33] Alexander Doty has argued against this model of connotation, suggesting that it keeps gay and lesbian concerns marginalized: "connotation has been the representational and interpretive closet of mass culture queerness for far too long . . . [This] shadowy realm of connotation . . . allows straight culture to use queerness for pleasure and profit in mass culture without admitting to it."[34] Accordingly, in many of these films, queerness is reduced to titillation, frisson, fashion, or fad. The "love that dare not speak its name" remains a shadowy Other which conversely works to bolster the equally constructed idea of a normative heterosexuality.

But it is also precisely this type of connotation (conscious or otherwise) which allows for and fosters the multiplicity of various readings and reading positions, including what has been called active queer (or gay, or lesbian) reading practices. If we adopt Roland Barthes's model of signification wherein the denotative meaning of any signifier is simply the first of many possible meanings along a connotative chain, then we can readily acknowledge that a multitude of spectators, some queer, some not, will each understand the "denotative" events of a visual narrative in different ways. For Doty, then, there is the (fourth) sense that any film viewed by a gay or lesbian spectator might be considered queer. The queer spectator's "gay-dar," already attuned to the possible discovery of homosexuality within culture-at-large, here functions in relation to specific cultural artifacts. As such, "Queer readings aren't 'alternative' readings, wishful or willful misreadings, or 'reading too much into things' readings. They result from the recognition and articulation of the complex range of queerness that has been in popular culture texts and their audiences all along."[35] In the case of horror films and monster movies, this "complex range of queerness" circulates through and around the figure of the monster, and in his/her relation to normality.

These approaches to finding homosexuals in and around the text are hardly mutually exclusive – in fact, these factors usually work in some combination to produce a text which might easily be understood as being "about" homosexuality. James Whale's *The Old Dark House* (1932), directed by and starring homosexual men, would be one such film that combines these approaches: while it might be possible for some spectators to miss the homosexual undercurrents which fuel the plot (since no character is forthrightly identified as overtly homosexual), for other spectators these themes readily leap off the screen. Conversely, other films which have no openly homosexual input or context might still be understood as queer by virtue of the ways in which they situate and represent their monster(s) in relation to heterosexuality. Ultimately, then, this project rests upon the variable and intersubjective responses between media texts and their spectators, in this case spectators whose individualized social subjectivities have already prepared and enabled them to acknowledge "the complex range of queerness" that exists in the English-language monster movie.

[. . .]

Notes

1 See John Wayne Plasek and Janicemarie Allard, "Misconceptions of Homophobia," in *Bashers, Baiters, & Bigots: Homophobia in American Society*, ed. John P. De Cecco (New York: Harrington Park Press, 1985) 23–38.

2 For more on the phenomenon, see Kellie Gibbs, "Fundamentalist Halloween: Scared All the Way to Jesus," *Out* 29 (February 1996) 20.

3 Some of these essays include: Ellis Hanson, "Undead," in *inside/out: Lesbian Theories, Gay Theories*, ed. Diana Fuss (New York: Routledge, 1991) 324–340; Andrew Parker, "Grafting David Cronenberg: Monstrosity, AIDS Media, National/Sexual Difference" and Katharine Park, "Kimberly Bergalis, AIDS, and the Plague Metaphor," both in *Media Spectacles*, eds Marjorie Garber, Jann Matlock, and Rebecca Walkowitz (New York: Routledge, 1993) 209–231 and 232–254.

Other writings on the connections between fictional monsters and homosexuality (not cited directly below) include: Terry Castle, *The Apparitional Lesbian: Female Homosexuality and Modern Culture* (New York: Columbia University Press, 1993); Rhona J. Berenstein, *Attack of the Leading Ladies: Gender, Sexuality, and Spectatorship in Classic Horror Cinema* (New York: Columbia University Press, 1996); Richard Dyer, "Children of the Night: Vampirism as Homosexuality, Homosexuality as Vampirism," *Sweet Dreams: Sexuality, Gender, and Popular Fiction*, ed. Susannah Radstone (London: Lawrence and Wishart, 1988) 47–72; Bonnie Zimmerman, "*Daughters of Darkness*: Lesbian Vampires," *Jump Cut* 24/25 (1981) 23–24; Martin F. Norden, "Sexual References in James Whale's *Bride of Frankenstein*," *Eros in the Mind's Eye: Sexuality and the Fantastic in Art and Film*, ed. Donald Palumbo (New York: Greenwood Press, 1986) 141–150; Elizabeth Reba Weise, "Bisexuality, *The Rocky Horror Picture Show*, and Me," in *Bi Any Other Name: Bisexual People Speak Out*, eds Loraine Hutchins and Lani Kaahumanu (Boston, MA: Alyson, 1991) 134–139; Patricia White, "Female Spectator, Lesbian Specter: *The Haunting*," in *inside/out: Lesbian Theories, Gay Theories*, ed. Diana Fuss (New York: Routledge, 1991) 142–172; Diana Fuss, "Monsters of Perversion: Jeffrey Dahmer and *The Silence of the Lambs*," in *Media Spectacles*, eds Marjorie Garber, Jann Matlock, and Rebecca L. Walkowitz (New York: Routledge, 1993) 181–205; Edward Guerrero, "AIDS as Monster in Science Fiction and Horror Cinema," *Journal of Popular Film and Television* 18:3 (Fall 1990) 86–93.

4 Simon Watney, *Policing Desire: Pornography, AIDS, and the Media*, second edition (Minneapolis: University of Minnesota Press, 1987) 42.

5 Many of these essays have been reworked and published in Robin Wood, *Hollywood: From Vietnam to Reagan* (New York: Columbia University Press, 1986) 79.

6 Tzvetan Todorov, *The Fantastic: A Structural Approach to a Literary Genre*, trans. Richard Howard (Ithaca, NY: Cornell University Press, 1973) especially 25–40; Sigmund Freud, "The Uncanny," in *The Standard Edition of the Complete Psychological Works of Sigmund Freud, Vol. XVII*, trans. James Strachey (London: The Hogarth Press, 1955) 219–252.

This trope of the genre has been theorized by a great many people in a variety of ways. For example, Noël Carroll has focused on rot, ooze, slime, and blood as generic motifs which suggest transition and transgression, concluding that "What horrifies is that which lies outside cultural categories" – in short, the queer (Noël Carroll, *The Philosophy of Horror, or Paradoxes of the Heart* (New York: Routledge, 1990) 35).

7 Louise Sloan, "Beyond Dialogue," *San Francisco Bay Guardian Literary Supplement* (March 1991), quoted in Lisa Duggan, "Making it Perfectly Queer," *Socialist Review* (April 1992) 19.

8 Sue Ellen Case, "Tracking the Vampire," *differences* 3:2 (Summer 1991) 3.

9 Case 3.

10 Alexander Doty, *Making Things Perfectly Queer: Interpreting Mass Culture* (Minneapolis: University of Minnesota Press, 1993) 15.

11 Eric Garber and Lyn Paleo, *Uranian Worlds: a Guide to Alternative Sexuality in Science Fiction, Fantasy, and Horror* (Boston, MA: G. K. Hall and Co., 1990) vii.

12 Quoted from Julia Kristeva, *The Powers of Horror: An Essay on Abjection*, trans. Leon S. Roudiez (New York: Columbia University Press, 1982), in Barbara Creed, "Horror and the Monstrous-Feminine: An Imaginary Abjection," Screen 27 (January–February 1986) 44–70. Expanding upon Kristeva's ideas, Creed notes that "definitions of the monstrous as constructed in the modern horror text are grounded in ancient religious and historical notions of abjection) – particularly in relation to the following religious 'abominations': sexual immorality and perversion; corporeal alteration, decay and death; human sacrifice; murder; the corpse; bodily wastes; the feminine body and incest." This list accurately describes the constellation of factors that surround and circulate through the social constructions of both the homosexual and the monster.

13 Richard Dyer, "Gays in Film," *Jump Cut* 18 (August 1978) 16.

14 For more on this and related points, see Barbara Creed, "Dark Desires: Male Masochism in the Horror Film," in *Screening the Male: Exploring Masculinity in Hollywood Cinema*, eds Steven Cohan and Ina Rae Hark (New York: Routledge, 1993) 118–133.

15 A brief note on terminology. Generally speaking, in the following pages I use the term "homosexual" in a somewhat clinical sense, to refer to a predisposition towards same-sex desire and sexual activity. I use the words "gay" and "lesbian" in reference to the specific twentieth-century construction(s) of that same desire and activity: gay and lesbian refer to *social* identities. "Queer" is the most multifarious term, encompassing homosexual, gay, lesbian and all other terms used for describing contra-straight sexuality; thus most of the monsters depicted in horror films are "monster queers" by virtue of their "deviant" sexuality. I also use queer to refer to a reading protocol, one described by aspects of textual coding and active spectatorship that question or go beyond normative, compulsory, white, male, heterosexist assumptions.

16 Margaret Tarratt, "Monsters from the Id," *Films and Filming* 17:3 (December 1970) 38–42 and 17:4 (January 1971) 40–42. Reprinted in Barry Keith Grant, ed., *Film Genre Reader* (Austin: University of Texas Press, 1986) 258–277.

17 For a brief narrative history of *Films and Filming*, see Anthony Slide, ed., *International Film, Radio, and Television Journals* (Westport, CT: Greenwood Press, 1985) 163–164. Slide notes the magazine's "definite homosexual slant" and also the mild controversy it caused in 1971 when some readers began to object. See also "Letters," *Films and Filming* (July 1971) 4.

18 See "Responsibilities of a Gay Film Critic," *Film Comment* 14:1 (January–February 1978), Reprinted in Bill Nichols, ed., *Movies and Methods, Volume Two* (Los Angeles: University of California Press, 1985) 649–660. One might wonder as to the degree his thinking about and writing on the horror film was related to this process.

19 Herbert Marcuse, *Eros and Civilization: A Philosophical Inquiry into Freud* (Boston, MA: Beacon Press, 1955), Gad Horowitz, *Repression: Basic and Surplus Repression in Psychoanalytic Theory: Freud, Reich, and Marcuse* (Buffalo: University of Toronto Press, 1977).

20 Watney 26.

21 Wood 79.

22 Michel Foucault, *The History of Sexuality*, trans. Robert Hurley (New York: Vintage Books, 1978) 12.

23 Foucault 27.

24 Foucault 114. Compare these thoughts with those of Herbert Marcuse in "Chapter Three: The Conquest of the Unhappy Consciousness: Repressive Desublimation," in *One-Dimensional Man: Studies in the Ideology of Advanced Industrial Society* (Boston, MA: Beacon Press, 1964) 56–83.

25 Foucault 100.

26 For an overview of the theoretical arguments which developed within and from the Birmingham Centre for Contemporary Cultural Studies, see Graeme Turner, *British Cultural Studies: An Introduction* (Boston, MA: Unwin Hyman 1990). Many of the most important original essays are collected in Michael Gurevitch, Tony Bennett, James Curran and Janet Woolacott, eds, *Culture, Society and the Media* (New York: Methuen, 1982) and Stuart Hall, Dorothy Hobson, Andrew Lowe, and Paul Willis, eds, *Culture, Media, Language* (London: Hutchinson, 1980).

27 Linda Williams, "When the Woman Looks," in *Re-Vision: Essays in Feminist Film Criticism*, eds Mary Ann Doane, Patricia Mellencamp, and Linda Williams (Los Angeles: University Publications of America, Inc., 1984) 83–99.

28 For an exploration of some of these issues, see Nick Browne, "The Spectator-in-the-Text: The Rhetoric of *Stagecoach*," in *Movies and Methods*, Vol. 2, ed. Bill Nichols (Los Angeles: University of California Press, 1985) 458–475.

29 Richard Dyer, "The Role of Stereotypes," in *The Matter of Images: Essays on Representation* (New York: Routledge, 1993) 11–18.

30 For a discussion of the Bakhtinian Carnival and how it relates to film (and briefly Halloween), see Robert Stam, "Chapter Three: Film, Literature, and the Carnivalesque," *Subversive Pleasures: Bakhtin, Cultural Criticism, and Film* (Baltimore: The Johns Hopkins University Press, 1989) 85–121. Although he doesn't specifically talk about horror films, several of the ten criteria he isolates for the cinematic expression of the Carnivalesque are highly relevant to the genre.

31 For an interesting account of how gay and lesbian actors get marginalized both within Hollywood narrative systems and industrial practice, see Patricia White, "Supporting Character: The Queer Career of Agnes Moorehead," in *Out in Culture: Gay, Lesbian, and Queer Essays on Popular Culture*, eds Corey K. Creekmur and Alexander Doty (Durham, NC and London: Duke University Press, 1995) 91–114.

32 For a fuller discussion of these issues, see Doty 17–38.

33 See Dyer, "Homosexuality and Film Noir," in *The Matter of Images: Essays on Representations* (New York: Routledge, 1993) 52–72.

34 Doty xi–xii.

35 Doty 16.

PART THREE

PRODUCING HORRORS

Introduction

In Parts I and II, the various extracts tried in different ways to relate the horror film to the cultural contexts within which it was produced. However, these were largely seen in rather general terms. Films were therefore related to general cultural structures such as capitalism or patriarchy.

Part III concentrates on rather more specific studies of the contexts within which films are produced. For example, in various different ways, each of these articles examines the specific economic and institutional systems within which horror films have been produced, although each extract, in its own way, relates these systems to other issues and processes.

In Chapter 8, Paul O'Flinn concentrates on the process of 'adaptation' through which Mary Shelley's classic novel, *Frankenstein*, came to be made into a film, James Whale's *Frankenstein* (1931). He starts out by considering the ways in which Mary Shelley's novel can be related to the cultural context within which it was written. While many studies present their cultural contexts as simple and inert backgrounds that were the foundations for more complex and dynamic texts, O'Flinn presents the context of *Frankenstein*'s production as one of complexity and contradictions. Here the cultural context is seen as a process of dialogue and debate which was not simply a background to Mary Shelley's novel, but rather a process within which the novel was a particular intervention.

However, when O'Flinn moves on to discuss the film, *Frankenstein*, which was produced by Universal Pictures, he moves on to consider the industrial conditions of its production. This does not involve a detailed study of the film's production history as more recent criticism has begun to do, but rather a more general criticism of mass culture. Mary Shelley's novel may have been a Gothic novel, which was 'pre-eminently a middle-class form in terms of authors and values as well as readership' (p. 109), but it was also a radical political statement. However, for O'Flinn, the Universal horror films were 'middle-class in none of these senses, produced as they are by large businesses in search of mass audiences' (p. 109), and so reproduce 'the dominant ideology in the 1930s' (p. 112). Two things are interesting here: first, that a middle-class audience is seen as compatible with radicalism while a mass audience is not; and second, that while it is deemed necessary to provide a critique of the political economy of a mass-audience film, there is no similar study of the political economy of book production in Mary Shelley's time. In other words, O'Flinn makes the familiar error of ignoring the political economy of legitimate culture, while simultaneously condemning the popular for its pursuit of profit (see, for example, Hollows, 1995).

Chapter 9 moves on from the Gothic horror films made at Universal Pictures in the 1930s to discuss those made at the British studio Hammer during the late 1950s through to the mid-1970s. In this extract, Peter Hutchings discusses the various ways in which critics have tried to relate these films to the national context of their production. In other words, Hutchings examines these films in relation to debates over British national cinema. In most of these accounts, the national culture is seen as something that is unique and indigenous to a people that can be expressed, in some form, within films. However, Hutchings proposes an alternative way of understanding a national film culture. Rather than an expression of some pre-existing national essence, Hutchings argues that Hammer's distinctive features were ways of distinguishing their products from those of other national cinemas. In other words, these features were not simply shaped by internal features, but through the relations of British film production to that of other national cinemas. The supposedly 'distinctive' features of British films can therefore be seen as the product of market differentiation in which the British film industry sought to compete with other national film industries by offering something different. As a result, it is also important to recognize that these films were made as much for an international market as for the home market.

Finally, in Chapter 10, Joan Hawkins raises questions about the context of horror production in another way. From Wood onwards, horror has usually been praised as a radical and transgressive genre, and this position has tended to privilege the low-budget horror film. A similar strategy can also be found in Clover's work on the slasher film:

> To a remarkable extent, horror has come to seem to me not only the form that most obviously trades in the repressed, but itself the repressed of mainstream filmmaking. When I see an Oscar-winning film like *The Accused* or the artful *Alien* with its blockbuster sequel *Aliens* or, more recently, *Sleeping with the Enemy* and *Silence of the Lambs*, and even *Thelma and Louise*, I cannot help thinking of all the low-budget, often harsh and awkward but sometimes deeply energetic films that preceded them by a decade or more – films that said it all, in flatter terms, and on a shoestring.
>
> (Clover, 1992: 20)

As a result, horror is often seen as an example of low culture: a radical, subaltern and even underground genre that is opposed to the middle-class mainstream. However, as Hawkins demonstrates, horror is not quite so simply an example of low culture, but on the contrary there is considerable traffic between the low horror and high avant-garde cinema. The line between the two in terms of both production and consumption is extremely blurred and unstable.

Indeed, the problem here is precisely that so many critics are attracted to horror exactly because it can be made to conform to avant-garde aesthetics, in which the low and high can be championed precisely through their difference from the mainstream or middlebrow. In many ways, throughout the history of both horror-film criticism and film studies more generally, it has not been low culture that has been the predominant problem, but rather the mainstream or middlebrow culture (Jancovich, forthcoming).

Production and reproduction 8

The case of *Frankenstein*

PAUL O'FLINN

Mary Shelley's Gothic novel *Frankenstein* was published anonymously in 1818. In the same year, a couple of other novels – Peacock's *Nightmare Abbey* and Jane Austen's *Northanger Abbey* – also appeared and their derisive use of Gothic conventions suggested that the form, fashionable for fifty years, was sliding into decline and disrepute. There seemed good reason to suppose that *Frankenstein*, an adolescent's first effort at fiction, would fade from view before its print-run was sold out.

Yet several generations later Mary Shelley's monster, having resisted his creator's attempts to eliminate him in the book, is able to reproduce himself with the variety and fertility that Frankenstein had feared. Apart from steady sales in Penguin, Everyman and OUP editions, there have been over a hundred film adaptations and there have been the Charles Addams cartoons in the *New Yorker*; Frankie Stein blunders about in the pages of *Whoopee* and *Monster Fun* comics, and approximate versions of the monster glare out from chewing gum wrappers and crisp bags. In the USA he forged a chain of restaurants; in South Africa in 1955 the work was banned as indecent and objectionable.[1]

None of these facts are new and some of them are obvious to anyone walking into a newsagent's with one eye open. They are worth setting out briefly here because *Frankenstein* seems to me to be a case where some recent debates in critical theory about cultural production and reproduction might usefully be centred, a work whose history can be used to test the claims that theory makes.[2] That history demonstrates clearly the futility of a search for the 'real', 'true' meaning of a work. There is no such thing as *Frankenstein*, there are only *Frankensteins*, as the text is ceaselessly rewritten, reproduced, refilmed and redesigned. The fact that many people call the monster Frankenstein and thus confuse the pair betrays the extent of that restructuring. What I would like to offer is neither a naive deconstructionist delight at the endless plurality of meanings the text has been able to afford nor a gesture of cultural despair at the failure of the Philistines to read the original and get it right. Instead I'd like to argue that at its moment of production *Frankenstein*, in an oblique way, was in touch with central tensions and contradictions in industrial society and only by seeing it in those terms can the prodigious efforts made over the last century and a half to alter and realign the work and its meanings be understood – a work that lacked that touch and that address could safely be left, as Marx said in another context, to the gnawing criticism of the mice.

Frankenstein is a particularly good example of three of the major ways in which alteration and realignment of this sort happens: firstly, through the operations of criticism; secondly, as a function of the shift from one medium to another; and thirdly as a result of the unfolding of history itself. The operations of criticism on this text are at present more vigorous than usual. When I was a student twenty years ago I picked up the *Pelican Guide to English Literature* to find the novel more or less wiped out in a direly condescending half-sentence as 'one of those second-rate works, written under the influence of more distinguished minds, that sometimes display in conveniently simple form the preoccupations of a coterie'.[3] *Frankenstein* may have been on T.V. but it wasn't on the syllabus. A generation and a lot of feminist criticism later and Mary Shelley is no longer a kind of half-witted secretary to Byron and Shelley but a woman writer whose text articulates and has been convincingly shown to articulate elements of woman's experience of patriarchy, the family and the trauma of giving birth.[4]

The second instance – the way a text's meaning alters as it moves from one medium to another – is something I'd like to look at in more detail [. . .] by examining the two classic screen versions: Universal's movie directed 1931 by James Whale and staring Boris Karloff, and Terence Fisher's picture for Hammer Films in 1957 with Peter Cushing. Literary criticism only metaphorically rewrites texts: the words on the page remain the same but the meanings they are encouraged to release differ. But a shift of medium means the literal rewriting of a text as novel becomes script becomes film. Scope for the ideological wrenching and reversing of a work and its way of seeing is here therefore even larger; some sense of the extent such changes can reach was evident not long ago in the BBC television serial of Malcolm Bradbury's *The History Man*, a novel set in 1972 and written in 1975. Its aggrieved author complained:

> By the time (the television adaptation) appeared in 1981, instead of being a needling critique of what exists, it is a satirical attack on what has already passed – and can therefore be misused by people who want to take it over from the Right, in order to turn it into an attack on sociology, universities, radicalism, in ways I deeply resented and disapproved of. If I'd known where 1981 was leading I might have doubted whether it should be turned into a television series.[5]

Bradbury's comment leads into the third category I suggested earlier – namely the way in which the movement of history itself refocuses a text and reorders its elements. *Frankenstein*, I'd like to argue, meant certain things in 1818 but meant and could be made to mean different things in 1931 and 1957, irrespective of authorial 'intention'. Brecht noted a similar effect in the case of his play *Life of Galileo*:

> My intention was, among others, to give an unvarnished picture of a new age – a strenuous undertaking since all those around me were convinced that our own era lacked every attribute of a new age. Nothing of this aspect had changed when, years later, I began together with Charles Laughton to prepare an American version of the play. The 'atomic' age made its debut at Hiroshima in the middle of our work. Overnight the biography of the founder of the new system of physics read differently. The infernal effect of the great bomb placed the conflict between Galileo and the authorities of his day in a new, sharper light.[6]

Mary Shelley's monster, in short, is ripped apart by one or more of at least three processes in each generation and then put together again as crudely as Victor Frankenstein constructed the original in his apartment. Faced with these processes traditional literary criticism can either, with a familiar gesture, pretend not to notice and insist instead that *Frankenstein* 'spanned time' with 'timeless and universal themes' that 'live beyond literary fashion'.[7] Or it can pay attention to those changes but slip past the power and the politics that they imply, so that shifts in the work's presentation become a plain mirror of human evolution: 'the Monster . . . is no longer separate, he is quite simply ourselves';[8] 'it is a magnified image of ourselves'.[9] Capitalism creates and recreates monsters; capitalist ideology then invites us to behold ourselves. I'd like to try to do something else.

First I'd like to argue that much of the strength in the text that continues to be released derives from certain issues in the decade of its composition, issues that the text addresses itself to in oblique, imaginative terms and that remain central and unresolved in industrial society. In that decade those issues erupted more turbulently than ever before: they were, briefly, the impact of technological developments on people's lives and the possibility of working-class revolution. Those issues fuel the Luddite disturbances of 1811–17 and the Pentridge rising of 1817.

There had been instances of machine-breaking before in British history but never with the same frequency and intensity. The size of the army marshalled to squash the Luddites – six times as big as any used previously for internal conflicts in the estimate of one historian[10] – is a measure of the extent to which the new technologies, in the first generation of the industrial revolution, threatened traditional livelihoods and provoked violent resistance. There is the same sort of new and disruptive energy evident in the Pentridge rising of June 1817, when 300 men marched towards Nottingham on the expectation of similar marches, designed to overthrow the Government, occurring across the country. The group was soon rounded up by Hussars and three of its leaders executed in November. The revolt ended, in shambles and failure but its significance for E.P. Thompson is epochal – it was 'one of the first attempts in history to mount a wholly proletarian insurrection, without any middle-class support'.[11]

[. . .]

Mary Shelley's interest in scientific questions has been well documented[12] and this interest is built into the very narrative structure of her novel. Frankenstein's story is itself framed by the story of Walton, the polar explorer whom Frankenstein meets and to whom he tells his tale. Through the twin narratives of Walton and Frankenstein Mary Shelley presents two models of scientific progress. Both men are obsessed by the urge to discover and both pursue that obsession, enticed by the possibility of 'immortality and power' that success would bring. In the end the pursuit kills Frankenstein whereas Walton survives. What is the difference?

The difference is the sailors on Walton's expedition ship. Frankenstein works alone but Walton works with a crew and it is the crew who force Walton to turn back when they realize that the reckless drive through the polar ice will cost everyone's lives. Several things are worth noting at this point. Firstly, Frankenstein makes a forceful speech aimed at changing the sailor's minds by reminding them of the honour that even failure will bring and still holding out the dream of heroic success. Secondly, Walton turns back not, as has been argued, for altruistic reasons or for the sake of his sister,[13] but simply because he is forced to by the threat of mutiny, to his own fury and frustration:

> The die is cast; I have consented to return, if we are not destroyed. Thus are my hopes blasted by cowardice and indecision; I come back ignorant and disappointed. It requires more philosophy than I possess, to bear this injustice with patience.
>
> (p. 215)

And thirdly Mary Shelley takes care to distance her reader's sympathies from both Frankenstein's pleas and Walton's anger by pushing those sympathies towards the sailors. Details about the crew must inevitably be few if the text is not to become overloaded and unbalanced but nonetheless she deliberately makes space to insert near the start of the novel in Letter II an otherwise pointless anecdote designed to illustrate the 'kindliness of heart' of the ship's master. The anecdote portrays him as 'generous' and 'wholly uneducated', a man of 'integrity and dauntless courage' and 'gentleness'. The anecdote's purpose can only be to enlist reader support for the master and his crew at the sole moment when they have any part to play in the plot – namely their threat of mutiny in Chapter 24, which is presented to Walton by a delegation of sailors elected by the crew.

What the text then appears to offer is a straightforward contrast. Scientific development subject to some form of strong democratic control – even in the violent form of mutiny – can avert the dangers its researchers encounter and save human beings from the possibly fatal consequences of those researches. That is Walton's story. But scientific advance pursued for private motives and with no reining and directing social control or sense of social responsibility leads directly to catastrophe. That is Frankenstein's story. The text does not, contrary to Christopher Small's claim, offer us hand-wringing about some abstracted and reified 'irresponsibility of science'.[14] Rather it sees scientific development as neutral, its results tolerable or disastrous entirely depending on the circumstances in which they are produced.

[. . .]

In the midst of this crisis, Mary Shelley picks up a way of seeing – the populace as a destructive monster – provided by Tory journalism and tries to re-think it in her own radical–liberal terms. And so in the novel the monster remains a monster – alien, frightening, violent – but is drenched with middle-class sympathy and given central space in the text to exercise the primary liberal right of free speech which he uses to appeal for the reader's pity and understanding. The caricatured people-monster that haunts the dominant ideology is reproduced through Mary Shelley's politics and becomes a contradictory figure, still ugly, vengeful and terrifying but now also human and intelligent and abused.

[. . .]

What I would like to do in the rest of this article is look at Universal's *Frankenstein* directed in 1931 by James Whale and starring Boris Karloff as the monster. [. . .]

[T]here seem to me to be at least three different types of shift that need to be borne in mind when looking at the gap between Mary Shelley's book and twentieth-century films; those shifts concern medium, audience and content. In the case of *Frankenstein*, the shift of medium is particularly important because it must inevitably obliterate and replace what is central to the novel's meaning and structure – namely the patterned movement through three narrators as the reader is taken by way of Walton's letters into Frankenstein's tale and on to the monster's autobiography before backing out through Frankenstein's conclusions to be left with Walton's last notes. That process cannot be filmed and so the very medium demands changes even before politics and ideology come into play.

The turning of novel into film also involves a change in the nature of the work's audience. David Punter has convincingly argued that the Gothic novel is pre-eminently a middle-class form in terms of authors and values as well as readership.[15] The films in question are middle-class in none of these senses, produced as they are by large businesses in search of mass audiences. That different site of production and area of distribution will again bear down on the work, pulling, stretching and clipping it to fit new needs and priorities.

Where this pulling, stretching and clipping appears most obviously is in the alterations in the third category mentioned earlier, namely the work's content, and I'd like to detail some of those in a moment. What needs emphasizing here is that the radical change in the class nature of producer and audience hacks away at the content of the original, so that the book is reduced to no more than an approximate skeleton, fleshed out in entirely and deliberately new ways. This makes it quite different from, for example, a BBC serial of a Jane Austen novel, where some attempt is made at a reasonably faithful reproduction of the text. It is therefore a traditional critical strategy in reviewing such serials to ask questions about how 'true' to the text, how 'accurate', is the portrayal of, say, Fitzwilliam Darcy or Emma Woodhouse. It is the failure to see this difference that makes one reviewer's querulous response to the 1931 film quite laughably beside the point:

> Shelley's story has artistic interest as an essay in German horrific romanticism and I think that if *Frankenstein* had been produced by a historically-minded German the result would have been much more interesting . . . What is the object of taking Mary Shelley's story and then removing the whole point of it before starting to make the picture?[16]

The object, of course, is precisely to remove the whole point of it – and substitute other ones.

Other ones are necessary for several reasons – not least because there are no immutable fears in human nature to which horror stories always speak in the same terms. There is not, for all David Punter's strenuous arguing, 'some inner social and cultural dynamic which makes it necessary for those images to be kept alive';[17] rather, those images need to be repeatedly broken up and reconstituted if they are to continue to touch people, which is one of the reasons why horror films that are thirty or forty years old can often seem simply boring or preposterous to a later audience.

The Universal movie was calculated quite precisely to touch the audiences of 1931. At that time Universal was not one of the front-rank Hollywood studios; its rather cautious and unimaginative policies had left it some distance adrift of the giants of the industry at the end of the 1920s, namely Famous Players, Loews and First National.[18] But a way out of the second rank seemed to offer itself with the huge box office success of Universal's *Dracula*, starring Bela Lugosi, which opened in February 1931 and soon grossed half a million dollars. In April Universal bought the rights of Peggy Webling's *Frankenstein: An Adventure in the Macabre*. The play had run in London in 1930 and its title already suggests a tilting of the work away from Mary Shelley's complex scientific and political statement towards those conventional terror terms for which *Dracula* had indicated a market. *Frankenstein*, filmed in August and September 1931, was an even bigger profit-maker than *Dracula*. Costing a quarter of a million dollars to make, it eventually earned Universal twelve million dollars, was voted one of the films of 1931 by the *New York Times* and confirmed a fashion for horror movies that was soon to include Paramount's *Dr. Jekyll and Mr. Hyde* and Universal's *The Murders in the Rue Morgue*.

In looking at the content of this movie I'd like to confine my comments to those three areas where the shifts from the novel seem to me most important in terms of the ideological and political re-jigging that they betray; those areas are the Walton story, the nature of the monster and the ending.

The point about the Walton story is a simple one: it's gone. It's not there in the immediate source of the movie, namely Peggy Webling's play, where its disappearance is partly prompted by the need to cram a novel into the average duration of a play. But the fact is that to take away half of Mary Shelley's statement is to change it. It was argued that the function of the Walton story within the text's meaning is to offer a different model of scientific and technological progress, one in which human survival is insured as long as that progress is under firm and effective popular control. Remove that narrative and the work collapses into Frankenstein's experience alone which can then be presented as a universal model, replete with the sort of reactionary moralizing about the dangers of meddling with the unknown and the delights of tranquillity which are implicit in that tale and made explicit at more than one point. The film can then more easily slide towards a wider statement about the perils of any kind of progress and change, feeding fears of the unknown that change brings and reinforcing those conservative values that stand in its way.

On the question of the nature of the monster, the most important revision here concerns the creature's brain. The film adds a new episode in which an extra character called Fritz, Frankenstein's assistant, is sent to a laboratory to steal a brain for the monster. In that laboratory are two such pickled organs, in large jars boldly labelled NORMAL BRAIN and ABNORMAL BRAIN. Before the theft, the audience hears an anatomy lecture from Professor Waldman in which he draws attention to various features of the normal brain, 'the most perfect specimen', and contrasts them with the abnormal brain whose defects drive its owner to a life of 'brutality, of violence and murder' because of 'degenerate characteristics'. Its original owner was, in fact, 'a criminal'. The lecture over, Fritz creeps in, grabs the normal brain and then lets it slip so that jar and contents are smashed on the floor. He is forced to take the abnormal brain instead.

The implications for the monster and his story are immense. A central part of Mary Shelley's thesis is to insist that the monster's eventual life of violence and revenge is the direct product of his social circumstances. The monster summarizes his own life in terms that the text endorses:

> Every where I see bliss, from which I alone am irrevocably excluded. I was benevolent and good; misery made me a fiend. Make me happy, and I shall again be virtuous.
>
> (p 100)

The film deletes this reading of the story through its insistence that the monster's behaviour is not a reaction to its experience but biologically determined, a result of nature, not nurture.

Most commentators on the film are bewildered by this change, one not found in Peggy Webling's play. It has been variously dismissed as an 'absurd and unnecessary sequence . . . a cumbersome attempt at establishing motivation', 'ridiculous' and 'the main weakness'.[19] If seen from Mary Shelley's stance, these comments are true; seen in terms of the film's ideological project, they miss the point. At one level in the text, Mary Shelley was concerned to suggest, in the imaginative terms of fiction, that Luddite violence was not the result of some brute characteristics of the nascent English working class but an understandable response to intolerable treatment. The Universal film, consciously or unconsciously, destroys the grounds for such a way of seeing with its radical political implications and instead sees violence as rooted in personal deficiencies, to be viewed with horror and to be labelled, literally, ABNORMAL and so sub-human. Bashing the monster ceases to be the problem but becomes instead the only way that the problem can be met and solved. So it is that Mary Shelley is stood on her head and *Frankenstein* is forced to produce new meanings for 1931.

This upending of Mary Shelley's book and its meaning explains two other profound changes in the monster's presentation that the film introduces. In the text, the monster spends Chapters 11 to 16 describing his life – a huge speech that is placed right in the centre of the novel and fills over twenty per cent of its pages. In the film the monster can't speak. Again, in the novel, the monster saves a child from drowning in Chapter 16; in the film, the monster drowns a child. Both reversals are of a piece with the Abnormal Brain scene and flow from it in that both deliberately seek to suppress audience sympathy for the monster. (Hence, when in the 1935 sequel *Bride of Frankenstein* the monster did speak, Boris Karloff protested that it made him seem 'more human' so that in the second sequel *Son of Frankenstein* in 1939 he is again wordless.) The changes sharpen a re-focusing which is itself part of the shift from novel to film: reading the book, we hear the monster at eloquent length but we don't see him except vaguely, in imagination, and so reader sympathy is easily evoked; watching the film, we hear nothing from him but instead we see a shambling goon with a forehead like a brick wall and a bolt through his neck, and so audience revulsion is promptly generated. Thus the novel makes him human while the film makes him sub-human, so that in the novel his saving of the drowning child is predictable while equally predictable is his drowning of the child in the film.

The way the film ends flows directly from the drowning of the child and so brings me to the third and last piece of ideological re-structuring in the Universal movie that I'd like to look at. In the novel, Frankenstein dies in his pursuit of the monster across the icy Arctic while the latter, in the final sentence, is 'borne away by the waves, and lost in darkness and distance'. In the film, the drowning of the child provokes the villagers to pursue the brute and trap it in an old windmill which is then burnt down; a brief, single-shot coda shows a recovered Frankenstein happily reunited with his fiancée Elizabeth. The politics of the mill-burning scene are overt: as the blaze engulfs the blades they form a gigantic fiery cross that deliberately suggests the Ku Klux Klan, virulently active at the time, and so, as Tropp crudely puts it, 'points up the mob violence that does the monster in'.[20] Similarly, another observer sees the film ending 'with what Whale called "the pagan sport of a mountain man-hunt"; at the finale, the film's sympathies are with the monster rather than with the lynch mob'.[21]

These may have been Whale's intentions but there is a wide gap between director's aims and the movie as distributed. In Whale's original version, in the drowning scene, the girl dies because the monster innocently tries to make her float on the water like the flowers they are playing with and then searches frantically for her when she sinks. But these moments were chopped from the print of the film put out for general release: there we simply see the monster reaching out towards the girl and then cut to a grief-stricken father carrying her corpse. Child rape and murder are the obvious assumptions, so that the immediate response of the community in organizing itself to eliminate the savage culprit comes across as a kind of ritual cleansing of that community, the prompt removal of an inhuman threat to civilized life which is comfortably justifiable within routine populist politics and at the same time provides the firm basis for and so receives its sanction from the conventionally romantic final scene of hero and heroine at last happy and free from danger. If Mary Shelley's monster alludes indirectly to working-class insurrection, one answer to that canvassed in the 1930s was counter-revolutionary mob violence.

Political readings of the film tend to see it either in simple reflectionist terms (Tropp, for example, regards the monster as 'a creature of the '30s shaped by shadowy forces beyond its control, wandering the countryside like some disfigured veteran or hideous tramp'[22] while another finds 'a world in which manipulations of the stock-market had recoiled on the manipulators; in which human creatures seemed to be abandoned by those who had called them into being and those who might have been thought responsible for their welfare'[23] or as escapist – 'Large sections of the public, having difficulty in dealing with the Depression, were glad to spend some time in the company of a monster that could more easily be defeated.'[24] Readings of that sort can only be more or a lot less inspired speculation. I'd prefer to look within the film and see it as a *practice*, as an intervention in its world rather than just a picture of it or a retreat from it, a practice whose extent is marked out by the reconstruction of the text that I have indicated. Certainly it was released in the depths of the Depression, depths which can shock even when seen from Thatcherite Britain. The value of manufactured goods and services produced in the USA in 1929 had stood at 81 billion dollars and output at 119 (1923 = 100); as the film criss-crossed the nation in 1932, the value of goods and services had more than halved to 40 billion dollars and output was down to 64. There were 14 million unemployed. How the film reflects that catastrophe or seeks to escape from it is less important than what it says to it. As we saw earlier it is historically at precisely such moments of crisis that Frankenstein's monster tends to be summoned by ideology and have its arm brutally twisted till it blurts out the statements that ideology demands. What Universal's *Frankenstein* seeks to say specifically to the mass audience at whom it is aimed concerns above all mass activity in times of crisis: where that activity might be assertive and democratic and beneficial (the Walton story), it is removed and concealed; where it is violent and insurrectionary (the monster's story), it is systematically denigrated; and where it is traditional and reactionary (the mill-burning), it is ambiguously endorsed. The extent to which the film powerfully articulates those familiar stances of the dominant ideology in the 1930s is measured by its box-office success.

[. . .]

Notes

1 Details from W.H. Lyles, *Mary Shelley: An Annotated Bibliography* (New York, 1975), and Peter Haining (ed.), *The Frankenstein File* (1977).

2 See in particular Tony Bennett, *Formalism and Marxism* (1979), Chapters 7, 8, and 9; Catherine Belsey, *Clinical Practice* (1980), Chapters 2 and 6; and Terry Eagleton, *Walter Benjamin: Or Towards a Revolutionary Criticism* (1981), Part II, Chapter 3.

3 D. W. Harding, 'The Character of Literature from Blake to Byron' in Boris Ford (ed.), *The Pelican Guide to English Literature: Volume 5 From Blake to Byron* (Harmondsworth, 1957), p.45.

4 See, for example, Ellen Moers, *Literary Women* (1977); Kate Ellis, 'Monsters in the Garden; Mary Shelley and the Bourgeois Family' in George Levine and U. C. Knoepflmacher (eds.),

The Endurance of Frankenstein: Essays on Mary Shelley's Novel (Berkeley, 1979); and Sandra M. Gilbert and Susan Gubar, *The Madwoman in the Attic: The Woman Writer and the Nineteenth-Century Literary Imagination* (Yale, 1979).

5 Quoted in Philip Simpson, 'Presentness Precise: Notes on *The History Man*', *Screen*, Vol. 23 no. 1 (May/June 1982), p. 25.

6 Bertolt Brecht, *Life of Galileo*, tr. John Willett (1980), p. 125.

7 Jane Dunn, *Moon in Eclipse: A Life of Mary Shelley* (1978), pp. 131 and 134.

8 Christopher Small, *Ariel Like a Harpy: Shelley, Mary and Frankenstein* (1972), p. 331.

9 Martin Tropp, *Mary Shelley's Monster* (Boston, 1976), p. 156.

10 Malcolm I. Thomis, *The Luddites: Machine-Breaking in Regency England* (1970), p. 144.

11 *The Making of the English Working Class* (Harmondsworth, 1968), p. 733.

13 See, for example, Tropp, p. 82, and Mary Poovey, 'My Hideous Progeny: Mary Shelley and the Feminization of Romanticism', PMLA, 95 (May 1980).

14 *Ariel Like a Harpy*, p. 328.

15 See the concluding chapter 'Towards a Theory of the Gothic' in Punter, *The Literature of Terror, A History of Gothic Fictions from 1765 to the Present Day* (1980).

16 *New Statesman* (30 January 1932), p. 120.

17 Punter, p. 424.

18 Information from J. Douglas Gomery, 'Writing the History of the American Film Industry: Warner Brothers and Sound', *Screen*, Vol. 17 no. 1 (Spring 1976). Facts about the making of the Universal Frankenstein in this Section are derived from Haining, *op. cit.*; Levine and Knoepflmacher, *op. cit.*; Paul M. Jensen, *Boris Karloff and His Films* (New Jersey, 1974); and Donald F. Glut, *Classic Movie Monsters* (New Jersey, 1978).

19 See, respectively, Tropp, pp 87 and 90; David Pirie, *A Heritage of Horror: The English Gothic Cinema 1946–1972* (1973), p. 69; and Jensen, p. 30.

20 Tropp, p. 97.

21 Jensen, p. 41.

22 Tropp, p. 93.

23 S. S. Prawer, *Caligari's Children: The Film as Tale of Terror* (1980), p. 22.

24 Jensen, p. 44.

The problem of British horror 9

PETER HUTCHINGS

[. . .]

Positive reports

David Pirie's claim in his groundbreaking work, A *Heritage of Horror*, that British horror was worthy of critical attention undoubtedly ran counter to the readings of British cinema dominant in the early 1970s when the book first appeared. However, Pirie himself denied that his work was a polemic, and indeed a close examination of it reveals that the two main strategies Pirie adopts to bring horror into the fold of critical respectability are closely connected to an already established way of understanding and valuing British cinema.

The first of these involves the construction of the horror genre as an important part of a national culture, with links to other aspects of British cinema, to literary traditions and also to a distinctive British character: 'it may be that the themes relate to certain psychopathological aspects of the English temperament'.[1]

The second entails bestowing upon Terence Fisher, Hammer's main film director, the status of auteur, someone with a vision that transcends commercial constraints: 'Indeed, once one begins to look at Fisher's films closely, it becomes clear that, unlike almost any other director working in the British commercial cinema, they appear to embody a recognisable and coherent Weltanschauung.'[2]

At the same time, Pirie is more sympathetic than other critics to Hammer's market-led production philosophy which, like Armes, he associates with Hollywood.

> There is a very slight echo of Ealing in the structure that emerged, but perhaps the most obvious analogy is with one of the small Hollywood studios of the 1930s and 1940s like Republic or Monogram; for almost overnight Hammer became a highly efficient factory for a vast series of exploitation pictures made on tight budgets with a repertory company of actors and a small, sometimes over-exposed, series of locations surrounding their tiny Buckinghamshire estate.[3]

A *Heritage of Horror* is full of valuable insights, and my own account of British horror is indebted to it. However, in his attempt to endow horror with a certain cultural respectability and worth, Pirie does not engage to any great extent with the reasons why the genre was disreputable in the first place. Also, while he includes an account of the economic circumstances within which Hammer was working, the implications this might have for the aesthetic and ideological properties of the films being made by Hammer are rarely taken up in his otherwise very provocative analyses of specific films. Generally, these analyses instead seek to locate the films in question within a longstanding gothic tradition or as products of an individual director's vision.

Writing in the early 1970s, Pirie was unable to avail himself of recent developments in film theory and history, with those concerning the relation of film aesthetics to the economic structures of the film industry especially pertinent to an understanding of British horror.[4] From the vantage point of today, the commercial nature of much film production seems less of an obstacle to a consideration of any film as a cultural artefact than perhaps it did in the past. Because of this, my own discussions of the aesthetic qualities of particular films will incorporate the fact that, without exception, these films were made primarily to make money.

It is surprising given the upsurge of critical interest in British cinema that has taken place in the 1980s that so little has been written on British horror outside of a few isolated essays and remarks in essays on other related subjects since A *Heritage of Horror*. One shift in attitudes that has taken place registers, albeit ambivalently, in one of the press reviews of *Hellraiser* (1987, d. Clive Barker): 'This, in fact, is a horror fantasy: the genre it has become fashionable to view as the repressed underside of British filmmaking.'[5]

The idea that British horror constitutes one aspect of what might be termed 'the dark side' of British cinema has been developed by Julian Petley in an article entitled 'The Lost Continent'. Petley argues that British films which are realistic have been valued by critics above all others. Consequent upon this, an awareness of other areas of British film production has been repressed. These areas are characterised by non-realistic or fantastic themes and styles: they include Gainsborough melodramas, the iconoclastic work of Michael Powell and Emeric Pressburger and, of course, the British horror film. This strain of fantasy permits the expression of that which is inexpressible elsewhere in British cinema. In so doing, it reveals the limitations of, perhaps even works to deconstruct, a critically privileged realist aesthetic.[6]

The metaphor of the dark side has provided a way of thinking about films which were not afforded much attention before. However, at this point we need to identify some of the shortcomings of this approach and, at the same time, indicate other possible ways of conceptualising British horror's position within British cinema. Two principal problems are apparent.

First, while it is clear that the realism/fantasy dichotomy upon which this metaphor depends is a central one in much critical writing on British cinema, it should also be clear that in an important sense the British horror film is operating in the same way as other, more realistic areas of British film production. The fact that horror films invariably come in the form of 80–120-minute fictional narratives peopled by psychologically individuated characters means that on a basic level and regardless of any aberrant or disreputable content they are unexceptional. For example, Hammer nearly always relied on straightforwardly conventional narratives. As Andrew Higson notes, 'Clearly, different films, and particularly different genres of film mark themselves as more realistic or more "fantastic" (this is particularly evident in British film culture), but it needs to be recognised that such marking is always in relation to a particular understanding of cinema.'[7]

Second, 'the dark side' offers itself as something which arises nightmarishly from within and is subservient to a dominant realist cinema. This fails to take account of the fact that these 'subterranean' films in themselves comprise an immensely popular cinema. When dealing with critical discourses that are primarily evaluative, it is often easy to lose sight of some of the commercial realities of British cinema. By any account, Hammer was a far more profitable enterprise (especially in the long term) than, say, the 1960s 'kitchen sink' productions from the likes of Woodfall and Bryanston, simply because more people saw its product than they did the products of the latter. In this sense, it is the dark side of British cinema rather than its realistic component that can be viewed, in the 1950s and 1960s at least, as dominant.

The contradiction between British horror's popularity, its centrality in the market place, and its critical marginalisation is not satisfactorily addressed by placing British horror on 'the dark side'. Looking at horror in this way, in its relation to realist discourses, can certainly be productive. However, it needs to be recognised that the horror genre as developed within this country has its own distinctive and complex history which encompasses a literary tradition (explored by Pirie), links with other horror movements and an aesthetic identity which in many instances is quite different from as opposed to deconstructive of a realist approach. What this means is that British horror does not merely reveal what is unsaid or repressed elsewhere in British cinema but is also capable of offering different ideas and a new way of seeing.

National cinema and genre

The main aim of this book is to explore the 'Britishness' of British horror, the way in which it functions within a specifically national context. It does seem that the various approaches outlined above, despite the usefulness of some, are in the end not fully adequate to this task. What is helpful at this stage is to think about British horror films as being part of a British national cinema, where this cinema is simultaneously a cultural and an economic institution which, in Geoffrey Nowell-Smith's words 'in some way signifies itself to its audiences as the cinema through which that country speaks'.[8]

Defining such a cinema is not as straightforward as one might suppose. This is readily apparent in *The British Film Catalogue 1895–1970: A Guide to Entertainment Films* where Denis Gifford lists a number of films which one does not usually think of as British; for example *The Haunting* (1963, d. Robert Wise) and *The Masque of the Red Death* (1964, d. Roger Corman).[9] Gifford's definition of what makes a film British depends on trade and legal designations, avoiding any consideration of theme or style and including films which might appear in their formal qualities to be more American or European. Conversely, films thought of as, say, unproblematically American can be shown to have had a significant British input in terms of the creative personnel who fashioned them. Charles Barr has shown this for the 1935 Universal horror film *The Bride of Frankenstein*.[10]

While an important component of a British national cinema must be its propensity to address specifically national issues and concerns, account also needs to be taken of films like *The Haunting* and *The Masque of the Red Death* which, while not connecting with a British context in any thematic or stylistic way, do testify to the importance of American-financed production in Britain throughout the 1960s. Similarly, that *The Bride of Frankenstein* can to a certain extent be seen as a British horror film in exile signifies rather pointedly the hostility of 1930s British film censors to the development of an indigenous horror genre.

Thinking about the similarities and differences between British and American horror films leads to another difficulty in our attempt to locate horror within a specifically national cinema: namely that the operations of the horror genre are not restricted to any one country or culture but rather are spread across much of the filmmaking world. What has to be considered here then is the role of this genre, and for that matter genre in general, within British cinema. For French critic (and later filmmaker) Jacques Rivette, this role is perfectly clear:

> British cinema is a *genre* cinema, but one where the genres have no genuine roots. On the one hand there are no self-validating genres as there are in American cinema, like the Western and the thriller . . . They are just false, in the sense of imitative, genres.[11]

Rivette's view (which in retrospect has a certain irony to it inasmuch as it was expressed in 1957, the year which saw the release of *The Curse of Frankenstein*, Hammer's first important colour horror film) can be contrasted with David Pirie's claim that the British horror film is in fact deeply rooted in British culture, 'the only staple cinematic myth which Britain can properly claim as its own, and which relates to it in the same way as the western relates to America'.[12] Is British horror 'rootless', merely a local example of a transnational cultural mode? If not, what relation does it bear to its American and European counterparts?

British horror's place in the standard accepted history of the horror genre lies in between American Cold War SF/horror and the modern American horror film (usually seen to have been initiated in 1968 with the release of *Night of the Living Dead* and *Rosemary's Baby*), with considerable overlaps at either end. In what is usually seen as a constant process of generic regeneration, Hammer and other British companies – alongside Italian filmmakers such as Mario Bava and Riccardo Freda and American filmmakers such as Roger Corman – introduce into the genre in the late 1950s colour as well as relatively graphic depictions of violence and sexuality, with all this played out in period settings. However, by the late 1960s gothic horror is superseded by a series of American films boasting modern settings and even more explicit images.

One factor that enables the construction of such a 'grand narrative' is the presence of 'horror' (regardless of how it is defined) as a distinct category within the organisation of different national film industries. But it is uncertain whether one can actually abstract from the extraordinarily wide range of horror films specific aesthetic elements or structures which can be seen to characterise the genre as a whole. Attempts that have been made, particularly in their insistence on the genre having either a fixed function or a central core of meaning ('the Ur-myth . . . a tale still hidden'),[13] have necessarily lifted films out of the national contexts within which they were produced, thereby evacuating them of much of their socio-historical significance.

Despite operating from different theoretical and methodological perspectives, many of these generalising approaches manifest a social conservatism. Horror tends to be identified as a means by which an audience comes to terms with certain unpleasant aspects of reality. For example: 'The horror film teaches an acceptance of the natural order of things and an affirmation of man's ability to cope with and even prevail over the evil of life which he can never hope to understand.'[14]

Psychiatric and psychological concepts have been especially influential in the development of the notion of horror as offering an essentially healthy and life-enhancing experience. Perhaps the baldest statement of this is found in Dr Martin Grotjahn's article 'Horror – Yes It

Can Do You Good': 'There is, perhaps, a healthy function in the fascination of horror. It keeps us on the task to face our anxieties and to work on them.'[15]

A related view of the genre has been argued at some length by James B. Twitchell who in his book on the genre writes:

> horror sequences are really formulaic rituals coded with precise social information needed by the adolescent audience. Like fairy tales that prepare the child for the anxieties of separation, modern horror myths prepare the teenager for the anxieties of reproduction.[16]

Drawing on Lacanian psychoanalysis, Steve Neale has offered a different approach to the genre. He argues that horror addresses the fascinations and anxieties of sexual difference, particularly as they register for the male spectator. In discussing horror's use of chiaroscuro lighting he notes that:

> all the elements involved here are central to the problematic of castration and . . . the horror film – centrally concerned with the fact and the effects of difference – invariably involves itself in that problematic and invariably mobilises specific castration anxieties.[17]

Horror is seen as 'centrally concerned' with questions of gender, not in the sense of providing role models but rather in its seeking to produce a secure spectatorial position for the male subject situated within a patriarchal social formation.

The insistent return in all the work cited above to an essential core of human experience or meaning enables their identification of horror as a distinctive body of work operating in a number of different social and historical situations. Even in Neale's apparently more socially aware approach, social specificity is acknowledged only inasmuch as the genre is seen to relate to a patriarchal society. The ahistorical qualities of his argument are clear from the examples he uses. These are picked, apparently at random, from British and American cinema of the 1930s, 1950s, 1960s and 1970s, the implicit assumption being that when reduced to their defining and invariant function these films are more or less the same.

It is also the case that those feminist critics of horror who have argued that the genre is an irredeemably misogynist area of culture, with its female characters functioning solely as victims, fail to grasp that particular horror films might – depending on the context in which they are produced and received – challenge or problematise certain patriarchal attitudes and definitions. For instance, the position of the woman in British horror from the mid-1960s onwards can be seen as offering a degree of resistance to an attempted male objectification of her. The forms this takes, and the extent to which it can be taken as a significant disruption of a male-centred narrative, can, however, only be determined through an analysis of specific films which does not presuppose the genre having fixed, immutable qualities.

One way of initiating a more comprehensively historical approach to horror is to see it as at any one time comprising a set of aesthetic conventions or norms (with these relating both to stylistic and thematic factors and narrative structure), the actual interplay and development of which takes place within particular national contexts. Jan Mukarovsky, in a discussion of aesthetic norms, provides a way of thinking about horror in these terms when he writes:

> we can state that the specific character of the aesthetic norm consists in the fact that it tends to be violated rather than to be observed. It has less than any other norm the

> character of an inviolable law. It is rather a point of orientation serving to make felt the degree of deformation of the artistic tradition by new tendencies . . . If we look at a work of art from this point of view, it will appear to us as a complex tangle of norms.[18]

What this suggests in the case of Hammer (and for that matter British horror in general) is that in its construction of horror within the context of 1950s Britain, it was negotiating with pre-existing generic norms, engaging in a process of product differentiation which necessarily involved 'common-sense' definitions of what a horror film actually was. The motivation for this differentiation can be found in the company's search for a new, expanded market.

This approach helps us in locating British horror as part of a specifically national cinema. The relation of British horror films to non-British horror, rather than arising from a shared generic identity, is instead constituted through a series of negotiations and differentiations, in effect through different interpretations of what horror actually is. This also has implications for our understanding of the internal development of British horror production, for, as will be shown, Hammer horror increasingly came to function in the 1960s as the 'norm' from which British horror filmmakers – including some working for Hammer itself – sought to differentiate their own work.

The norms in relation to which Hammer initiated its own distinctive horror cycle were primarily those of the American cinema, and particularly the type of horror associated with Universal Studios throughout the 1930s and 1940s and featuring stars such as Boris Karloff, Bela Lugosi and Lon Chaney Jnr (with some of these films still proving popular in British cinemas in the 1950s). This is most apparent in Hammer's producing films centred on monsters already established in film horror by Universal: Frankenstein, Dracula, the Mummy and the Wolfman.[19]

Both Dracula and Frankenstein were 'stars' on the stage before the 1930s.[20] Universal's main innovation was to place them in cycles of films, in so doing removing them even further from the novels in which they first appeared. This cyclical structure, which was reproduced in the subsequent Mummy and Wolfman cycles, helped the studio to make the most of its limited resources: sets, costumes and, in some cases, footage could be reused. But this also had implications for the type of monster that was being produced. In particular, the relationship between the monster's creation and its eventual destruction changes when it is assumed (both by filmmakers and audiences) that the monster will return in a later film. It would seem that the elements of spectacle associated with these moments on the stage become even more important in the movies. As Steve Neale has noted, the horror film is often marked by a fascination with the appearance and disappearance of the monster, turning as these do on a 'fetishistic division of belief.[21] These moments, codified for the first time in serial Universal horror production, are usually linked with a display of cinematic techniques (make-up, special effects, set design, etc.), so that not only the monster but aspects of cinema itself are involved in the spectacle. It is within such a conception of horror that Hammer, initially at least, operates, most visibly in its Frankenstein and Dracula films but also throughout the rest of its horror production in the 1950s and the first part of the 1960s.

As has already been indicated, British horror in the late 1950s was also part of a much wider renaissance of the genre: this included films from Italy (Riccardo Freda's *I Vampiri* in 1956 and Mario Bava's *La Maschera del Demonio* in 1960), America (Roger Corman's *The Fall of the House of Usher* in 1960 and his subsequent Poe adaptations, Hitchcock's *Psycho* in the same year) and Spain (Jesus Franco's *Gritos en la Noche* in 1962). All of these exploited a general relaxation of censorship through an increased explicitness in their representations of sex and violence, while many also utilised the relatively cheap colour systems that had just become available. They also, to a limited extent, shared some creative personnel. (This was mainly the case with actors: for example, British cult actress Barbara Steele made films in Italy, America and Britain.)

However, the ways in which British, Italian and American cinema responded to these common elements were in the main determined by factors operative within their respective national contexts. Moreover, while there was undoubtedly an international market for horror at this time (an important consideration for filmmakers), with films from the countries listed above regularly distributed in other countries, it is most unlikely that the response of the various audiences was a uniform one. As will be shown in subsequent chapters, many of the issues with which British horror was working were of specific relevance to British life, and, because of this, certain aspects of the films would simply have lacked resonance for non-British audiences. This does not mean that audiences in America and Europe (where British horror, initially at least, proved very popular) were 'misreading' these films; rather that they were locating them within and making sense of them in relation to their own national cultures. The extent to which a film lends itself to this process determines its international success or failure.

When the horror genre is viewed in this way as a collection of different horror cinemas, the relations between which are mediated via numerous national institutions, it becomes much easier to think about British horror both as an important intervention into the international horror genre and as a significant part of the post-war British cultural scene.

Entertainment value

> when the National Film Theatre gave us a two-week season I was horrified. I thought if they made us respectable it would ruin our whole image. When one reads all those criticisms such as the ones that appear in the NFT programme and the little ones that appear in *Time Out* when one of our films appears on TV, one is simply amazed.
>
> (Michael Carreras, Hammer executive and filmmaker)[22]

Carreras's words are a salutary reminder of the fact that the vast majority, if not all, of British horror films were intended primarily as 'just entertainment'. However, this begs the question of what the nature and function of entertainment for profit actually is. While this book will identify some of the economic factors at work in the production of horror, these factors in themselves do not wholly explain the forms which the films take. This is because films do not arise naturally, ready-made, from the conditions of their production, but are instead imagined by groups of individuals working within particular institutions. An account of the 'entertainment value' of British horror needs to discover what was entailed in the imaginative work done by the filmmakers. It will become clear that in seeking to make horror attractive to an audience, these filmmakers necessarily had to address what they perceived to be the lived experiences, fears and anxieties of that audience, with the terms of this engagement both aesthetic and ideological. In fact the history of horror in Britain can in part be read as a number of attempted (re)identifications of an audience, the nature of which (because of demographic factors and changing definitions of youth, class and gender) was unstable.

British horror films did not merely reflect or reproduce socially specific trends and issues but instead imaginatively transformed whatever they incorporated. For example, in the case of Hammer in the 1950s, its work can be seen to have involved seizing upon aspects of a contemporaneous social reality that were not naturally connected – in particular, shifts in gender definition and changing notions of professionalism – and weaving these into an aesthetic unity in the interests of making horror relevant to a British market. While it is clear that much of this work would have been unconscious, this does not render any of these creative processes any less effective. Only through an awareness of such activities is one able to engage with both the conditions of British horror's existence and the nature of that existence.

Notes

1 David Pirie, *A Heritage of Horror: the English Gothic Cinema 1946–1972*, London, p. 11.
2 Ibid., p. 51.
3 Ibid., p. 42.
4 For example, David Bordwell, Janet Staiger and Kristin Thompson, *The Classical Hollywood Cinema: Film Style and Mode of Production to 1960*, London, 1985.
5 The *Guardian*, 10 September 1987.
6 Julian Petley, 'The Lost Continent' in Charles Barr (ed.), *All Our Yesterdays: 90 Years of British Cinema*, London, 1986, pp. 98–119.
7 Andrew Higson, 'Critical Theory and "British Cinema"', *Screen*, 24, no. 4–5, July–October 1983, p. 91.
8 In Pam Cook (ed.), *The Cinema Book*, London, 1985, p. 36.
9 Denis Gifford, *The British Film Catalogue 1895–1970: a Guide to Entertainment Films*, Newton Abbot, 1973.
10 Charles Barr, 'Amnesia and Schizophrenia' in Barr (ed.), *All Our Yesterdays*, pp. 9–10.
11 Quoted in Jim Hillier (ed.), *Cahiers du Cinéma: Volume I*, London, 1985, p. 32.
12 Pirie, *A Heritage of Horror*, p. 9.
13 James B. Twitchell, *Dreadful Pleasures: an Anatomy of Modern Horror*, New York, 1985, p. 99.
14 R. H. W. Dillard, 'The Pageantry of Death' in Roy Huss and T. J. Ross (eds), *Focus on the Horror Film*, New Jersey, 1972, p. 37.
15 Martin Grotjahn, 'Horror – Yes, It Can Do You Good', *Films and Filming*, November 1958, p. 9.
16 Twitchell, *Dreadful Pleasures*, p. 7.
17 Steve Neale, *Genre*, London, 1980, p. 43.
18 Jan Mukarovsky, *Structure, Sign and Function*, New Haven and London, 1978, p. 52.
19 An important connection between the British and American 'schools' of horror lies in the copyright agreement struck between Hammer and Universal permitting the former's 'remakes' of Universal horror classics. This was only one of a series of agreements between UK and US companies that signalled the importance attached by British film producers to the US market. In this respect, it makes sense that Hammer should turn to Americanised models of horror, if only to transform them.
20 For a discussion of stage adaptations of Mary Shelley's *Frankenstein*, see Radu Florescu, *In Search of Frankenstein*, London, 1977, pp. 163–71; Albert J. Lavalley, 'The Stage and Film

Children of *Frankenstein*' in George Levine and U. C. Knoepflmacher (eds), *The Endurance of Frankenstein: Essays on Mary Shelley's Novel*, Berkeley and London, 1975, pp. 243–89. See Donald F. Glut, *The Dracula Book*, Metuchen NJ, 1975, and *Dracula: Universal Filmscripts Series: Classic Horror Films – Volume* 13, Absecon NJ, 1991 for details of stage adaptations of Dracula.

21 Neale, *Genre*, p. 45.

22 Quoted in John Brosnan, *The Horror People*, London, 1976, p. 118.

Sleaze mania, Euro-trash, and high art

10

The place of European art films in American low culture

JOAN HAWKINS

Open the pages of any U.S. horror fanzine—*Outré, Fangoria, Cinéfantastique*—and you will find listings for mail order video companies which cater to afficionados of what Jeffrey Sconce has called "paracinema" and trash aesthetics.[1] Not only do these mail-order companies represent one of the fastest-growing segments of the video market,[2] their catalogues challenge many of our continuing assumptions about the binary opposition of prestige cinema (European art and avant-garde/experimental films) and popular culture.[3] Certainly, they highlight an aspect of art cinema which is generally overlooked or repressed in cultural analysis, namely, the degree to which high culture trades on the same images, tropes, and themes which characterize low culture.

In the world of horror and cult film fanzines and mail order catalogues, what Carol J. Clover calls "the high end" of the horror genre[4] mingles indiscriminately with the "low end." Here, Murnau's *Nosferatu* (1921) and Dreyer's *Vampyr* (1931) appear alongside such drive-in favorites as *Tower of Screaming Virgins* (1971) and *Jail Bait* (1955). Even more interesting, European art films which have little to do with horror—Antonioni's *L'avventura* (1960), for example—are listed alongside movies which Video Vamp labels "Eurociné-trash." European art films are not easily located through separate catalogue subheadings or listings. Many catalogues simply list film titles alphabetically, making no attempt to differentiate among genres or subgenres, high or low art. In *Luminous Film and Video Works Catalogue* 2.0, for example, Jean-Luc Godard's edgy *Weekend* (1968) is sandwiched between *The Washing Machine* (1993) and *The Werewolf and the Yeti* (1975). Sinister Cinema's 1996–97 catalogue, which organizes titles chronologically, lists Godard's *Alphaville* (1965) between *Lighting Bolt* (1965) and *Zontar, the Thing from Venus* (1966).[5] [. . .]

In addition to art, horror, and science-fiction films, "paracinema" catalogues "include entries from such seemingly disparate genres" as badfilm, splatterpunk, mondo films, sword-and-sandal epics, Elvis flicks, government hygiene films, Japanese monster movies, beach party musicals, and "just about every other historical manifestation of exploitation cinema from juvenile delinquency documentaries to . . . pornography" (Sconce, 372). As Sconce explains, this is an "extremely elastic textual category," and comprises "less a distinct group of films than a particular reading protocol, a counter-aesthetic turned subcultural sensibility devoted to all manner of cultural detritus. In short, the explicit manifesto of paracinematic culture is to valorize all forms of cinematic 'trash' whether such films have been either explicitly rejected or simply ignored by legitimate film culture" (372).

This valorization is achieved, he argues, largely through heavily ironized strategies of cinematic reading. Connoisseurs of trash cinema are always on the lookout for movies that are so awful they're good. But they also consume films which are recognized by "legitimate" film culture as masterpieces. And catalogue descriptions do attempt to alert the consumer that such films might require a different reading strategy—less heavily ironized—than other films listed in the catalogue.[6] Sinister Cinema's description of *Vampyr* is a good example: "If you're looking for a fast-paced horror film with lots of action go to another movie in our listings. If you like mood and atmosphere this is probably the greatest horror movie ever made. The use of light, shadow, and camera angles is translated into a pureness of horror seldom equaled, in this chilling vampire-in-a-castle tale. One of the best.[7]

Clearly, the description serves an important economic purpose. Customers are less likely to be disappointed, to return tapes, if they understand clearly what they're getting. But the delineation of important stylistic elements is instructional as well as cautionary. It tells the collector what to look for, how to read a film which might seem lugubrious or boring. The fact that the catalogue lists two versions of the film—a longer, foreign-language version and a shorter version with English subtitles—marks the company's economic stake in serious collectors and completionists (people who collect many versions of the same title—the U.S. theatrical release, the director's cut or uncut European version, the rough cut, etc.). But it also gives the catalogue a curiously academic or scholarly air, which links Sinister Cinema to more upscale "serious" video companies like Facets.

While paracinema catalogues often tag art films as films which require a different reading strategy than *Reefer Madness* (1939) or *Glen and Glenda* (1953), they also tag certain B movies as films which can be openly appreciated on pure aesthetic grounds. In the same catalogue which characterizes *Vampyr* as "one of the best," for example, the reader can also find a listing for *Carnival of Souls* (1962), a B-grade American horror film which *The Encyclopedia of Horror Movies* calls "insufferably portentous." The script, the *Encyclopedia* tells us, "harks back to those expressionistic dramas which solemnly debated this life and the next with heavy-breathing dialogue."[8] For Sinister Cinema catalogue patrons, however, the film is described in terms not unlike the ones used to describe *Vampyr*: "A riveting pipe-organ music score. Seldom have the elements of sight and sound come together in such a horrifying way. A haunting film that you'll never forget. Original uncut 80-minute version."[9] Although this description does not praise *Carnival of Souls*' use of "light, shadow, and camera angles," its observation that "sight and sound come together in a . . . horrifying way" is a tribute to the film's formal style. And the use of the word "haunting" in the next-to-last line reminds the reader that schlock, too, can be beautiful. Like the Surrealist film critic Ado Kyrou, the writers for paracinema publications continually remind readers that low budget horror can sometimes be "sublime."[10]

Negotiating paracinema catalogues often calls, then, for a more complicated set of textual reading strategies than is commonly assumed. Viewing/reading the films themselves—even the trashiest films—demands a set of sophisticated strategies which, Sconce argues, are remarkably similar to the strategies employed by the cultural elite.

> Paracinematic taste involves a reading strategy that renders the bad into the sublime, the deviant into the defamiliarized and in so doing, calls attention to the aesthetic

> aberrance and stylistic variety evident but routinely dismissed in the many subgenres of trash cinema. By concentrating on a film's formal bizarreness and stylish eccentricity, the paracinematic audience, *much like the viewer attuned to the innovations of Godard* . . . foregrounds structures of cinematic discourse and artifice so that the material identity of the film ceases to be a structure made invisible in service of the diegesis, but becomes instead the primary focus of textual attention.
>
> (388, emphasis mine)

Since Sconce is mainly interested in theorizing trash aesthetics, he doesn't take the "high" art aspects of the catalogues' video lists into account. So he does not thoroughly discuss the way in which the companies' listing practices erase the difference between what's considered trash and what's considered art through a deliberate leveling of hierarchies and recasting of categories. But his comments about "the viewer attuned to the innovations of Godard" help to explain the heavy representation of Godard's films in these catalogues. As Godard himself repeatedly demonstrated, there is a very fine line between the reading strategies demanded by trash and the reading strategies demanded by high culture.

Earlier I mentioned that the design of paracinema mail order catalogues—which list titles alphabetically or chronologically, and make no attempt to differentiate between high and low genres—encourages a kind of dialectical cultural reading. Certainly, it highlights an aspect of art cinema generally overlooked or repressed in cultural analysis, namely, the degree to which high culture trades on the same images, tropes, and themes that characterize low culture. "Film is a vivid medium," as Steven Shaviro notes.[11] And there is something vividly scandalous and transgressive about the films of Peter Greenaway, Derek Jarman, Luis Buñuel, Jean-Luc Godard, and the other European filmmakers mentioned above. In fact, European art cinema has followed a trajectory in the United States not unlike that of pure exploitation cinema, in that historically it has been seen as delving "unashamedly into often disreputable content," often "promoting it in . . . [a] disreputable manner."[12]

As Peter Lev notes, *Open City* (1945), "the first foreign-language film to earn more than a million dollars in the United States, is certainly not sexually explicit by contemporary standards. But some observers felt that *Open City*'s success in the United States was based on a salacious advertising campaign." Similarly, throughout the 1960s, the advertisements for Jean-Luc Godard's films tended to feature scantily clad women, images which were, American distributors felt, in keeping with the impression most Americans had of French cinema, as something sexy.[14] And as late as 1972, Pauline Kael felt it necessary to distinguish *Last Tango in Paris*'s eroticism from that of exploitation films and to stress the movie's links to the world of high culture.[15]

While Michael Mayer gives a long list of reasons for the rise in popularity of foreign films in the U.S. after the war—the Paramount decision, which had the effect of decreasing the number of films produced in the U.S., the increased American interest in all things foreign, the end of political isolationism, more travel opportunities, the increased sophistication of the viewing public ("the public no longer requires complete clarity on film")—most interesting for our purposes is the importance he places on the "violent" change in Americans' sexual mores.[16] Certainly, this is the "lesson" which Hollywood learned from the rise of art cinema. As Kristin Thompson and David Bordwell note in *Film History*, "one way of competing with television, which had extremely strict censorship," as well as with European art films, "was to make films with more daring subject matter. As a result, producers find distributors pushed the code further and further."[17]

For many Americans, however, throughout the late 50s and early 60s, European art cinema retained a scandalous reputation which marked its difference from Hollywood cinema (even a Hollywood cinema dedicated to "push[ing] the code further and further"). In 1960, the residents of Fort Lee, New Jersey, protested the opening of a "film art house" in their community. "It is a known fact that many of the foreign films are without doubt detrimental to the morals of the young and old," one pastor maintained. Apparently, the president of the Borough Council agreed. "I would not hesitate to pass an ordinance barring all future theatres from Fort Lee," he claimed, "if that's the only way to keep this one out."[18] And both Janet Staiger and Douglas Gomery stress the degree to which the audience for art films in the U.S. has always been a "special interest group."[19] Hollywood's need to compete for art film audiences, then, should be seen more as an indication of changing audience demographics (mainstream audiences were going less and less frequently to the movies; special interest groups were going more and more) than as an index of changing mainstream tastes. The moviegoing audience was not only becoming segmented, as Janet Staiger claims,[20] it was becoming polarized (into mainstream and "alternative" or "fringe" audiences). Interestingly, the majority of historical titles on horror and exploitation-video mail order lists are drawn from films made during the era when this polarization became pronounced. Agreeing with Richard Kadrey that "everything interesting is out at the edges," the catalogues celebrate the two extreme tastes of the postwar, youthful filmgoing public: low-budget horror, sci-fi, and exploitation films on the one hand; art-film "classics," on the other.

In addition to these, there is an interesting array of films which, put quite simply, are difficult to categorize. Films with high production values, European art-film cachet, and enough sex and violence to thrill all but the most jaded horror fan: Roger Vadim's *Blood and Roses* (1960), Stanley Kubrick's *Clockwork Orange* (1971), Harry Kuemel's *Daughters of Darkness* (1971), Georges Franju's *Eyes Without a Face* (1959), Roman Polanski's *Repulsion* (1965) and *The Tenant* (1976), to name just a few. There are films, like Tod Browning's *Freaks* (1932), which began their career as horror or exploitation films and were later revived as art films; films, like Paul Morrissey's *Andy Warhol's Frankenstein* (1973) and *Andy Warhol's Dracula* (1974) which belong to New York avant-garde culture as well as to horror; and experimental films, like the Surrealist classic *Un chien andalou* (1929), which contain sequences as shocking as those in any contemporary splatter film.[22] These are films which promise *both* affect and "something different"; films which defy the traditional genre labels by which we try to make sense of cinematic history and cultures, films which seem to have a stake in both high and low art.

Unlike *Nosferatu* or *Vampyr*—films which I earlier designated "the high end of horror"—these films still directly engage the viewer's body. Like the slasher films which Clover analyzes, many of them are "drenched in taboo" and encroach "vigorously on the pornographic."[23] All of them meet both Linda Williams' and William Paul's criteria for lower cinematic forms. In *Laughing Screaming*, Paul writes:

> From the high perch of an elitist view, the negative definition of the lower works would have it that they are less subtle than higher genres. More positively, it could be said they are more direct. Where lower forms are explicit, higher forms tend to operate more by indirection. Because of this indirection the higher forms are often regarded as being

> more metaphorical and consequently, more resonant, more open to the exegetical analyses of the academic industry.[24]

This concurs with Williams' characterization of body genres as physically excessive, viscerally manipulative genres. For both Williams and Paul, so-called "low" genres lack "proper aesthetic distance" (Williams, 144). In fact, the title of Paul's book, *Laughing Screaming*, specifically foregrounds the kind of undistanced involuntary response—what Williams might call the ecstatic response—which direct, body-genre films evoke from the audience. As Williams notes, "aurally, excess is marked by recourse not to the coded articulations of language but to inarticulate cries" (143)—laughing, screaming—both onscreen and in the audience.

The films listed above are nothing if not direct. There may be a "metaphorical" significance to the slashing of a woman's eye in *Un chien andalou*—in fact, feminist film theory would argue that there's a profound metaphorical significance to such an act—but that significance is very much bound up with the immediate physical jolt experienced by the spectator. Similarly, when Dracula vomits blood in *Andy Warhol's Dracula*, when Dr. Génessier peels the skin from a woman's face in *Eyes Without a Face*, and when Stephan, in *Daughters of Darkness*, whips his wife in an excess of sadistic sexual frenzy, the directness of the image, as Paul points out, "makes metaphoric significance seem secondary to the primary power" of the image itself (32).

Which is not to say these films don't simultaneously operate at the high end of the horror spectrum. They do. The pacing, the blatant disregard for the cause–effect logic of classical Hollywood cinema, the strategic use of discontinuous editing, the painterly composition of certain scenes all serve to mark these films as art cinema.[25] The fact that the films seem to operate at both ends of the horror spectrum is at least partly responsible for the fact that the best of them were so poorly received at the time of their release. *Daughters of Darkness* was so unsuccessful in finding a generic niche, *The Encyclopedia of Horror Movies* notes, that it never received the attention it deserved. This "unsettlingly intelligent" and uncommonly beautiful film was not well received "by any of the established audiences for art cinema, horror or camp movies" (242).

A film which had an even more difficult time staking out its generic territory is Tod Browning's *Freaks* (1932). Initially made as a mainstream horror film at MGM, the film caused a scandal. Described in reviews as "loathsome" and "unwholesome," the film was pulled from mainstream distribution shortly after its initial release and leased to Dwain Esper (the prolific exploitation filmmaker), who showed it, under a variety of titles, on the exploitation circuit. Like *Daughters of Darkness*, however, the film had trouble finding an appropriate audience. Too sensational for mainstream filmgoers, the film simply wasn't sensational enough for many exploitation fans. As David Friedman notes, *Freaks* nearly caused a riot when Dwain Esper showed it to a North Carolina drive-in audience under the sensational title *Forbidden Love*. Led by the title and advertising to expect a softcore treatment of "love" between "a beautiful women and a midget," the crowd had no patience with a movie which Raymond Durgnat later compared to the European art films of Buñuel.[26] Esper managed to pacify the drive-in patrons by showing them a black-and-white nudist colony one-reeler that he had tucked in the trunk of his car, a film that apparently came much closer to satisfying their expectations than did Browning's creepy classic.[27] Interestingly enough, *Freaks* was revived 30 years later as an "art film" and did very well, attracting favorable reviews by Raymond Durgnat and John Thomas, and captivating such notable patrons as Emile de Antonio and Diane Arbus.[28] By 1967, David J. Skal notes, the film "had made it to the Museum of Modern Art" (21).

Finally, Michael Powell's art-horror masterpiece, *Peeping Tom* (1960), which *The Encyclopedia of Horror Movies* calls "one of the best and most disturbing films to be made in Britain," not only shocked audiences, it almost ruined the director's career (135). Known for making films like *The Life and Death of Colonel Blimp* (1943), *Black Narcissus* (1947), and *The Red Shoes* (1948), Powell had previously flirted with the sensational in his work, but never so graphically and disturbingly as he did in *Peeping Tom*. The film disgusted reviewers. Derek Hill's now infamous review for the *Tribune* perhaps best sums up the critical response. "The only really satisfactory way to dispose of *Peeping Tom*," Hill writes, "would be to shovel it up and flush it swiftly down the nearest sewer. Even then the stench would remain."[29] Interestingly, the film is now shown in art houses as well as in horror venues, and it is frequently taught—as an example of some of the best of British filmmaking—in university courses treating the history of British cinema.

In a way, hybrid genres like art-horror films simply point up the problems which have historically characterized all attempts at genre definition. As S. S. Prawer notes,

> (i) Every worthwhile work modifies the genre [horror] to some extent, brings something new to it, and therefore forces us to rethink definitions and delimitations.
> (ii) There are borderline cases, works that belong to more than one genre—the overlap between the "fantastic terror" film and the "science fiction" film is particularly large.
> (iii) Wide variations in quality are possible within a given genre.
> (iv) There are works which as a whole clearly do not belong to the genre in question but which embody references to that genre, or contain sequences that derive from, allude to, or influence it. The first dream sequence in Bergman's *Wild Strawberries* . . . clearly . . . [belongs] in that category.[30]

While Prawer is speaking here mainly of horror films, his remark—as he himself points out—can be adapted to fit "genre studies in any medium" (37). Certainly, they can be adapted to fit other film genres. Film noir, the thriller, and melodrama have a great deal of overlap with other genres. Avant-garde cinema is just as divergent in scope and quality as horror cinema. The European art film is so diverse that it is generally not represented as a genre at all. And, as Jim Collins maintains in *Architectures of Excess*, the '80s and '90s have been marked by the increasing number of "eclectic, hybrid genre films": films such as *The Road Warrior* (1981), *Blade Runner* (1982), *Blue Velvet* (1986), *Near Dark* (1988), and *Thelma and Louise* (1991), which "engage in specific tranformations across genres."[31] In fact, genre overlap and instability is so common, Robin Wood maintains, that the tendency to treat genres as discrete has been one of the major obstacles to developing what he calls a synthetic definition of the term.[32]

Not only is there slippage between genres, there is slippage between evaluative classifications as well. As Eric Schaefer pointed out to me, if *Dementia* (*Daughter of Horror*, 1955) or *Carnival of Souls* (1962) had been made in Europe they would probably be considered art, or at least art-horror, films, instead of drive-in classics. Similarly, if *Eyes Without a Face* had been made in the United States, it would probably be considered a low-budget horror film. That is, in evaluative terms, the films would occupy not only a different generic niche, they would occupy a different artistic category or "class." The instability of film categorization (as high or low art) in all genres was illustrated when the July—August 1997 issue of *Film Comment* published a list of the top 30 unreleased foreign-language films of the '90s. Drawing upon a poll which queried such film scholars and critics as David Bordwell, Roger Ebert, Jonathan Rosenbaum, and Robert Sklar, Gavin Smith (writing for *Film Comment*) listed *Les Amants du*

Pont Neuf (Leos Carax, 1991) as the second-best unreleased art house flick of the '90s.[33] Thus the film was categorized as high art. In 1996, however, before the *Film Comment* poll results were published, the film was listed in a special paracinema company mailing, *Video Vamp Presents Celebrity Skin Videos*, as a "French sleaze classic." Clearly, as Jameson suggests, we need to rethink the emphasis we have placed on evaluation and essentialized categorization and replace it with a mode of assessment that's a little more dynamic.

As I've suggested, horror is not the only genre/category which is hard to pin down and it's not the only genre/category which continually flirts with the possibility of existing simultaneously as high and low art.[34] To some degree, as William Paul asserts, all film still has something disreputable about it,[35] all film still has to struggle to be seen as art at all. And yet, we do, as he also notes, consistently make distinctions between good cinema and bad, between artistic films and films that are "just entertainment." Even within as democratic a medium as film, we worry about "taste," a phenomenon which, social critics from Pierre Bourdieu to V. Vale and Andrea Juno maintain is always already bound up with questions of class.[36]

But while it is not the only popular genre which continually flirts with a kind of high-art double—in this case, the European art film or prestige import cinema—horror is perhaps the best vantage point from which to study the cracks that seem to exist everywhere in late twentieth-century "sacralized" film culture. Precisely because it plays so relentlessly on the body, horror's "low" elements are easy to see. As Joe Bob Briggs is fond of reminding us, fans of low horror are drawn by the body count ("We're talking two breasts, four quarts of blood, five dead bodies . . . Joe Bob says check it out").[37] And as catalogues from mail order video companies remind us, prestigious films, too, can play relentlessly on the public's desire—or at least its willingness—to be physically affronted. Like the lowest of low horror, European art films can "leave audiences gagging."

Notes

A shorter version of this article was presented at the 1997 Society for Cinema Studies Conference. I would like to thank Chris Anderson, Carol J. Clover, Skip Hawkins, Eric Schaefer, Ann Martin, and the Editorial Board of *Film Quarterly*, all of whom read earlier versions of the essay and made helpful suggestions. Also, a special thanks to Eric Schaefer for his sensitive reading of the piece and the references he gave me.

1 See Jeffrey Sconce, "'Trashing' the Academy: Taste, Excess, and an Emerging Politics of Cinematic Style," *Screen* 36:4 (Winter 1995), 372. Michael Weldon calls this cinema "psychotronic." See Michael Weldon, *The Psychotronic Encyclopedia* (New York: Ballantine Books, 1983); Michael Weldon, *The Psychotronic Video Guide* (New York: St. Martin's Griffin, 1996). Subsequent references to these three works will be given in the text. See also Michael Weldon, ed., *Psychotronic Video* (serial, Narrowsburg, New York).

2 Remarkably little has been written on the low end of the mail order video business. Fanzines and mass-market horror publications periodically publish addresses and lists. But, since they're preaching to the converted, they provide very little analysis of the phenomenon. At the time of this writing, Sconce's "'Trashing' the Academy" remains the only article which attempts to theorize the phenomenon and the aesthetic it

represents. The best general interest articles on mail order video were published in the July—August 1991 issue of *Film Comment*. See Elliot Forbes, "The 'Lost' World"; Maitland McDonagh, "The House by the Cemetery"; and Peter Hogue, "Riders of the Dawn," *Film Comment* 27 (July–Aug. 1991), 41–49. See also Richard Kadrey, "Director's Cuts," *World Art* 3/1996, 64–68, which discusses the aesthetic of bootlegs. Tony Williams' "Resource Guide: Video Sales and Rentals," *Jump Cut* 37 (1992), 99–109, and "Mail Order and Video Companies II," *Jump Cut* 41(1994), 110–118, mainly list companies. It's interesting, though, that in an article geared mainly toward teachers and film professionals, Williams mentions paracinema companies as well as more upscale, traditional sources.

3 For years, scholars have been challenging the binary opposition of high art and popular culture, and have been problematizing the uninflected use of the two terms. But the 1993 General Agreement on Tariffs and Trade (GATT) discussions over audiovisual products illustrated the degree to which the North American mainstream press continues to reproduce and valorize a dichotomy which cultural scholars and fans of paracinema find problematic. See Matthew Fraser, "A Question of Culture: The Canadian Solution Resolves a GATT Standoff," *MacLean's* v. 106 n. 52 (Canada, Dec. 27, 1993), 50; David Lawday, "France Guns for Clint Eastwood," *U.S. News and World Report* v. 115 n. 23 (Dec. 13, 1993), 72; and Daniel Singer, "GATT and the Shape of Our Dreams," *The Nation* v. 258 n. 2 (Jan 17, 1994), 54.

4 Carol J. Clover, "Her Body, Himself: Gender in the Slasher Film," *Representations* 20 (Fall 1987), 187.

5 While most art-cinema mail order companies separate films into generic categories, Home Film Festival simply lists titles alphabetically—to similarly startling effect. In *Program Guide* #12, for example, George Romero's *Night of the Living Dead* (1968) comes between Charles Laughton's *The Night of the Hunter* (1955) and Paolo and Vittorio Taviani's *The Night of the Shooting Stars* (1982). *Home Film Festival Program Guide* #12, 140.

6 This is the only qualitative distinction which the catalogues make—films which require ironized strategies of reading and those which don't. It's important to note, however, that films which don't are not considered better (or worse) than the ones that do—just different.

7 *Sinister Cinema Catalogue*, 12.

8 The reviewer does admit that "Harvey's direction has a weird flair, sometimes suggesting a throwback to the silent days and drawing a kind of awkward honesty out of the actors." Phil Hardy, ed., *The Encyclopedia of Horror Movies* (New York: Harper and Row, 1986), 147. Subsequent references will be given in the text.

9 *Sinister Cinema Catalogue*, 21.

10 Kyrou wrote, "Je vous en conjure, apprenez à voir les 'mauvais' films, ils sont parfois sublimes" ("I beg you, learn to see 'bad' films; they are sometimes sublime"). Ado Kyrou, *Le Surréalisme au cinéma*, 276. Translation mine.

11 Steven Shaviro, *The Cinematic Body* (Minneapolis: University of Minnesota Press, 1993), vii.

12 This is part of the "exploitation" definition given by Thomas Doherty, in *Teenagers and Teenpics: The Juvenilization of American Movies in the 1950s* (Boston: Unwin Hyman, 1988), 8.

13 Peter Lev, *The Euro-American Cinema* (Austin: University of Texas Press, 1993), 8.

14 That impression persists to this day. "People see 'French video' in the phone book," Donna Sayada, the owner of Video France, said in a 1996 interview, "and they think it's either highbrow cultural stuff or it's porno. . . . You should hear some of the calls we get." Peter

M. Nichols, "A Hard Sell, Those Little French Films," *New York Times* (Sunday, June 23, 1996), H29.

15 See Pauline Kael, "*Last Tango in Paris*," in Pauline Kael, *For Keeps* (New York: Dutton, 1994), 450; reprinted from Kael, *Reeling* (1976).

16 Michael F. Mayer, *Foreign Films on American Screens* (New York: Arco, 1965), 1–3.

17 Kristin Thompson and David Bordwell, *Film History: An Introduction* (New York: McGraw-Hill, 1994), 386.

18 "Parochial Uproar in Ft. Lee; Panics Before 'Foreign Art Films,'" *Variety* (Wednesday, Feb. 24, 1960), 24, 3.

19 In fact, Hollywood's attempt to compete for art film audiences has much to do with the fact that the traditional moviegoing base had been eroded. Staiger points out that younger, better-educated people were more likely to go to the movies than older, less-educated people. These people had very different tastes from the "masses." As Staiger notes, "while the 'masses' were not especially attracted to 'realism' or message' pictures, art-house audiences were typified as preferring those films." Janet Staiger, *Interpreting Films: Studies in the Historical Reception of American Cinema* (Princeton: Princeton University Press, 1992), 185. Douglas Gomery concurs, noting that audience studies "found that art theatres attracted persons of above-average education, more men than women and many solitary moviegoers. This was the crowd who attended the opera, theatre, lectures and ballet." Douglas Gomery, *Shared Pleasures: A History of Movie Presentation in the United States* (Madison: Wisconsin University Press, 1992), 189.

20 Staiger, *Interpreting Films*, 184.

21 Richard Kadrey, *Covert Culture Sourcebook*, (New York: St. Martin's Press, 1993), 1.

21 A few minutes into *Un chien andalou*, a man—played by Luis Buñuel—slices open a woman's eye with a razor. To gauge from student responses when I show the film in class, the segment has lost none of its power to shock and horrify the spectator, to act directly on the spectator's body.

23 Carol J. Clover, *Men, Women and Chain Saws: Gender in the Modern Horror Film* (Princeton: Princeton University Press, 1992), 21.

24 William Paul, *Laughing Screaming: Modern Hollywood Horror and Comedy* (New York: Columbia University Press, 1994), 32. Subsequent citations will be given in the text.

25 Lack of cause and effect, and strategic use of discontinuous editing, also links these films with exploitation cinema, which, as Eric Schaefer points out, can utilize similar techniques because of their reliance on forbidden spectacle. And it's a key feature of almost all European horror films made during the 1956–84 period. As Cathal Tohill and Pete Tombs point out, "Linear narrative and logic are always ignored in a *fantastique* [horror] film." Cathal Tohill and Pete Tombs, *Immoral Tales: European Sex and Horror Movies 1956–1984* (New York: St. Martin's Griffin, 1994), 5.

26 See Raymond Durgnat, "*Freaks*," *Films and Filming* vol. 9, no. 1 (Aug. 1963), 23.

27 See David F. Friedman (with Don DeNevi), *A Youth in Babylon: Confessions of a Trash-Film King* (Buffalo, N.Y.: Prometheus Books, 1990).

28 See David J. Skal, *The Monster Show: A Cultural History of Horror* (New York: W. W. Norton, 1993), and Patricia Bosworth, *Diane Arbus* (New York: Alfred A. Knopf, 1984). I have written at greater length on the film elsewhere. See "One of Us: Tod Browning's *Freaks*," in Rosemarie Garland Thomson, ed., *Freakery: Cultural Spectacles of the Extraordinary Body* (New York: New York University Press, 1996), 265–76; and David J. Skal and Elias Savada, "Offend

One and You Offend Them All," in Skal and Savada, *Dark Carnival: The Secret World of Tod Browning* (New York: Anchor Books, 1995) 159–82. Future citations of *The Monster Show* will be given in the text.

29 Derek Hill, "Cheap Thrills," *Tribune* (London: April 29, 1960), 11.

30 S. S. Prawer, *Caligari's Children: The Film as Tale of Terror* (New York: Da Cape Press, 1980), 37–38.

31 Jim Collins, *Architectures of Excess: Cultural Life in the Information Age* (New York: Routledge, 1995), 131.

32 Robin Wood, "Ideology, Genre, Auteur," in Gerald Mast, Marshall Cohen, and Leo Braudy, eds., *Film Theory and Criticism*, fourth edition (New York: Oxford University Press, 1992), 478.

33 Gavin Smith, "Foreign Affairs: Which Foreign Films Must Be Seen At All Costs," *Film Comment* vol. 33, no. 4 (July–Aug. 1997), 40–41.

34 Comedy, thrillers, sci-fi, and melodrama all have this ability. Jim Collins has done an excellent job of analyzing the way "the eclecticism of the contemporary genre films involves a hybridity of conventions that works at cross-purposes with the traditional notion of genre as a stable, integrated set of narrative and stylistic conventions." *Architectures of Excess*, 126.

35 See Paul, *Laughing Screaming*.

36 See Pierre Bourdieu, *Distinction: A Social Critique of the Judgement of Taste*, trans. Richard Nice (Cambridge, MA: Harvard University Press, 1984); William Paul, *Laughing Screaming*; and V. Vale and Andrea Juno, "Introduction," in Jim Morton (guest editor), *Incredibly Strange Films*, RE/SEARCH #10 (San Francisco: RE/SEARCH, 1986), 4–6.

37 Quoted in *Men, Women and Chainsaws*, 21. See also note, 22.

PART FOUR

CONSUMING FEARS

Introduction

One of the problems with production-based accounts is that they imply that the meaning of a text is determined by its conditions of production. However, not only do different audiences read films in different ways, but the meaning of a film can actually change over time. For example, while many critics today regard the horror film as a genre that is predominantly produced and consumed by men, extracts in this final part of the book demonstrate not only that there is a significant group of female fans of the genre, but also that many classic horror films were targeted at both male and female audiences.

In Chapter 11, for example, Rhona Berenstein looks at the marketing of horror films in order to understand the ways in which the industry presented films to audiences, and so framed their readings in different ways. Of course, audiences were not obliged to read films in particular ways, but advertising campaigns were designed in part to present a range of possible ways of reading films. They present audiences with the terms of reference with which to makes sense of, and derive pleasure from, a film. However, in its desire to appeal to a broad and diverse audience, the industry marketed the films in different ways to different groups. Far from being solely targeted to a male audience, Berenstein therefore demonstrates that many horror films were marketed through campaigns that not only presented the films differently to different audiences, but also actively courted the female viewer.

By studying the marketing of films, we do not gain direct access to how audiences understood specific films, but we can demonstrate that texts may have had a range of meanings and pleasures that we simply cannot deduce from the text itself and that can be reconstructed only through an analysis of the intertexts that surrounded it within a period.

This concern with the intertexts that surround films is also central to Chapter 12, in which Mark Jancovich examines the critical reception of *The Silence of the Lambs*. While marketing and promotion are, to a large extent, part of the industry's own practices, the meanings of films are also shaped by the range of critical commentary that surrounds them in reviews, articles, star profiles, etc. However, these are often in publications over which the industry has less control. Certainly, the industry does try to manage the media that comment upon them, but they cannot exert too much control without threatening to invalidate the supposed autonomy of these publications. After all, the assumption is that a review is somehow independent of the producing company, at least to some limited extent, and it is this that gives it a sense of authority and also distinguishes it from mere advertising.

This autonomy, however, means that films may be discussed in ways that are different from the terms that the producing institutions have used to market it. For example, it may be judged according to different terms of reference. Jancovich's extract therefore concentrates on *The Silence of the Lambs* and the different ways in which it was evaluated. In the process, he demonstrates that not only did different sections of the media frame the film in different ways, but that this process was also related to the ways in which it was generically categorized. Thus, while some critics have seen it as a horror film, others studiously avoided an association with the genre, or sought to distinguish it from certain perceptions of the genre. The study of reviews and features therefore tells us much about the struggles over the meanings of films, and the cultural politics that underpin them.

However, while these extracts concentrate on the different intertexts that surround a film, in Chapter 13, Linda Williams focuses on the contexts of exhibition. People do not simply watch films, but watch them within very specific social contexts. Watching a film in the cinema is not the same experience as watching a film on video within the home. Different social relations are in place that create different relationships to the film. Indeed, it could be claimed that historically many people did not go to see specific films, but rather 'went to the cinema', and in many cases, the least important aspect of this activity may have been the film that was showing.

However, Williams studies the specific strategies used in the exhibition of Alfred Hitchcock's *Psycho*, strategies that, she argues, were unique within the exhibition of films at the time. Most significantly, *Psycho* was shown in separate performances. This practice may now be common, but it was not in 1960; and for Williams, these practices of exhibition were used to discipline the audience and produce a particular type of spectator for the film. In other words, through exhibition practices, audiences were taught how to watch a film.

However, while Williams emphasizes that the practice of showing films in separate performances was uncommon, as Joan Hawkins has pointed out, it was only uncommon in the exhibition of *popular* films. In the art cinema, it was the norm and was born out of a very different set of tastes and values associated with the social groups who made up the art-cinema audience. In other words, modes of exhibition are directly tied to issues of social distinction and taste.

Finally, in Chapter 14, Brigid Cherry presents an ethnographic study of actual female horror fans. While the study of marketing, critical reception and exhibition can all help us to understand how films were framed for audiences, they cannot give us direct access to how audiences will actually relate to films and cinema more generally.

Indeed, Cherry's work is a critique of many textual studies of the horror film that demonstrates that we cannot deduce how audiences will interpret a film from an analysis of its formal features, and that while this practice has often led critics to claim that horror is predominantly consumed by men, the genre has a significant female fan-base. A study of their tastes and preferences therefore has much to tell us, not only about the films, but also about the social contexts that produce their specific competences and dispositions. Indeed, if we are to understand how audiences understand and use films within their everyday lives, it is necessary to move beyond questions of textual analysis.

11 Horror for sale

The marketing and reception of classic horror cinema

RHONA BERENSTEIN

> Take the girl friend and by the middle of the first reel she'll have both arms around your neck and holding on [*sic*] for dear life.
>
> (James E. Mitchell, Review of *Doctor* X (Warner Bros., 1932))

I

What did a man have to do to be a good horror viewer in the 1930s? According to James E. Mitchell in his review of *Doctor* X for the *Los Angeles Examiner*, he had to take his girlfriend to the movies and subject himself to her hysterical clutches. Like the standard model of film and horror spectatorship, Mitchell casts men as the genre's brave patrons, while women cower in their seats and hold on to their dates as if their lives depend on it. In the dark of the theater, Mitchell seems to suggest, horror movies provide women with a socially sanctioned reason to grab on to their boyfriends, to hold tight with all their might.

But was holding a quivering woman the only thing a man had to do to be a horror viewer in the 1930s? Not quite. In an effort to open this chapter with the conventional version of spectatorship, I preempted Mitchell's words at a crucial moment: "Take the girl friend and by the middle of the first reel she'll have both arms around your neck and holding on [*sic*] for dear life. *And you'll be giggling hysterically, too, trying to convince her you are not scared to death, either*" (emphasis added).[1] Mitchell's direct address to horror's male viewer not only relies on traditional gender dynamics—women are terrified and men are called upon to be brave—but confirms that gender traits can be performed. Just as social mandates invited women in the 1930s to cling to men while screening horror movies, thus encouraging them to display conventionally feminine behavior as a means of garnering male attention, so, too, did the male viewer, at least according to Mitchell, use female fear, as well as his own traditional display of bravery, to disguise *his* terror behind a socially prescribed behavior.

Mitchell's recognition that male spectators perform traditional gender behaviors adds yet another element to horror viewing. For, according to Mitchell, not only is male courage acted out in the dark of the movie theater, so, too, are the traditional ground rules for heterosexual coupling performed by patrons. Mitchell's 1932 commentary reinforces the findings of Norbert

Mundorf et al.'s recent study of horror spectatorship which found that contemporary horror movies offer prime arenas for teenagers of both sexes to play out the conventional mandates of gender roles and heterosexual coupling. The socially prescribed behaviors that Mitchell details in his review of *Doctor X* are, then, markers of the degree to which traditional gender traits can be mobilized in a specific social setting—such as a movie theater, and for particular cultural purposes—such as abiding by gender expectations and performing heterosexual dating rituals as expected. Whether as gender play, dating ploy, or both, the performance of bravery on the part of the male spectator to whom Mitchell addresses his review underscores the degree to which traditional signs of masculinity and heterosexual coupling can be constructed. [. . .]

My intent is to present and situate original documents both as a means of tracing the historical twists and turns of classic horror reception—specifically, as it pertains to gender—as well as a vehicle for suggesting that theatrical role-play, which I have attributed to imputed spectators, was elicited by studio and theater marketing ploys, and in film reviews in the 1930s. Thus, the performative dimensions that I align with spectatorship in theoretical terms are framed here in historical terms.

My focus on the gender dynamics of Production Code reports, popular film reviews, and marketing tactics derives from my belief that the textual and extratextual levels of classic horror movies should be studied as parallel modes of expression, as meaning systems that toyed with gender repeatedly, yet also appealed to assumptions about appropriate gender behavior as a selling ploy. Whether the parallels between horror's on- and offscreen representations of gender were intended by those who produced them in the 1930s (such as publicity departments and directors) is of less interest to me than is tracing the genre's address to viewers on the basis of gender expectations. Offscreen mentions of horror's appeal to women or its ability to terrify them, for example, found parallel representations in movies that portrayed heroines who were positively transformed while under a monster's sway, or who swooned when faced with terrors too horrible to bear. Horror movies were sites of negotiation and contradiction when it came to their portrayals of and assumptions about gender, and similar efforts at negotiation and signs of contradiction were at work in the publicity ploys used to market them to male and female viewers in the 1930s.

Believing that the textual and extratextual levels are connected however, is not the same as pinpointing the exact impact their convergence had on viewers. Much as I would like to claim that the gender behaviors that appear or are promoted on- and offscreen fully determine spectators' interpretations of classic horror, doing so would be an exercise in analytic projection, not precision.

[. . .]

What I do know is that their reactions were contested in reviews, [. . .] hoped for and promoted in Pressbooks, and overtly manipulated in exhibition ploys. How men and women were believed to react to horror movies was given contradictory attention by reviewers and promoters.[2] Precisely what spectators did with those diverse messages remains a matter of speculation—my guess is that they responded with a matching dose of contradiction and complexity, at least when behind theater doors.

Many horror reviews from the 1930s addressed spectators in unspecified terms. Reporters used gender-neutral language such as "horror fans" and "audiences." As Mordaunt Hall remarked of *Dracula* (Universal, 1931): "It is a production that evidently had the desired effect upon many in the audience yesterday afternoon, for there was a general outburst of applause when Dr. Van Helsing produced a little cross that caused the dreaded Dracula to fling his cloak over his head and make himself scarce."[3] The *Motion Picture Herald*'s reviewer, McCarthy, made similarly unspecified claims regarding *Mark of the Vampire* (MGM) four years later: "This is a picture that should give the horror fans all they want. It's full of shrieks and screams, gasps and shudders."[4] Edwin Schallert was convinced that *Frankenstein* elicited a range of affective responses from spectators when the film ran at the RKO Orpheum in 1932, but the audience remains a genderless mass for him: "This weird shiver feature seems to cause the audience not only to experience the spinal chills, but also to laugh, cry and otherwise express hysteria of the moment."[5]

While Louella O. Parsons gave viewership a more dramatic flair in her review of *King Kong* (RKO, 1933), she was equally vague when it came to gender: "Breathless with suspense, nervous with suppressed emotion and thrilled with continued horrors, the audience greeted 'KING KONG' at the Chinese Theatre last night, as something entirely new in the way of motion picture entertainment."[6] This lack of gender specification in a good portion of reviews is instructive, for it suggests that while assumed differences in male and female spectatorship are crucial to more recent scholarship on horror cinema, they were of less concern to critics when classic horror first appeared. What mattered most consistently to reporters was whether or not films were good, and whether they were suitable for children.

Despite the focus on other criteria, gender was referenced in a number of reviews. Critics usually offered one of three perspectives:[7] (1) they remark upon the terrors endured by both men and women in the audience; (2) they are surprised or convinced that women respond well to horror movies; and (3) they suggest that male and female viewers appreciate different aspects of films. Leo Meehan's 1931 review of *Frankenstein* in the *Motion Picture Herald* is a good example of the first critical perspective on gender: "Women come out trembling, men exhausted. I don't know what it might do to children, but I wouldn't want my kids to see it."[8] One reviewer for Warner Bros.'s *The Mystery of the Wax Museum* (1933) painted an almost identical portrait two years later: "Adults of both sexes will find more than enough in the way of startling excitement to interest them, but because of its gruesomeness, *Wax Museum* is a little too strong for juvenile patronage."[9]

In one of the few instances in which a reporter was revealed to be a woman, she assumed she could speak for all members of her sex when she made the following remarks about *Doctor X*: "All we can tell you—and we'll grant that our sisters will agree, and let the boyfriends do the real figuring in this case—is that 'Doctor X' moves swiftly from start to finish [and] it's an amusingly creepy way of spending an afternoon or evening."[10] As late as 1935, when the first horror cycle neared its end, reviewers continued to emphasize horror's draw to men, women and children: "In 'The Bride of Frankenstein,' Boris Karloff comes again to terrify the children, frighten the women and play a jiggling tune upon masculine spines."[11]

Like the other critics cited, *Time* magazine's reporter responded to *White Zombie* in 1932 by affirming that men, like women, are scared of monsters, but went a step further by critiquing the star's performance: "Bela Lugosi looks like a comic imbecile, [and] can make his jawbones rigid and show the whites of his eyes. These abilities qualify him to make strong men cower and women swoon."[12] The anonymous reviewer's critical tone suggested disdain not only for the movie and its star, but also for patrons who respond with fear in spite of Lugosi's botched performance. In fact, *White Zombie* is an excellent example of a horror movie that fared poorly among critics but well with the public. As Michael Price and George Turner note: "*White Zombie* opened on Broadway at the Rivoli Theatre. No movie ever received a more thorough critical scourge, although the public loved it and it brought in a great deal of money."[13] *White Zombie* is a reminder that 1930s reviews are limited gauges of spectatorship. Since classic horror films were released during an era when audience studies were scarce,[14] historical research can describe the environment for spectatorship but not the minutiae of viewer reactions.

The second approach to gender evidenced by reporters—surprise or conviction that horror movies delighted female patrons—was articulated in a *Variety* review for *Dracula* in 1931. As Rush noted: "Here was a picture whose screen fortunes must have caused much uncertainty as to the femme fan reaction. As it turns out all the signs are that the woman angle is favorable and that sets the picture for better than average money at the box office."[15] Universal had a hand in eliciting female interest in the film. The studio released *Dracula* with an explicitly romantic campaign targeted at women. The movie opened in New York City on February 14, 1931—Valentine's Day—accompanied by suggestive cutlines: "The Story of the Strangest Passion Ever Known;"[16] "The Strangest Love Story of All;"[17] and "The Strangest Love a Man Has Ever Know."[18]

The assumption that women might have a romantic stake in vampire movies may not have been surprising at the time, given that fiends often sweep heroines off their feet. But the same *Variety* reporter thought female patrons hooked on *Frankenstein* as well: "Appeal is candidly to the morbid side and the screen effect is up to promised specifications. Feminine fans seem to get some kind of emotional kick out of this sublimation of the bedtime ghost story done with all the literariness of the camera." Although Rush did not elaborate upon why he or she thought women were drawn to James Whale's movie, a more general viewer profile was provided: "The audience for this type of film is probably the detective story readers and the mystery yarn radio listeners."[19]

Who were those detective readers and mystery listeners? Rush did not say. Yet clues appeared in two industry magazines geared toward exhibitors: the *Motion Picture Herald* (MPH) and its predecessor, the *Exhibitors Herald-World* (EHW). In a 1933 issue of the MPH, the following headline appeared: "Girls Want Mystery; Boys War Pictures." The brief article announced the results of an Edinburgh, Scotland, study of children's spectatorial preferences. The gender lines were drawn between mystery and war movies but, noted the report, neither group liked romance films.[20] The column went on to suggest that girls will, eventually, become women with a continued investment in mysteries. That they might also grow up to crave romance was an assumption made by the motion picture industry at the time.

That assumption was articulated in a 1930 article in the EHW entitled, "B. O. Explodes Idea That Women Dislike War and Crook Pictures. Feminine Attendance at Four Productions Classed as Lacking in Love or Romantic Interest Averages 61 Per Cent of Total at Matinees and 59 Per Cent at Night." Although the films cited were war and gangster pictures, the unconventional results predicted female horror attendance—*Dracula* debuted and was a box-office success only five months later. "Smashing a traditional theory of the box office," the article continued, "investigation has brought to light some pertinent facts to disprove the idea that women, who decide the fate of motion pictures, object as a rule to war pictures, crook dramas, and films in which the love or romantic interest is conspicuous by its absence.'[21] While the percentage of men attending matinees increased in the early part of the 1930s, due to rising unemployment rates, women remained a significant viewing force. Thus, the study's announcement of female interest in gangster and war films was also a promising sign of horrific things to come.

Although the EHW article encouraged exhibitors to quell their anxieties about female attendance at rough-and-tumble movies, classic horror marketing rarely took women for granted. Films often included romance at the narrative level, which was promoted as a selling point to women viewers. In McCarthy's review of *The Mummy* (Universal, 1932) in the MPH, for example, he or she articulated the gender divide assumed in spectator tastes: "It has that type of romance, which, although far-fetched and entirely visionary, is nevertheless fascinating to feminine patrons, while the mystic unrealism should provide the men folk something new.[22] Men and women may enjoy horror movies, McCarthy claimed, but their pleasures are found in divergent aspects of films. Furthermore, McCarthy thought that the source of fascination for women was decidedly unimpressive, "far-fetched" romance in the reporter's own words.

Not surprisingly, given the goal of as wide a viewership as possible, classic horror movies were made and marketed with a general audience in mind. As an MPH reviewer noted of *King Kong* in 1933, the film "has everything—romance, drama, spectacle, unrealism, thrill terror and 'love interest.'"[23] The same combination of disparate themes was proclaimed in a 1931 MPH advertisement for *Dr. Jekyll and Mr. Hyde*. As the cutline notes: "PARAMOUNT BRINGS YOU THE THRILLER OF ALL THRILLERS!—PLUS A GREAT LOVE STORY." Later in the same advertisement, diverse promotional possibilities were emphasized: "Swell cast; great director and a fascinating story. Mystery and horror! Heart-warming romance and intense-drama! Everything! Its appeal is unlimited.'[24] Just in case that appeal was divided along gender lines, *Variety* ran what David J. Skal calls a "split-personality review" [. . .]. A sidebar commentary entitled "The Woman's Angle" recasts some of the film's supposed failures in the horror department as draws for female spectators. As *Variety*'s reporter remarked: "Classic shocker loses much of its stark horror and consequent unpleasantness for women, by growing logical with psychoanalytical motivation and daringly presented sex appeal. Latest version made enticing instead of repellent to the girls."[25]

Along the same lines, one exhibitor of Paramount's film literally split his lobby display in two and separated the horror from the romance theme. As the MPH reported:

> In connection with one of the recent so-called "Horror" pictures, "Dr. Jekyll and Mr. Hyde," contrasting lobby displays were most effectively used by George Laby, manager of the Washington Street Olympia Theatre, Boston, Mass.; so effectively, in fact, that the displays were thought to be a contributing factor obtaining the highest weekly gross over the period of the year. The accompanying photo speaks for itself. At the left, now the famous "Doctor" in characteristic poses of himself and other self, treated from the "horror" angle. At the right are featured characters representing the romantic side of the picture.[26]

The romantic side consisted of a poster of actresses Miriam Hopkins and Rose Hobart flanking heartthrob Fredric March, who stars in the eponymous role. The dual-focus display parallels the film's dual theme and highlights exhibitor assumptions about male and female spectatorial preferences. Thus, although some reviewers claimed that women and horror were a fine match, others believed that female patrons had to be courted with romance themes and promotional stunts.

II

Classic horror's promotional gimmicks took various forms, including updating techniques from the silent era. The ambulance parked outside the theater door, for example, was a popular ploy in the 1920s and was refurbished by exhibitors in the next decade. As the MPH reports, the following sign was displayed in front of the Princess Theatre in Aurora, Mississippi, for performances of *Bride of Frankenstein* (Universal) in 1935: "No parking here, space reserved for ambulance."[27] Holden Swinger, manager of the Palace Theatre in Akron, Ohio, went a step further—he "stationed an ambulance at his curb during his 'Bride of Frankenstein' date with lobby easel and sign on ambulance calling attention to the free emergency service for those who 'couldn't take it.'"[28] Both stunts, used earlier in the decade for *Frankenstein* (Universal, 1931), are variations on a ploy listed by John F. Barry and Epes W. Sargent in their 1927 guide to exhibitors, *Building Theatre Patronage: Management and Merchandising*.

Barry and Sargent had clear ideas about the appeals of the ambulance to motion-picture theater managers and, by extension, to spectators:

> A standard comedy stunt is the ambulance parked in front of the theatre to carry out those who may be overcome with laughter. The ambulance may be paraded through the streets with signs to the effect that the occupant is being rushed to the hospital because he nearly died laughing at the named comedy. If you can get a man who can laugh naturally and infectiously, it will not hurt to have him stagger from the house, and be helped into the ambulance, laughing all the way.[29]

While the ideal comedy stunt participant, according to Barry and Sargent, is a man whose laughter is infectious, horror exhibitors preferred women for exploitation purposes in the 1930s.

For example, in order to draw as many patrons to *Mark of the Vampire* (MGM, 1935) as possible, a first-aid stretcher was placed in the lobby of the Loew's Colonial Theatre in Reading, Pennsylvania. The in-house stunt was accompanied by advertisements in the town's daily newspapers addressed to "women who are not afraid." The notices recounted the film's storyline and challenged female viewers to attend a screening. As the copy for the advertisement suggests, the contest winner was expected to respond *against* her conventional gender role; she was supposed to be brave.[30] A year later, the Wicomico Theatre in Salisbury, Maryland, devised a tie-in prize for *The Invisible Ray*, which targeted women again. A free permanent was offered by the town's leading beauty salon to any woman willing to sit alone in the theater and watch the film at midnight. According to the MPH, there were twenty applicants for the stunt and "crowds gathered at the theatre to watch the gal enter."[31] Both exhibitor efforts used women as prototypical viewers, drew upon stereotypes that assumed that female patrons will be frightened by watching horror and invited women to defy those stereotypes as a means of garnering prizes and proving their prowess as spectators.

In an analysis of the relationship between women and early exhibition tactics, Diane Waldman mentions that the manager of New York's Rialto Theatre took pride in promoting horror movies to a predominantly male clientele. Waldman uses the manager's claim as a springboard to analyze horror's sadistic address to women in the early 1940s:

> If other theatres showing horror films were anything like the Rialto, one piece of exploitation aimed at women takes on ominous tones: a theatre exhibiting Universal's *Frankenstein Meets the Wolf Man* (1943) offered a prize to any woman who would sit through the midnight show alone. It is not clear whether the danger was supposed to derive from the terrors of the screen or from the other patrons of the theatre. This stunt, then, made explicit the connection between horror films and the terrorizing of women, capitalizing on one of women's most common experiences: fear of harassment when alone, especially at night, in a public place heavily frequented by men.[32]

While Waldman is right to take note of the midnight terrors endured by women in American society, she reduces the Rialto stunt to vulgar sexism and assumes that it fully encapsulates horror's relationship to women. Waldman is not far off in claiming that the choice of a female patron resulted from conventional assumptions about women in a patriarchal culture, but she is wrong to assert that the choice only connoted attack and harassment.

Women were classic horror's central stunt participants because they were thought to personify the genre's favored affect: fear. The upshot was that if women could survive the viewing of a horror film and, moreover, if they could respond bravely, then other patrons, meaning *men* can do the same. While Waldman's claim has some validity, it was not exhibitors' primary motivation. Given that the woman chosen was expected to view *Frankenstein Meets the Wolf Man* alone in the theater, harassment by men was not part of the contest's requirements, but solitary bravery was. Female responses to horror were used by exhibitors to prove that the films should and could be seen by all patrons and to highlight the performative elements of terror. For if women were asked over and over again to *act* out or refuse to act out their fears in front of crowds or to garner prizes, their gender roles—though conventional and promoted—were also highly theatricalized.

Take the efforts of the Loew's Majestic Theatre in Bridgeport, Connecticut, for instance. During screenings of *Mark of the Vampire* in 1935, "[a] woman was planted in the audience at each show to scream and faint, after which she was carried out to an ambulance parked in front of the theatre and whisked away."[33] While the female scream is a popular on-screen trope, it was also promoted heavily as a horror gimmick, a performance intended to incite viewer response. So powerful was the female scream for audiences that Marquis Busby claimed it sparked his reaction to *Dracula* at the beginning of the decade: "I wasn't really scared until some lady in the audience let out a piercing scream. Maybe it was just a pin, but it was disconcerting to the rest of the audience."[34] Maybe it *was* just a pin, maybe she was a plant, maybe the viewer was terrified, or maybe she pretended to be. Whichever explanation holds true, the sound of a woman's scream promoted fear, guaranteed the genre's effectiveness, and linked female gender behavior to an overwrought performance.[35]

While some theaters addressed female patrons with tame ploys—for example, the Capitol in Dallas premiered Universal's *The Black Cat* (1934) with a contest for the most beautiful cat[36]—others tried to create as large a ruckus as possible. Owners of the Palace Theatre in Chicago, for example, placed advertisements in newspapers noting, "EMOTION TEST HITS ON '[BRIDE OF] FRANKENSTEIN.'" The exhibitors remodeled a lie-detector exam to register the affective roller coaster experienced by viewers. The prototypical spectators chosen for the stunt were two female subjects, aged five and twenty-five respectively, who were hooked up to the contraption as they screened the film. A first-aid booth was placed in the lobby to dramatize the health hazards of horror viewing. The promotional efforts were rounded out by a tie-up with the Loop department store, which utilized "a professional mannikin [sic] modeling evening gowns, surrounded by color enlargements from the picture."[38] As was true of other stunts, female responses to horror were promoted vociferously and used to gauge the genre's ability to frighten, amuse, and satisfy patrons.

Although department store tie-ins were initiated by local theater managers, they were also suggested in Pressbooks. The promotional materials distributed for *The Mystery of the Wax Museum*, for instance, include a full-page game plan for linking the film to a local department store. Exhibitors were advised to approach a store as follows: "Here is a tie-up that is a natural for any store that uses the finer grade of lifelike wax models for gown displays. Offer to furnish the store with such equipment, the services of an experienced gown model, and one that in general dimensions, sizes up to the wax models to be used."[39] The idea was for the store to announce a window fashion show, at which time the live model would pose with the wax figurines, stand frozen for a few moments, and surprise the audience by smiling and bowing. The logic ran as follows: exhibit beautiful gowns at local department stores to pique women's interest in the latest horror film, and they will arrive at the next showing with their dates and friends in tow.

Although the exhibition ploys listed thus far appeal to women as prototypical horror viewers and consumers of feminine wares, other promotional tactics were developed. One popular technique was to link women with monstrosity, as well as suggest their desire for a fiend. The RKO Theatre in Los Angeles, for example, sent masked women into the streets to hand out "Beware" notices announcing the premiere of *The Invisible Man* (Universal, 1934).[40] While the announcements targeted male as well as female patrons, women were used to promote the picture as fiendish doubles—like the film's monster; their identities remain hidden. The MPH added yet another dimension in its advice to exhibitors for the same film: "There are a million more [exploitation angles] you can concoct, not the least of which are those that can be applied to women to stir their curiosity. How would they like to be embraced, kissed, by an invisible lover?"[41] Here, the MPH urged managers to address women in terms of their desire *for* the invisible man, and not their resemblance to him.

The publicity ploys for *Island of Lost Souls* (Paramount, 1933) also targeted female patrons in dual terms. Prior to the release of the movie, Paramount conducted a nationwide search for the Panther Woman of America. Basing the competition on the female monster in Erle C. Kenton's screen adaptation of H. G. Wells's novel *The Island of Dr. Moreau* (1895), the search gained public attention and boosted pre-release interest in the film. Paramount chose a winning entrant for each state and decided on a national victor amid fanfare in Chicago. The winner received a prize, the Panther Woman of America title, and the promise that Laughton would turn her into a beast.[42] The contest was mentioned in newspapers across the country and *Photoplay* hinted at it in a review: "A thriller of thrillers. Among the monstrosities created is *Lota*, the much publicized 'Panther Woman'" (emphasis in original).[43] The movie's Pressbook is filled with references to Kathleen Burke's prize-winning portrayal of the Panther Woman. Theater managers were advised to plant stories regarding her contest travails in local newspapers two days before the film's release. Proposed headlines include: "A STAR BEFORE SHE STARTS! 'PANTHER WOMAN' ACHIEVES NEW OVERNIGHT FILM SUCCESS" and "WINS 60,000 TO ONE SHOT! OFFICE GIRL CAPTURES 'PANTHER WOMAN' ROLE"[44]

Other publicity materials for *Island of Lost Souls* tempered the horror theme through an appeal to stardom. In the February 1933 issue of *Photoplay*, a three-page story was devoted to Charles Laughton who played the mad doctor of Kenton's film. The profile, which included glossies of Laughton in and out of costumes, and a still of him posing with his thespian-wife Elsa Lanchester in a moment of conjugal bliss, presented him to *Photoplay*'s readership as a character actor of great versatility and a husband of exceeding warmth. This piece appeared in the same month that *Island of Lost Souls* was reviewed and advertised in the magazine. Laughton may have played a horrid man in the film, fans were told in the ads, but he was a gentleman in real life, according to the star profile.[45]

A full-page advertisement for *Island of Lost Souls* appeared near the beginning of the same *Photoplay* issue. Depicting a drawing of a partially clad woman surrounded by wild animals, the cutline intoned: "HE TOOK THEM FROM HIS MAD MENAGERIE . . . NIGHTS WERE HORRIBLE WITH THE SCREAMS OF TORTURED BEASTS . . . FROM HIS HOUSE OF PAIN THEY CAME RE-MADE. . . . HIS MASTERPIECE—THE PANTHER WOMAN THROBBING TO THE HOT FLUSH OF LOVE."[46] The publicity simultaneously positions the mad doctor as a sadist, a passion-inspiring figure, and a man capable of transforming women in terrifying and desirable ways. *Photoplay*'s readers were invited to view Lota, the monstrous Panther Woman, as both tortured and positively transformed by Laughton, her equally monstrous creator.

The doubling of heroines and fiends persisted in publicity for other films as well. A striking advertisement for *Svengali* (Warner Bros., 1931)[47] appeared in *Photoplay* in July of 1931 and positioned John Barrymore, who played the title role, as a simultaneous object of fear and desire for Marian Marsh's Trilby, as well as a double for her: "HE IS GENIUS—MADMAN—LOVER! HIS HYPNOTIC SPELL REACHES OUT OF DARKNESS CONTROLLING LOVE—HATE—LIFE ITSELF. SHE IS THE BEAUTY WHO HAD ALL PARIS AT HER FEET—WHO WINS MEN WITH A SMILE—WHO HATES SVENGALI THE SINISTER LOVEMAKER—UNTIL HIS MAGIC SPELL FORCES EVEN HER TO BEAT HIS MANUFACTURED LOVE!" (emphasis in original)[48] In a mimicry of Svengali's hypnotic abilities, Trilby, the advertisement proclaims, is not only subject to the fiend's control but exhibits her own brand of hypnosis—she has Paris at her feet and wins men with a smile.

Like *Photoplay*'s presentation of *Island of Lost Souls* two years later, this advertisement banks on multiple modes of address to, primarily, female readers. The cutline aligns fiend with heroine, suggests they desire each other *and* introduces stardom into the mix. Cut across the center of the layout, in capital letters, are the following words: "JOHN BARRYMORE AS 'SVENGALI' THE HYPNOTIST." The typeface is largest for the actor's last name—it literally slices the advertisement in half and draws the most visual attention.

[. . .]

Notes

1 James E. Mitchell, "Mad Scientists, Cannibalism, Bodies—Gosh!" *Los Angeles Examiner*, August 12, 1932.

2 While *Attack of the Leading Ladies* is filled with references to original reviews, most of these reviews are either unsigned, signed by initials only, or signed with pseudonyms. It is therefore impossible to determine whether these reviews were written by male or female reporters. As a result, what might have proven to be a compelling element of this book—addressing the ways in which male and female reviewers responded to the genre—must remain a good idea but one it is impossible to elaborate. I have therefore made some preliminary and brief comments—both in the text and the notes—when the reporter is a

woman, and I assume that the rest of the reviewers (for example, Bige, Char, and McCarthy) will forever remain a mystery in gender terms. One of the other issues I was aware of when conducting my research was that of differentiating reviews that appeared in industry magazines from those geared toward the public at large. I initially assumed that industry reviews would be on the whole less critical than those appearing in general publications. I was wrong. Bad reviews for horror movies were as likely to appear in the *Hollywood Reporter*, *Film Daily*, and *Variety* as in the *Nation*, the *New York Times*, and the *New Yorker* (which was ruthless in its dismissals of 1930s horror). As a result, I have chosen to include reviews from different sources side by side. Although the intended readership of publications may have differed, each individual publication's overall attitude toward films remained consistent.

3 Mordaunt Hall, "Bram Stoker's Human Vampire," *New York Times* (February 13, 1931): 21.

4 McCarthy, "Mark of the Vampire," *Motion Picture Herald* 191, no. 1 (April 6, 1935): 48.

5 Edwin Schallert, "'Frankenstein' a Hit," *Los Angeles Times* (January 4, 1932).

6 Louella O. Parsons, "Horror, Thrills and Suspense Fill Picture," *Los Angeles Examiner* (March 25, 1933).

7 I found only one direct mention of horror's incompatibility with female patrons in my research, which appeared in a letter to the editor in the *Motion Picture Herald*. The letter reads as follows: "THEY HAVE OVERLOOKED THE WOMEN. The producers find that in some of the larger cities where their overhead is highest, horror pictures, weird and gruesome pictures . . . have taken their fair sized grosses. From this as a beginning they have figured that the whole country wants this type of film fare. In this they are very erroneous. . . . [T]he women have been almost entirely overlooked" (Letter to the Editor, signed F. M. A. Litchard, Morse Theatre, Franklin, Mass., *Motion Picture Herald* 111, no. 4 [April 22, 1933]: 50). The glut of horror and gangster films produced during the early 1930s were, according to Litchard, drawing "large numbers of unemployed men who have nothing to do." They were not pulling in the more important urban *and* rural patrons, namely women. Although Litchard's letter is the only direct complaint I located about horror's lack of appeal to women, the polarization of gender in viewership was commented on in a review for *Murders in the Zoo* (1933), a Paramount mystery film. As McCarthy noted in the *Motion Picture Herald*: "The men in the preview audience seemed to appreciate the ruthless Gorman and the comic Yates, with the animal element. The women, as could be expected, did the gasping, and according to their comments, they seemed to agree that it was a little too brutal for feminine appreciation" ("Murders in the Zoo," *Motion Picture Herald* 110, no. 11 (March 11, 1933): 19). Of course, it is possible to read the responses of female patrons as ambiguous—their gasps may have indicated their appreciation of the film in line with gender norms, and their comments to the reviewer may have favored more conventional gender expectations.

8 Meehan, "Frankenstein," *Motion Picture Herald* 105, no. 7 (November 14, 1931): 40.

9 McCarthy, "Wax Museum," *Motion Picture Herald* 110, no. 2 (January 7, 1933): 23.

10 Irene Thirer, "Doctor X," *New York Daily News* (August 4, 1932). Fay Wray Collection, University of Southern California Cinema Archives.

11 "At the Roxy," *New York Times* (May 11, 1935): 21.

12 "White Zombie," *Time* (August 8, 1932).

13 Michael Price and George Turner, "*White Zombie*—Today's Unlikely Classic," *American Cinematographer* (February 1988): 36.

14 Although Leo Handel's audience studies in the 1940s suggest that men liked horror more than women, the variance in preferences was less significant than might be expected, given popular assumptions about the relationship between gender and generic tastes. On the whole, the research reported by Handel for a 1942 study suggested that neither women nor men counted horror among their top four choices when they were asked to rank the story types they liked the most. Mystery and horror pictures were ranked as men's fifth favorite type, behind war pictures, adventure action pictures, musical comedies, and westerns. Women ranked mystery and horror movies (which were listed as a pair in the survey) as number seven out of a possible twenty-one options, after love stories, musical comedies, serious dramas, war pictures, sophisticated comedies, and historicals and biographies. It should be noted, however, that when ranking story types according to their dislikes, horror and mystery films ranked second behind westerns for women (and tied with G-men and gangster movies), while men rated the genre as the eighth most disliked (again, in a tie with G-men and gangster films). It is noteworthy that Handel's results also varied according to age—younger audiences from twelve to twenty-nine liked mystery and horror films far more than those viewers aged thirty to forty-four. (*Hollywood Looks at Its Audience: A Report of Film Audience Research* (Urbana: University of Illinois Press, 1950), p. 124.

15 Rush, "Dracula," *Variety* (February 18, 1931).

16 *Motion Picture Herald* 102, no. 2 (January 10, 1931): 39.

17 Michael J. Murphy, *The Celluloid Vampire: A History and Filmography*, 1897–1979 (Ann Arbor, Mich.: Pierian, 1979), p. 21.

18 Alan Frank, *Horror Movies: Tales of Terror in the Cinema* (London: Octopus, 1974), p. 14.

19 Rush, "Frankenstein," *Variety* (December 8, 1931).

20 Bernard Charman, "Girls Want Mystery; Boys War Pictures," *Motion Picture Herald* 111, no. 4 (April 22, 1933): 47.

21 Charles S. Aaronson, "B.O. Explodes Idea That Women Dislike War and Crook Pictures. Feminine Attendance at Four Production Classed as Lacking in Love or Romantic Interest Averages 61 Per Cent of Total at Matinees and 59 Per cent at Night," *Exhibitors Herald-World* no. 10 (September 6, 1930): 24.

22 McCarthy, "The Mummy," *Motion Picture Herald* 109, no. 10 (December 3, 1932): 27.

23 McCarthy, "King Kong," *Motion Picture Herald* 110, no. 9 (February 25, 1933): 37, 40.

24 *Motion Picture Herald* 105, no. 13 (December 26, 1931): 28.

25 Rush, "Dr. Jekyll and Mr Hyde," *Variety* (January 5, 1932).

26 "Lady's Effective Lobby Display," *Motion Picture Herald* 106, no. 5 (January 30, 1932): 68.

27 "Swinger Offers First Aid," p. 64.

28 "Swinger Offers First Aid," *Motion Picture Herald* 120, no. 11 (September 14, 1935).

29 John F. Barry and Epes W. Sargent, *Building Theatre Patronage: Management and Merchandising* (New York: Chalmers, 1927), p. 222. In her excellent study of early marketing stunts, "From Elephants to Lux Soap: The Programming and 'Flow' of Early Motion Picture Exploitation," *The Velvet Light Trap* 25 (Spring 1990), Jane Gaines mentions Barry and Sargent's ambulance ploy and adds: "The ambulance was also used threateningly to convey the message that audiences attended horror films at their own risk" (36). Since she only footnotes Barry and Sargent after this comment and since the exhibitors did not mention the usefulness of the ambulance for horror showings, my guess is that Gaines's reference points forward to the 1930s when ambulances and medical care became a promotional staple for the genre.

30 *Motion Picture Herald* 120, no. 1 (July 6, 1935): 99.

31 "Free Permanent Given for 'Invisible Rau,'" *Motion Picture Herald* 124, no. 3 (July 18, 1936): 85.

32 Diane Waldman, "From Midnight Shows to Marriage Vows: Women, Exploitation, and Exhibition," *Wide Angle* 6, no. 2 (1984): 41.

33 "'When Will She Wake?' Rosy Asks Bridgeport," *Motion Picture Herald* 119, no. 13 (June 29, 1935): 91. The fainting female patron was, it seems, a fixture of classic horror stunts in the 1930s. In some cases, however, she may have been an unintended by-product of exhibitor efforts. According to Maury Foladare, one of *King Kong*'s publicists, a female patron in the Pacific Northwest was so distraught by a stunt that she fainted and sued for damages. As he noted many years later: "I got a big guy and rented an ape costume from Western Costume. I had the big ape walk into the Wenatchee (WA) Department Store. This one woman fainted. Later, she sued me and the studio (RKO) for $100,000." Eventually, the matter was settled without payment (Beverly Beyette, "Dean of Hollywood Publicists, 79, Keeps Plugging Away Honest," *Los Angeles Examiner* (September 21, 1986)).

34 Marquis Busby, "'Dracula' Better Film Than Stage Play at Orpheum," *Los Angeles Examiner* (March 28, 1931).

35 In some instances it was less what women did than what they *did not* do vis-à-vis horror that was remarked upon. A reporter for the *New York World-Telegram* had the following to say about *Doctor X* in 1932: "As far as the eyes of this conscientious reporter could detect, not one woman in the audience fainted" (August 4, 1932).

36 "Louise Charnisky Stages Swell *Black Cat* Show," *Motion Picture Herald* 116, no. 2 (July 7, 1934): 74.

37 Despite reviewer warnings that children and youths should not attend films, exhibitors encouraged their attendance quite enthusiastically by mid-decade.

38 "Emotion Test Hits on 'Frankenstein,'" *Motion Picture Herald* 119, no. 7 (May 18, 1935): 79.

39 *The Mystery of the Wax Museum* (Warner Bros., 1932) Pressbook, Library of Congress microfiche file, Washington, D.C.

40 McCarthy, "The Invisible Man," *Motion Picture Herald* 113, no. 6 (November 4, 1933): 37.

42 Kurt Singer, *The Laughton Story: An Intimate Story of Charles Laughton* (Philadelphia: John C. Winston, 1954), p. 105.

43 "Island of Lost Souls," *Photoplay* 43, no. 3 (February 1933): 58.

44 *Island of Lost Souls* (Paramount, 1932) Pressbook, Library of Congress microfiche file, Washington, D.C.

45 Barbara Barry, "Such a Naughty Nero," *Photoplay* 14, no. 3 (February 1933): 46–47, 95–96.

46 *Photoplay* 43, no. 3 (February 1933): 4.

47 Whether or not *Svengali* is a horror film has been debated for a number of years. Phil Hardy does not include it in his *Encyclopedia of Horror*, but William K. Everson contextualized it in relation to Hollywood's horror cycle in "Svengali" in 1973 (*The New School Program Notes* (June 26, 1973)). The film has a strong link to vampire and zombie films, with its hypnosis focus and the construction of the eponymous character as a fiend. *Svengali*'s status as a horror movie is merely assumed by Ellen Draper in an article on films in which fiends mesmerize heroines. According to Draper, *Svengali*, like the classic horror movie *White Zombie* (1932), depicts the victimization of women so well that it proves Laura Mulvey right about the sadistic male gaze. For Draper, however, *Svengali* and a number of other films go one step further: they overstate female suffering to the point that patriarchy's misogynistic machinations are laid bare. See Draper's "Zombie Women: When the Gaze

is Male," *Wide Angle* 10, no. 3 (1988): 52–62. As I will argue, the hypnosis film's visual dynamics cannot be reduced to the sadistic male gaze, even one that reveals its own power structures, as Draper would have it.

48 *Photoplay* 40, no. 2 (July 1931): 7.

Genre and the audience 12

Genre classifications and cultural distinctions in the mediation of *The Silence of the Lambs*

MARK JANCOVICH

In a recent article on *film noir*, James Naremore has commented on the difficulty of defining the term. This difficulty, he argues, arises because the definition 'has less to do with a group of artefacts than with a discourse – a loose evolving system of arguments and readings, helping to shape commercial strategies and aesthetic ideologies'.[1] Not only have understandings of *film noir* changed, but in the process specific films and filmmakers have acquired different meanings in relation to the term. *The Lost Weekend*, once regarded as a central reference point in early discussions of *film noir*, has been completely excluded from later constructions of the field.

As Naremore argues, it is not so much the case that a group of texts simply exist in some relation to one another, however obscure that relation might be, but that 'the Name of the Genre . . . functions in much the same way as the Name of the Author'.[2] He cites Michel Foucault's analysis of 'the author function' to substantiate the parallel between these systems of classification. For Foucault, the author function creates 'a relationship of homogeneity, filiation, authentication of some texts by use of others'.[3] But this technique of classification does not simply identify some pre-existing essence. Instead, it produces what it purports to identify. It is the product of a desire and projection, of a need to believe that there is 'a point where contradictions are resolved, where incompatible elements are at last tied together or organised around a fundamental original contradiction'.[4]

As a result, and as Andrew Tudor has also argued, the pursuit of the 'Factor X' that defines a specific genre is both essentialist and ultimately futile. Naremore and Tudor both argue that genres are not defined by a feature that makes all films of a certain type fundamentally similar; rather, they are produced by the discourses through which films are understood. While Naremore considers how the meaning of the term *film noir* changes historically, Tudor defines the horror genre as 'what we collectively believe it to be', and sets out to study historical shifts in the patterns of those films understood to belong to the genre, and in the social concerns that have been expressed by and about them.[5]

Both types of work provide vital contributions to the study of genre and illustrate the point that genre definitions are not simply of academic interest, but have far greater currency and significance. Both also emphasise that genre definitions are produced more by the ways in which films are understood by those who produce, mediate and consume them, than they are by the internal properties of the films themselves. The historical focus of these two critics tends to obscure one problem, however. Both authors presuppose the existence of a collective consensus – about the definition of particular genres within any given period. But such a collective consensus may not have actually existed. We need, therefore, to study not only how definitions of genre change over time, but also how they operate within the intense struggles between different taste formations that are present at a given historical moment.

Differences in taste are never neutral. The varying definitions of any given genre used by different social groups do not imply a pluralistic ideal of variety and heterogeneity. Ien Ang has observed that it is not the *fact* of differences but 'the meanings of differences that matter', and that these meanings 'can only be grasped . . . by looking at their contexts, social and cultural bases, and impacts'.[6] Issues of cultural authority and power are normally inextricably bound up with the conflict between different taste formations. [. . .]

Such conflicts over the definition of a genre occur among both its consumers and its detractors. There are at least three levels at which struggles over the cultural authority inherent in distinctions between genres take place among audiences. One cultural position identifies genre with popular film, and aligns itself with an art cinema which is either seen as 'free' from genre or else as subverting the genres of 'mainstream commercial cinema'. A second position does not reject genre *per se*, but instead constructs hierarchies of genre, by which *film noir*, for example, is likely to be seen as a more 'legitimate' genre than horror, or the western as more important than 'feminine' genres such as the romantic comedy. Even consumers of genres with low-cultural status will often find themselves in competition with one another. As Bourdieu has contended: 'Explicit aesthetic choices are in fact often constituted in opposition to the choices of the groups closest in social space, with whom competition is most direct and immediate'.[7] It is perhaps not surprising that those who seek to distance themselves from the consumers of a particular genre may have a very different sense of the genre from those who were either its untroubled, casual viewers or its enthusiastic fans. There can, however, be violent disagreements among the consumers of a specific genre over their respective constructions of the field, and this constitutes the third level at which struggles over genre definitions take place.

It is common for some horror fans to make a bid for greater legitimacy by distancing themselves from the denigrated image of the gory horror movie and its fans, and to privilege films, such as *The Innocents* (1961) and *The Haunting* (1963), that are said to work through 'atmosphere' and 'suggestion'.[8] In contrast, other horror fans, as represented by such publications as *Fangoria* and *Gorezone*, specifically privilege films of gory 'excess', and present the emphasis on 'atmosphere' and 'suggestion' as a 'cop out'; an essentially feminised preference for the predictable, safe and untroubling.

In these debates, notions of authenticity often become central, with each group defining themselves as superior to other fans who are constructed as a mindless, conformist horde associated either with mass, middlebrow culture or with a lowbrow, illegitimate form. By the same process, each group distinguishes between the 'real' and 'authentic' examples of a genre and its 'inauthentic' appropriation. On occasions, this distinction becomes a matter of exclusion from the category. Within horror fandom, there are major disagreements over the status of films such as *Alien* and *Aliens*. For some horror fans, these films are included within the horror canon as works of immense importance, while others exclude them altogether, dismissing them as representing all the impoverishments of the science fiction film. Other groups distinguish vampire literature and films as separate from the general category of horror.[9]

Genres cannot, therefore, simply be defined by the expectations of 'the audience', because the audience is not a coherent body with a consistent set of expectations. Different sections of the audience can have violently opposed expectations. Not only can the generic status of an individual film change over time, it can also be the object of intense struggles at a particular moment. A film which, for some, may seem obviously to belong to one genre may, for others, clearly belong to another genre altogether.

A case in point is Jonathan Demme's *The Silence of the Lambs*, which critics such as Jonathan Lake Crane and Carol Clover identify unequivocally as a horror film.[10] For years, I have done so quite happily as well, but I have gradually come to realise that most of my present-day students find this classification bemusing. While I remember *The Silence of the Lambs* as the first horror film to sweep the major awards at the Oscars, for most of my students the film's status as an Oscar winner defines it as a 'quality drama' – a grouping frequently preferred by people who claim not to like 'genre films'. While this seemed puzzling to me at first, research on the film's promotion established that, even on its initial release, the distributors of *The Silence of the Lambs* had tried to negotiate a special status for the film as distinct from the 'ordinary horror film', capable of appealing to those who identified themselves as far removed from 'the horror fan'. The final part of this essay examines this strategy by analysing the cover story of the March 1991 US edition of *Premiere* magazine, 'A Kind of Redemption' by Fred Schubers.[11]

Before examining this article, however, it is necessary to engage with some of the insights provided by historical reception studies, an approach to the study of film that has placed particular emphasis on the study of subsidiary publications such as reviews, interviews and feature articles. Theoretical accounts of historical reception studies acknowledge that there is no 'immanent meaning in a text' and that 'receptions need to be related to specific historical conditions as *events*'.[12] Janet Staiger, whose book, *Interpreting Films*, provides the most sustained conceptual elaboration of historical reception studies, is critical of types of film studies which assume that meaning is an inherent quality existing in the forms of the text. Staiger insists that meaning is produced by audiences on the basis of the knowledge and discourses they bring to the film, and that each interpretation is therefore an event, an act of meaning production. Reception studies must, therefore, reinsert the film into the system of social relations that sustains it, and analyse not only the material conditions of its production, but also what Bourdieu terms 'the symbolic production of the work, i.e. the production of the value of the work or, which amounts to the same thing, of belief in the value of the work' – a symbolic production undertaken by, among others, the agencies of publicity, criticism and the academy.[13]

According to Barbara Klinger, however, historical reception studies has exhibited a tendency

> to concentrate on single practices within the original moments of reception. Thus, much of this research . . . has not systematically explored the fuller range of effects that historical context might have on cinematic identity. Films clearly circulate beyond their encounter with any one institutional or social sphere. How can we conceive of the relationship between history and cinema to address this more extensive sense of circulation, to examine the issue of meaning in a *comprehensive*, that is, transhistorical, transcontextual manner?[14]

Klinger also emphasises the need to look not only at how the meanings of a film change over time, but also at the different meanings which a film can have within a specific time-period. Her work expands the horizons of historical reception studies, which has on occasion done little more than practise a historical version of reader-response theory, in which the task of the critic is to unearth the 'appropriate' competences necessary for the interpretation of films. While historical reception studies has been principally concerned to discover how audiences are 'expected' to fill in gaps within texts and what knowledge they are 'required' to bring with them to the interpretation of films, it has shown relatively little interest in the ways in which issues of taste produce not only different readings of a text within a given historical period, but conflicts between the proponents of these different readings.

Klinger's work suggests that it is also necessary to strive for a more complex and nuanced understanding of historical receptions, and the competing discourses which make them possible. In practice, historical reception studies have relied on the analysis of published materials such as reviews, on the grounds that other evidence is often unavailable, while acknowledging that the public status of these artefacts makes them suspect. In her article on *The Silence of the Lambs*, for example, Staiger refers to reviews as *traces* of the event, as ways of reconstructing reception events, while also using them to identify the discourses that *produce* these events. Other critics have seen reviews as providing very different kinds of evidence: Robert C. Allen and Douglas Gomery for example, point to the agenda-setting function of reviews that may not tell 'audiences what to think so much as . . . what to think *about*'.[15] As part of the process of contextualisation by which interpretations are framed and incorporated in struggles between different taste formations, reviews cannot be read as giving automatic or unproblematic access to the ways in which audiences interpret films. Any review, or any other act of criticism, is in itself 'an affirmation of its own legitimacy', a claim by the reviewer of his or her entitlement to participate in the process by which cultural value is defined and distinguished, and thus to take part not only in a legitimate discourse about the film, but also in the production of its cultural value.[16] Reviews cannot, then, simply be taken as *traces* of readings, nor as providing a straightforward access to the discourses that produce interpretations; rather, they give a sense of the very different ways in which people are supposed to 'talk' about films. The importance of distinguishing between the activity of consuming films and the activity of talking about them is clearly demonstrated in Ien Ang's work on *Dallas*. She found that many of those who wrote to her were fully aware of the ways in which their consumption of the show could be judged by others, and constantly positioned what they said about the show in relation to a public discourse on the distinction between legitimate and illegitimate taste, and to what Ang calls 'the ideology of mass culture'.[17]

Articles and reviews can most usefully be understood as one of the ways in which people learn to position themselves within hierarchies of taste. As Klinger contends, reviews

> signify cultural hierarchies of aesthetic value reigning at particular times. As a primary public tastemaker, the critic operates to make, in Pierre Bourdieu's parlance, 'distinctions'. Among other things, the critic distinguishes legitimate from illegitimate art and proper from improper modes of aesthetic appropriation.[18]

Although Klinger is principally discussing the construction of hierarchies of legitimate taste, a similar argument can be made about the role of popular publications in constructing cultural hierarchies and proper modes of aesthetic appropriation in matters of popular taste. In both cases, reviews and feature articles set agendas for audiences by drawing attention to what is taken to be interesting or noteworthy about a film. They also reflect the differing attitudes of different sections of the media to varying taste formations. In the process, they focus their attention on different features and employ wildly different notions of cinematic value.

In her analysis of the reviews of Douglas Sirk's films during the 1950s, Klinger identifies three different and opposed taste formations in operation. The first, which she identifies as 'the liberal sources', routinely ignored mainstream Hollywood products in favour of an avant-garde aesthetic. The second shared tastes similar to those addressed by Universal's sales campaigns for Sirk's movies, while the third was associated with a broadly realist aesthetic related to the upper end of the middlebrow and the lower end of legitimate culture:

> Appearing mainly in East Coast and otherwise urban periodicals and newspapers, these reviews offered negative evaluations of Sirk's melodramas, in part influenced by a dominant canon of the time that endorsed realism in dramas. This general critical context supervised value judgements for drama, including the adult melodrama, that genre to which Sirk's films belonged at the time.[19]

As Klinger demonstrates, reviews are products of specific taste formations, and also function specifically as gate-keepers or guardians of specific taste formations, mediating between texts and audiences and specifying particular ways of appropriating or consuming texts. As such, they are part of a complex process involving a series of media which we must recognise as neither monolithic nor monological. As both Klinger and Charlotte Brunsdon have shown, the different taste formations which underpin different publications will lead those publications to discuss films, and to address their own readers, in very different ways.[20] There are deep struggles not only *between* many of the media but also *within* specific media. Newspaper and magazine reviewing, for example, embraces very different taste formations with very different agendas: one would hardly expect *Fangoria* or *Gorezone* to share the same terms of reference as, say, *The New Republic* or *Sight and Sound*; indeed, *Fangoria* and *Gorezone* share different taste formations from one another. Examining a range of publications addressing a variety of readerships will reveal very different interests and preoccupations in any given film, and even clarify the contexts within which these publications are themselves meaningful as texts.

Staiger's discussion of *The Silence of the Lambs* clearly demonstrates an interest in discursive struggles over meaning, but her analysis concentrates on reviews of the film in publications addressing a middle-class, educated intelligentsia: the *Village Voice*, *Los Angeles Times*, *Wall Street Journal*, *New Republic*, *New Yorker*, *Rolling Stone*, *Vanguard* and *The Nation*. Within this audience, which corresponds to the first of Klinger's three taste formations, debates about the meaning of *The Silence of the Lambs* had, by the film's fifth week of the release

> solidified into a set of propositions: 1) that whether or not Jonathan Demme had intended to create a homophobic film, the character of the serial murderer had attributes associated with stereotypes of gay men; 2) that in a time of paranoia over AIDS and increased violence directed towards gays in the United States, even suggesting connections between homosexuals and a serial murderer was irresponsible; but 3) that

> the character of Clarice Starling played by Jodie Foster was a positive image of a woman working in a patriarchal society and, thus, empowering for women viewers.[21]

The struggle that Staiger analyses is, however, also bound up with a debate over the film's cultural and generic status, a debate that was given particular inflection in the different media outlets addressing different taste formations. Attempts to emphasise the status of Starling as a 'positive image' often relied on distinguishing the film from the generic category of 'the slasher movie', while attacks on the film's supposed homophobia usually sought to associate the film with the horror genre in a manner that both drew upon and reproduced assumptions about the genre's status as an example of popular cinema. In contrast to many other critics, Carol Clover does not present *The Silence of the Lambs* as either a radical reversal of the sexual politics of the slasher movie, or as proof of the horror film's inherently reactionary nature. For her:

> When I see an Oscar-winning film like *The Accused* or the artful *Alien* and its blockbuster sequel *Aliens* or, more recently *Sleeping with the Enemy* and *The Silence of the Lambs*, and even *Thelma and Louise*, I cannot help thinking of all the low-budget, often harsh and awkward but sometimes deeply energetic films that preceded them by a decade or more – films that said it all, and in flatter terms, and on a shoestring. If mainstream film detains us with niceties of plot, character, motivation, cinematography, pacing, acting, and the like, low or exploitation horror operates at the bottom line, and in so doing reminds us that every movie has a bottom line, no matter how covert or mystified or sublimated it may be.[22]

It is therefore important to address the ways in which debates over the film's gender politics were bound up with issues of class taste and its legitimating functions, and it is this association which will be the focus of my analysis of Fred Schubers's article in *Premiere*.

When *The Silence of the Lambs* was released in the United States (on St Valentine's Day, 1991) sections of the press scrupulously avoided any direct association of the film with the horror genre. Many reviews established the film's association with horror, but then deflected or neutralised it. In place of generic classifications, reviewers deployed ambivalent adjectives: 'terrifying', 'brutally real', 'chilling', 'macabre', 'dark', and as having 'an atmosphere of Gothic gloom'.[23] Apart from this reference to the Gothic, the only generic identification I have been able to find in reviews and commentary published in mainstream, middle-class or quality publications describes the film as a 'suspenseful drama'.[24]

The Silence of the Lambs was nevertheless associated with the horror genre in reviews which emphasised the 'ordeal' involved in watching the film in a manner that drew directly upon the traditional 'dare' of horror movie promotion. *Playboy*, for example, declared that: 'If you can handle it, *The Silence of the Lambs* is a paralysing suspense drama, the kind of movie to watch by peeking through your fingers . . . Audiences are likely to sit tight . . . and gasp with relief when it's over'.[25] *Premiere*'s short review observed: 'If it's a choice between this and chocolates for Valentine's Day, the bonbons might be a better bet, but then again, *The Silence of the Lambs* promises to be so terrifying, you're bound to end up in your sweetheart's arms'.[26]

The main strategy of many of the reviews is simultaneously to present the film as offering the pleasures associated with the horror movie – that it will be gripping, terrifying, shocking, etc. – while also legitimating the film through its distinction from the genre. This sense of distinction is constructed in two main ways: first, through claims about the film's aesthetic 'quality', and, second, through claims about its politics, which are generally defined in terms of feminism.

The first of these strategies can be seen in the article by Fred Schubers, published in *Premiere* in 1991, which tries to negotiate a position for the film by emphasising both the horrific nature of its material and the auteur status of its director, Jonathan Demme:

> The zesty auteur of such recent light operas as *Something Wild* (which did have corrosive later stages) and *Married to the Mob* did not seem temperamentally ideal for novelist Thomas Harris's brutally real, often macabre version of a pair of serial killers who, respectively, skin and consume their victims.[27]

The role of promotional materials in framing the film for reviewers before reviewers frame films for audiences is indicated by the striking similarity between this passage and one which appears in the *Playboy* review, which observes: 'Director Jonathan Demme, more often associated with lightweight fare (*Something Wild* and *Married to the Mob*), brings touches of dark humour as well as cinematic style to this adaptation . . . of Thomas Harris's novel'.[28] Both passages emphasise Demme's status as an auteur director who is to be taken seriously (so countering one problem) while also stressing that he is known for making light, likeable films (so countering another). On the other hand, they ignore Demme's background in 'exploitation' movies, such as the women-in-prison drama, *Caged Heat*, which he made for Roger Corman.

The Schubers article in *Premiere* also continued this project by presenting Demme's motivations for making *The Silence of the Lambs* as simultaneously aesthetic and political: 'If somebody had asked me if I would be interested in doing a movie about a young woman who goes after a man who mutilates and murders young women, I would have said absolutely not. But the people at Orion said, "We've got this script we're really excited about – just read it"'.[29] Without any attempt at a transition, the article continues: 'Given the choice, says Demme, "I'd much rather see a strong story with a lead character as a women than the lead as a man. Because the odds are stacked higher against the woman"'.[30] This again emphasises the 'horrific' nature of the materials while maintaining a sense that Demme was attracted to the quality of the script – its 'strong story' – and the presence of a female rather than a male lead, which is at the core of the film's supposedly feminist politics. While many discussions of the film suggested that the presence of a heroic female lead distinguished it from other horror movies, the slasher movie is usually characterised by the presence of a strong female hero, the figure whom Carol Clover identifies as the 'final girl'.[31] In plot terms, the presence of Clarice Starling as the heroic protagonist associates the film with the slasher genre, rather than distancing it.

Other distinctions between *The Silence of the Lambs* and the horror genre were constructed by invoking Demme's auteur status and emphasising his discreet handling of the film's violence. The *Time Out Film Guide* observed: 'Although Demme does reveal the results of the killer's violence, he for the most part refrains from showing the acts themselves; the film could never be accused of pandering to voyeuristic impulses' – reference to the supposedly voyeuristic nature of the horror film in general, and the slasher movie in particular.[32] Once again, the message was clear: the film could offer the thrills of a horror movie without middle-class audiences either having to feel guilty or questioning their sense of their own distinction from that monstrous other, the troubling and disturbing figure of the slasher movie viewer.

The most overt and sustained way in which these distinctions were constructed, however, was through the star image of Jodie Foster. A particular construction of Foster's star image was used to legitimate the film as a whole and the character of Clarice Starling in particular. By presenting Foster in particular ways, Schubers' article endorses certain readings of Clarice as a character. This process also works reciprocally. Foster is presented as actively investing the character with meaning (strength) and in the process, her own star image and her credentials as an actor are re-established and given an explicitly political dimension. At one point, Schubers informs us that Demme had originally considered Michelle Pfeiffer for the part of Clarice, but that he had soon changed his mind because 'feminist fellow-traveller Demme understood that [Foster's] commitment would give Starling the backbone the part requires'.[33]

This notion of backbone, articulated through an emphasis on professional and political commitment, is central to the image of Foster constructed by the article. Her status as a serious actor is established through an account of her dedication to realism: 'In the service of authenticity, Foster spent several days simulating the life of a trainee at the FBI in Quantico'.[34] Quite what 'several days' actually amounted to, and quite how 'authentic' it might have made Foster's performance, is not elaborated. Rather, the reader is supposed to relate this information to a concept of acting established through Method performance, demonstrated predominantly by male stars such as Robert De Niro and Dustin Hoffman, who seek to distinguish themselves from the supposed 'inauthenticity' of popular culture – an inauthenticity which is usually associated with feminisation – and to associate themselves with a masculine, legitimate culture.[35] In Foster's case, these notions of commitment and the suggestions of the work involved in constructing the star's performance are given a political dimension through the claim that the performance is itself an act of *political* labour. Some of the film's promotional material structures her performance as part of a broader struggle underpinning Foster's entire career, which arises from her personal and political commitment to feminism. As the *Premiere* contents page states, in *The Silence of the Lambs* Foster 'once again confronts the victimisation of women'.[36] This involves a rereading of Foster's previous films, in order to present them as being *a commentary upon* victimisation, rather than simply (as could be argued) *an instance of* victimisation.

The suggestion that Starling is not just a victim but a heroic female character is used to establish the film's distinction from the popular. Schubers' article quotes Foster: 'What's great about this character is that her lot in life, as the hero, is to save the underdog, because she's lucky enough not to be the underdog anymore. I feel like there's never been a female hero who uses femininity as a warrior thing, and not like Rambo – Rambette – in underwear. This is not some male version of a female hero'.[37] In saying this, Foster was trying to distinguish the film from a range of female action heroes, of whom the most famous is Ripley in the *Alien* films. Indeed, after the release of *Alien* there were several references which associated Ripley with Rambo, most obviously in the word 'Fembo'.[38] As a result, Foster as an actor was perhaps legitimated through an association with masculinity and realism, as opposed to the popular, the fantastic and the generic.

The title of Schubers' article – 'A Kind of Redemption' – emphasises the idea of Foster's performance as an act of feminist struggle. It derives from Foster's comment that

> I realise that I play certain characters to redeem them. I think in some ways what my makeup is, and my lot in life, is that I've used fiction to save women who otherwise would have been spat upon or passed off, not paid attention to. To reverse a certain negative

> history. That's why I've always played those people, to make them human. It has reverberations in my life, how I feel about my family and how I feel about the literature I studied and the things that I do.[33]

Schubers draws attention to Foster's education: her 'Yale major was literature (with a concentration on African-American works), Toni Morrison her thesis subject'.[40] Suggesting that Foster 'seems to see her work in *Silence* as the actor's equivalent of a slim, pithy novel', the article constructs another link between the film and legitimate culture.[41] [. . .]

Foster's comments also refer to her own life and particularly the way in which 'I feel about my family'. Schubers stresses that Foster's family lacked a father and revolved around a strong maternal figure, while Foster herself supported the family financially throughout her childhood. This discussion of her family background presents Foster as the strong daughter: the brilliant young actress whose talent, intelligence and hard work rendered a male bread-winner unnecessary, combining ideas of female strength and independence with the image of Foster as a serious artist. For example, the supposedly semi-autobiographical features of her directorial debut, *Little Man Tate*, serve to establish her not only as a serious actress, but also as an auteur director through the supposedly personal nature of the material as well as through the 'sensitivity' of its handling.

Schubers's article presents the film as having all the pleasures of a horror film without threatening the self-image of those audience members who distinguish themselves from 'the horror fan'. Most significantly, it seeks to detach the film from the horror genre's associations with voyeurism, misogyny and formulaic simplicity. At the time of the film's initial release, the quality press, much of the promotional material, and even the film's own mise-en-scène all sought to evoke an association with the terms 'Gothic' and 'terror', rather than horror.[42] These terms engage a familiar set of distinctions by which 'the Gothic novel' and 'the tale of terror' are not constructed as the other to legitimate culture (as they have been in other contexts) but rather are associated with legitimate culture through a series of distinctions in which 'horror' is constructed as their own other.

The mediation of *The Silence of the Lambs* illustrates the ways in which genre distinctions operate not to designate or describe a fixed class of texts, but as terms that are constantly and inevitably in a process of contestation. Imbricated in that contest are questions of cultural value, privilege and the authority to determine cultural legitimacy through the act of genre definition. Rather than horror having a single meaning, different social groups construct it in different, competing ways as they seek to identify with or distance themselves from the term, and associate different texts with these constructions of horror. [. . .] From such a critical perspective, the reductive project of trying to define whether *The Silence of the Lambs* is a horror film or something else is replaced by the much more interesting tasks of interrogating how such a definition is constructed and contested, and examining what forms of cultural authority are at stake in the process of generic definition.

Notes

1 James Naremore, 'American *Film Noir*: The History of an Idea', *Film Quarterly*, vol. 49. no. 2 (winter 1995–6), p. 14. Naremore enlarges on his discussion in Chapter 1 of his book, *More than Night: Film Noir in Its Contexts* (Berkeley, CA: University of California Press, 1998), pp. 9–39.

2 Ibid.
3 Ibid.
4 Ibid., p. 14.
5 See, for example, Andrew Tudor, 'Genre', in Barry K. Grant (ed.), *The Film Genre Reader* (Austin: University of Texas Press, 1986), pp. 3–10; and Andrew Tudor, *Monsters and Mad Scientists: A Cultural History of the Horror Movie* (Oxford: Blackwells, 1989).
6 Ien Ang, 'Wanted: Audiences. On the Politics of Empirical Audience Studies in Ellen Seiter *et al.* (eds), *Remote Control: Television Audiences and Cultural Power* (London: Routledge, 1989), p. 107.
7 Pierre Bourdieu, *Distinction: A Social Critique of the Judgement of Taste*, trans. Richard Nice (Cambridge, MA: Harvard University Press, 1984), p. 60.
8 For a corroboration of this view, see Brigid Cherry, 'Refusing to Refuse to Look: Female Viewers of the Horror Film', in Melvyn Stokes and Richard Maltby (eds), *Identifying Hollywood's Audiences: Cultural Identity and the Movies* (London: BFI, 1999), pp. 190–205.
9 Ibid.
10 Jonathan Lake Crane, *Terror and Everyday Life: Singular Moments in the History of the Horror Film* (Thousand Oaks, CA: Sage, 1994); and Carol Clover, *Men, Women and Chain Saws: Gender in the Modern Horror Film* (London: BFI, 1992).
11 Fred Schubers, 'A Kind of Redemption', *Premiere*, US edition (March 1991), p. 52.
12 Janet Staiger, 'Taboo and Totem: Cultural Meanings of *The Silence of the Lambs*', in Jim Collins *et al.*, (eds), *Film Theory Goes to the Movies* (New York: Routledge, 1993), p. 143.
13 Pierre Bourdieu, 'The Field of Cultural Production, or: The Economic World Reversed', in Pierre Bourdieu, *The Field of Cultural Production: Essays on Art and Literature*, ed. Randal Johnson (Oxford: Polity Press, 1993), p. 37.
14 Barbara Klinger, *Melodrama and Meaning: History, Culture and the Films of Douglas Sirk* (Bloomington: Indiana University Press, 1994), p. xvii.
15 Robert C. Allen and Douglas Gomery, *Film History: Theory and Practice* (New York: Knopf, 1985), p. 90.
16 Bourdieu, 'The Field of Cultural Production', pp. 35–6.
17 See Ien Ang, *Watching 'Dallas': Soap Opera and the Melodramatic Imagination* (London: Methuen, 1985).
18 Klinger, *Melodrama and Meaning*, p. 70.
19 Ibid., p. 71.
20 Charlotte Brunsdon, *Screen Tastes: Soap Opera to Satellite Dishes* (London: Routledge, 1997).
21 Staiger, 'Taboo and Totem', p. 142.
22 Clover, *Men, Women and Chain Saws*, p. 20.
23 'Review', *Premiere* (February 1991), p. 12; Schubers, 'A Kind of Redemption', p. 52; 'Review', *Playboy* (April 1991), p.24; 'Review', *Radio Times* (12–18 October 1996).
24 'Review', *Playboy* (April 1991), p. 24.
25 Ibid.
26 'Review', *Premiere*, February 1991, p. 12. Compare this to the review of Dr X by James E. Mitchell in the *Los Angeles Examiner* in 1932: 'Take the girl friend and by the middle of the first reel she'll have both arms around your neck and holding on for dear life'. Cited in Rhona J. Berenstein, *Attack of the Leading Ladies: Gender, Sexuality, and Spectatorship in Classic Horror Cinema* (New York: Columbia University Press, 1996), p. 60.
27 Schubers, 'A Kind of Redemption', p. 52.

28 'Review', *Playboy* (April 1991), p. 24.
29 Schubers, 'A Kind of Redemption', p. 52.
30 Ibid.
31 Amy Taubin, 'Killing Men', *Sight and Sound*, vol. 1: issue 1 (1991), pp. 14–18; Clover, *Men, Women and Chain Saws*, esp. pp. 35–42.
32 *Time Out Film Guide* (Harmondsworth: Penguin, 1989), p. 666.
33 Schubers, 'A Kind of Redemption', p. 53.
34 Ibid.
35 Richard Dyer, *Stars* (London: BFI, 1979) and *Heavenly Bodies* (London: BFI, 1987).
36 'Contents', *Premiere* (March 1991), p. 7.
37 Schubers, 'A Kind of Redemption', p. 52.
38 Harvey R. Greenberg, 'Fembo: *Aliens* Intention', *Journal of Popular Film and Television*, vol. 15, no. 4, (winter 1988), pp. 165–71.
39 Ibid., p. 53.
40 Ibid.
41 Ibid.
42 Compare, for example, the 'Gothic' dungeon in which Clarice encounters Lecter in Demme's film with Michael Mann's presentation of the modernist/postmodernist asylum in which Will Graham confronts Lecktor [sic] in *Manhunter*, a film based on *Red Dragon*, the Thomas Harris novel which immediately precedes *The Silence of the Lambs*.

Learning to scream

13

LINDA WILLIAMS

Talk to psychoanalytic critics about *Psycho* and they will tell you how perfectly the film illustrates the perverse pleasures of cinema. Talk to horror aficionados about *Psycho* and they will tell you the film represents the moment when horror moved from what is outside and far away to what is inside us all and very close to home.

But talk to anyone old enough to have seen *Psycho* on its release in a movie theatre and they will tell you what it felt like to be scared out of their wits. I vividly remember a Saturday matinee in 1960 when two girlfriends and I spent much of the screening with our eyes shut listening to the music and to the audience's screams as we tried to guess when we might venture to look again at a screen whose terrors were unaccountably thrilling.

Most people who saw *Psycho* for the first time in a theatre have similarly vivid memories. Many will recall the shock of the shower murder and how they were afraid to take showers for months or years afterwards. But if it is particularly remembered that *Psycho* altered the bathing habits of a nation, it is less well recalled how it fundamentally changed viewing habits.

When the purposeful, voyeuristic camera eye investigating Marion Crane's love affair and theft of $40,000 "washed" down the drain in a vertiginous spiral after the shower murder, audiences took pleasure in losing the kind of control they had been trained to enjoy in classical narrative cinema. With *Psycho*, cinema in some ways reverted to what the critic Tom Gunning has described as the "attractions" of pre-classical cinema – an experience that has more of the effect of a rollercoaster ride than the absorption of a classical narrative.

Anyone who has gone to the movies in the last 20 years cannot help but notice how entrenched this rollercoaster sensibility of repeated tension and release, assault and escape has become. While narrative is not abandoned, it often takes second place to a succession of visual and auditory shocks and thrills which are, as Thomas Schatz puts it in 'The New Hollywood' "'visceral, kinetic, and fast paced, increasingly reliant on special effects, increasingly 'fantastic' . . . and increasingly targeted at younger audiences". Schatz cites *Jaws* (1975) as the precursor of the New Hollywood calculated blockbuster, but the film that set the stage for the "visceral, kinetic" appeal of post-classical cinema was *Psycho*.

From the very first screenings, audience reaction, in the form of gasps, screams, yells, even running up and down the aisles, was unprecedented. Although Hitchcock later claimed to have calculated all this, saying he could hear the screams when planning the shower montage, screenwriter Joseph Stefano counters, "he was lying . . . We had no idea. We thought people would gasp or be silent, but screaming? Never." Contemporary reviews were in no doubt that audiences were screaming as never before: "So well is the picture made . . . that it can lead audiences to do something they hardly ever do any more – cry out to the characters, in hopes of dissuading them from going to the doom that has been cleverly established as awaiting them" (Ernest Callenbach, *Film Quarterly*, Fall 1960).

But having unleashed such reactions, the problem Hitchcock and every theatre manager now faced was how to keep them from getting out of hand. According to Anthony Perkins, the entire scene in the hardware store following the shower murder, the mopping up and disposal of Marion's body in the swamp was usually inaudible thanks to leftover howls from the previous scene. According to Stephen Rebello in *The Making of Psycho*, Hitchcock even asked Paramount to allow him to remix the sound to allow for the audience's reaction. Permission was denied.

Hitchcock's unprecedented "special policy" of allowing no one into the theatre once the film had begun was one means both of encouraging, and handling, the mayhem. It also ensured that audiences would fully appreciate the shock of having the rug pulled out from under them so thoroughly in the surprise murder of the main character in the shower. Most importantly, however, it transformed the previously casual act of going to the movies into a much more disciplined activity of arriving on time and waiting in an orderly line.

Hitchcock's insistence that no one be admitted late to the film supposedly came to him during the editing: "I suddenly startled my fellow-workers with a noisy vow that my frontwards-sidewards-and-inside-out labors on *Psycho* would not be in vain – that everyone else in the world would have to enjoy the fruits of my labor to the full by seeing the picture from beginning to end. This was the way the picture was conceived – and this was how it had to be seen" (*Motion Picture Herald*, 6 August 1960). In a narrow sense, this simply meant that having worked so hard to set up the surprise of the shower murder, Hitchcock wanted to make sure that it was fully appreciated. In the larger sense, however, his demand that the audience arrive on time would eventually lead to the set show times, closely spaced screenings, elimination of cartoons and short subjects and patient waits in lines that are now standard procedure.

Critics obliged Hitchcock by promoting the new policy: "At any other entertainment from ice show to baseball games, the bulk of the patrons arrive before the performance begins. Not so at the movies which have followed the policy of grabbing customers in any time they arrive, no matter how it may impair the story for those who come in midway" (*View*). Columnist Stan Delaplane describes in detail the experience of going to see *Psycho* and captures something of the psychological undertones of the new film-viewing discipline.

"There was a long line of people at the show – they will only seat you at the beginning and I don't think they let you out while it's going on . . . A loudspeaker was carrying a sound track made by Mr. Hitchcock.

"He said it was absolutely necessary – he gave it the British pronunciation like 'nessary'. He said you absolutely could not go in at the beginning.

"The loudspeaker then let out a couple of female shrieks that would turn your blood to ice. And the ticket taker began letting us all in.

"A few months ago, I was reading the London review of this picture. The British critics rapped it. 'Contrived.' they said. 'Not up to the Hitchcock standards.'

"I do not know what standards they were talking about. But I must say that Hitchcock . . . did not seem to be that kind of person at all. Hitchcock turned us all on.

"Of all the shrieking and screaming! We were all limp. And, after drying my palms on the mink coat next to me, we went out to have hamburgers. And let the next line of people go in and die.

"Well, if you are reading the trade papers, you must know that *Psycho* is making a mint of money.

"This means we are in for a whole series of such pictures." (*Los Angeles Examiner*, 9 December 1960).

Obviously the audience described by Delaplane was docile. Their fun was dependent upon this docility. Yet we can see an element of playful performance at work in this evocation of the exhilaration of a group submitting itself to a thrilling sensation of fear and release. In this highly ritualised masochistic submission to a familiar "master", we see shrieking and screaming understood frankly as a "turn on", followed by a highly sexualised climax ("go in and die"), a limp feeling, and then a renewal of (literal and metaphorical) appetite. This audience, despite its mix of class (mink and hamburgers) and gender, has acquired a new sense of itself as bonded around certain terrifying sexual secrets. The shock of learning these secrets produces both a discipline and, around that discipline, a camaraderie, a pleasure of the group that was both new to motion pictures and destabilising to the conventional gender roles of audiences.

Another important tool in disciplining the *Psycho* audience were the promotional trailers. All three hinted at, but unlike most "coming attractions" refrained from showing too much of, the film's secrets. In the most famous of these, Hitchcock acts as a house-of-horrors tour guide at the Universal International Studios set of the Bates Motel and adjacent house (now the Universal Studios Theme Park featuring the *Psycho* house and motel). Each trailer stresses the importance of special discipline: either "please don't tell the ending, it's the only one we have", or the need to arrive on time.

But there was another trailer, not seen by the general public yet even more crucial in inculcating discipline into the audience. Called "The Care and Handling of *Psycho*", this was not a preview but a filmed "press book" teaching theatre managers how to exhibit the film and police the audience.

The black and white film begins with the pounding violins of Bernard Herrmann's score over a street scene outside the DeMille Theater in New York, where *Psycho* was first released. A long line waits on the sidewalk for a matinee. An urgent-sounding narrator explains that the man in the tuxedo is a theatre manager in charge of implementing the policy for exhibiting the film – a policy which has placed him out on the sidewalk directing traffic for the "blockbuster". The film then explains the key elements of the procedure, beginning with the broadcasting, in Hitchcock's own sly, disembodied voice, of the message that "this queuing up is good for you, it will make you appreciate the seats inside. It will also make you appreciate *Psycho*." The mixture of polite inducement, backed up by the presence of Pinkerton guards and a life-size lobby cardboard cut-out of Hitchcock sternly pointing to his watch, seem comical today because we have so thoroughly assimilated the lessons of punctuality and secret-keeping.

Part of the fun of the film is Hitchcock's playfully sadistic pose mixed with an over-solicitous concern for the audience's pleasure. He asks the waiting crowd to keep the "tiny, little horrifying secrets" of the story because he has only their best interests in mind. (According to Rebello, the strategy succeeded – when shaken spectators leaving the theatre were grilled by those waiting in line, they answered only that the film had to be seen.) He then insists on the democracy of a policy that will not make exceptions for the Queen of England or the manager's brother.

Punctuated by short glimpses of a screaming woman (who isn't Janet Leigh – could it be her double?) and Herrmann's unsettling score, this training film is a fascinating record of the process by which film-going became both a more gut-wrenching experience and a more disciplined act. Exploiting his popular television persona of the man who loves to scare you, Hitchcock also went one better than television by providing the kind of big-jolt ride the small screen could not convey. And he obtained the kind of rapt attention that would have been the envy of a symphony orchestra from an audience more associated with the distractions of amusement parks than with the disciplines of high culture.

In *Highbrow/Lowbrow*, Lawrence Levine has written compellingly about the taming of American audiences during the latter part of the nineteenth century. Levine argues that while American theatre audiences in the first half of the century were a highly participatory and unruly lot, arriving late, leaving early, spitting tobacco, talking back to the actors, stamping feet and applauding promiscuously, they were gradually taught by the arbiters of culture to "submit to creators and become mere instruments of their will, mere auditors of the productions of the artist". Certainly Hitchcock asserts "the will of the artist" to "tame his audience, but this will is in the service of producing visceral thrills and ear-splitting screams rather than the passivity and silence Levine describes. Hitchcock's disciplining of the audience is a more subtle exercise of power, productive rather than repressive, in Michel Foucault's sense of the term, merging knowledge and power in the production of pleasure.

In the discipline imposed by Hitchcock, the efficiency and control demonstrated outside the theatre need to be viewed in tandem with the patterns of fear and release unleashed inside. And this discipline, not unlike that demanded by the emerging theme parks, was not based on the division of audiences into high and low, nor, as would later occur through the ratings system, was it based on the stratification of different age groups. In Hitchcock's assumption of the persona of the sadist who expects his submissive audience to trust him to provide a devious form of pleasure, we see a new bargain struck between artist and audience: if you want me to make you scream in a new way and about these previously taboo sexual secrets, then line up patiently to receive the thrill.

While the training film offers us a look at the audience for *Psycho* outside the theatre, photographs taken with infra-red cameras during screenings at the Plaza Theatre in London and issued in an oversized press kit by Paramount, the film's distributor, provide an insight into what went on inside. The intense-looking audience, jaws set, stares hard at the screen, with the exception of a few people with averted eyes. The somewhat defensive postures indicate anticipation – arms are crossed, while several people hold their ears, suggesting the importance of sound in cueing terror.

On the whole the men are looking intently, some with hands up towards their face or chin. One man is dramatically clutching his tie while holding it out from his body; another bites his fingers while the young man next to him both smokes a cigarette and grabs his cheek. It is women in these pictures who look down, including the woman whose hand covers her mouth sitting next to the cool male smoker.

How are we to interpret these images of an audience showing its fear? Is it possible that a discipline, albeit of a different kind, operated inside as well as outside the theatre? Of course we have no way of knowing at what point in the movie these shots were taken. But do we know that the film's scariest moments occur before and during the appearances of "Mrs Bates" and that these appearances result in the highly feminised terror first of Marion, then of subsequent victims.

The terrified female victim is a cliché of horror cinema: both the display of sexual arousal and the display of fear are coded as quintessentially feminine. As Carol J. Clover puts it in *Men, Women and Chain Saws*, "abject fear" is "gendered feminine". The image of a highly sexualised and terrified woman is thus the most conventionally gendered of the film.

Much less conventional is the ostensible of this terror: "Mrs Bates". Apparently gendered feminine, yet equipped with a phallic knife, "Mrs Bates" represented a new kind of movie monster. But Hitchcock's decision to turn the traditional monster of horror cinema into a son who dresses up as his own mummified mother was not so much about giving violent power to a castrating 'monstrous feminine' as about deploying the sensational pleasures of a sexually indeterminate drag.

"He's a transvestite!", says the District Attorney in a famously inadequate attempt to explain the roots of Norman's behaviour. Certainly Norman is no mere transvestite – that is, a person whose sexual pleasure involves dressing up as the opposite sex – but rather a much more deeply disturbed individual whose whole personality, according to the psychiatrist's lengthy discourse, has at times "become the mother". Yet in the scene that supposedly shows us that Norman has "become" the mother, what we in fact see is Norman, now without wig and dress, sitting alone and reflecting, in the most feminine of the many voices given "Mrs Bates", on the evil of "her" son. In other words, while ostensibly illustrating that Norman now "is" the mother, the scene provides a visual and aural variation on Norman's earlier sexual indeterminacy. The shock of this scene is the combination of young male body and older female voice: it is not the recognition of one identity overcome by another that fascinates so much as the tension between masculine and feminine. The penultimate shot of Norman's face, from which briefly emerges the grinning mouth of Mrs Bates' corpse, drives this home.

The psychiatrist's contention that Norman is entirely his mother is therefore unproven. Instead, these variations of drag become an ironic, and by this point almost camp, play with audience expectations that gender is fixed. Norman is not a transvestite, but transvestism – an incomplete assimilation to one or the other pole of the gender binary – is an attraction of these scenes.

But if gender performance is a newly important element within the film, how does it also figure for the audience in viewing *Psycho*? I would argue that a destabilisation of gender roles takes place both on screen *and* in the theatre, and that even the most classic-seeming masculine and feminine forms of behaviour take on parodic elements of performance that destabilise gender-fixed reactions.

Thus while the men in the audience look conventionally masculine, while they appear to stay cool in the face of danger and to look steadily at the screen, there is something just a little forced about their poses. In the face of the gender-confused source of terror on screen, their dogged masculinity seems staged. The more masculine they try to appear – as with the man clutching his tie – the more it is clear that a threat of femininity has been registered.

The cringing and ducking women, on the other hand, assume classic attitudes of frightened femininity. Yet here too the exaggeration suggests a pleasurable and self-conscious performance. I once interpreted this classic women's reaction as a sign of resistance: that women resisted assault on their own gaze by refusing to look at the female victims of male monstrosity. However, this notion of resistance simply assumed a masculine monster and the displeasure of horror for female spectators. Now I am more inclined to think that if some of the women in the audience were refusing to look at the screen, then they were also, like my girlfriends and I, at the early stages of assimilating a discipline that was teaching us *how* to look – emboldening us to look as the men did, in the interest of experiencing greater thrills.

We also need to recognise what these photographs cannot show us: that these disciplines of gender performance evolved over time and, though they *seem* fixed here, were actually thrown into flux by *Psycho*. Male and female spectators who either stared stoically or clutched themselves, covered eyes, ears, and recoiled in fear at the shower murder may have been responding involuntarily, and quite conventionally, the first time, to an unexpected assault. But by the film's second assault, this audience was already beginning to play the game of anticipation and to repeat its response in either gender conventional or gender transgressive – but in both cases increasingly performative – gestures.

By the time the game of slasher-assault had become a genre in the mid- and late 70s, by the time a film like *The Rocky Horror Picture Show* took on its own performative life, by the time the erotic thriller had become a newly invigorated genre in the 80s and 90s, this disciplined performing audience was to give way to the equivalent of the kids who raise their hands in rollercoaster rides and call out, "Look Ma, no hands!"

The dislocations between masculine and feminine, between normal and psychotic, between eros and fear, even between the familiar Hitchcockian suspense and a new, gender-based horror were new in *Psycho*. And it is these qualities that make it the precursor to the kinds of thrill-producing visual "attractions" that would become fundamental to the New Hollywood. After making *Psycho*, Hitchcock boasted of his power to control audience response, saying that if you "designed a picture correctly in terms of its emotional impact, the Japanese audience would scream at the same time as the Indian audience". It might seem that the photographs of the *Psycho* audience bear him out – certainly they exhibit his power to elicit response – yet there is reason to suspect a level of calculation behind his emotional engineering. We have seen that Hitchcock was in fact taken aback by the screams *Psycho* produced. Perhaps his elaborate attempts to stage the experience of the film's screenings were simply bids to regain control over an audience response which scared even him.

Special thanks to Michael Friend of the Academy Library for showing me the cinema managers' training film "The Care and Handling of Psycho". Psycho *is available on CIC Video*

Refusing to refuse to look 14

Female viewers of the horror film

BRIGID CHERRY

Most studies of the horror film that have considered questions of gender and spectatorship have concerned themselves with a theoretical male spectator, usually identifying the monster's gaze as male, and the heroine-victim as the subject of that gaze.[1] From such a critical perspective, Linda Williams describes the female spectators gaze at the monster as representing 'a surprising (and at times subversive) affinity between monster and woman' that acknowledges their 'similar status within patriarchal structures of seeing'.[2] Williams does not, however, regard this female gaze as a pleasurable one: despite their affinity, female spectators do not find pleasure in the figure of the monster, and the act of looking is punished. For Williams, this explains why the female viewer of horror films refuses to look, often physically blocking or averting her eyes from the screen.

Whether most female spectators actually behave like this is another question: in my own study of female horror film fans and followers, only 19 per cent of participants claimed frequently to avert their gaze in some way, while 67 per cent claimed they only rarely or never refuse to look. In some segments of the audience, then, there are female viewers who do take pleasure in viewing horror films and who, in what could amount to an act of defiance, refuse to refuse so look.

[. . .]

Critics such as Williams who observe displeasure in the female viewer may be underestimating the pleasures inherent in this type of film for at least some female viewers. If female viewers do not always refuse to look, what kinds of horror film do they attend and what pleasures do they derive from seeing them? What is at stake for the female fans and followers of the horror film? These questions about the consumption of the horror film cannot be answered solely by a consideration of the text–reader relationship or by theoretical models of spectatorship and identification. A profile of female horror film fans and followers can be developed only through an audience study. Jackie Stacey's study of female film-goers of the 1940s and 1950s provides a useful model and highlights the need to interpret generic films in relation to their audience.[3] Since the horror genre is also the subject of fan discourses, my study also aimed to investigate female participation in fan practices, drawing on the work of Henry Jenkins.[4]

While heeding Tanya Modleski's warning of the dangers of producing a celebratory and uncritical account of popular culture and pleasure, the value of 'demonstrating the invisible experiences of women with popular culture' was demonstrated by the very large proportion of respondents in this study who expressed their delight and thanks in having an opportunity to speak about their experiences.[5] My study of female horror film viewers allows the voice of an otherwise marginalised and invisible audience to be heard, their experiences recorded, the possibilities for resistance (if any) explored, and the potentially feminine pleasures of the horror film identified.[6] [. . .]

One proposition that this study confirms is that these horror film fans and followers tend to keep their liking for the genre private, and either view alone or with one or two people close to them who also like the genre. Cinema-viewing was the most infrequent format for viewing horror films. This may be related to the infrequency with which horror films are released as well as the less regular attendance of people over twenty-five at all forms of cinema, but the 11 per cent who never watched horror films at the cinema, together with the 67 per cent who watched at the cinema less than once a month, reinforced the idea of an invisible female horror film audience. These female horror film viewers watched horror films on television or, more frequently, on video cassette. Seventy-two per cent of the respondents watched a horror video at least monthly, while 56 per cent watched several times a month; 17 per cent watched a horror film on television at least once a week, 37 per cent two or three times a month and 19 per cent once a month. Overall, 12 per cent watched a horror film two or more times per week, 34 per cent once or twice a week and 41 per cent two or three times a month; thus, just under half of the participants watched a horror film at least once a week. Fourteen per cent viewed fairly infrequently, although only 1 per cent watched less than one horror film a month.

The survey confirms Clover's suggestion that there is a larger female audience for certain horror film types than for others.[7] By far the most popular type of horror film was the vampire film: 92 per cent of the respondents liked all or most vampire films. This was followed in popularity by occult/supernatural films (liked by 86 per cent), psychological thrillers (81 per cent), Hammer films (76 per cent), and science-fiction/horror films (74 per cent). The least well-liked horror film type by far was the slasher film, liked by only 25 per cent of the participants. It was also the most disliked horror film type. Fifty-four per cent of respondents disliked all or most examples of the type. The second and third most disliked types were the serial killer film at 25 per cent and horror-comedies at 22 per cent but these types were liked by 53 per cent and 59 per cent of participants respectively, so that the slasher film seems to be unique in its low appeal to female viewers.

The comments of respondents who liked this film type revealed a significant contradiction in the tastes and responses of these female fans. Surprisingly, perhaps, there was no significant difference between age groups in their preferences for these films. Those respondents classing themselves as fans, however, were more likely to admit to liking slasher films, suggesting that they may have more appeal to the more dedicated female horror film viewer. Many respondents tended to excuse their taste in some way, typically by stating that they like particular examples of the genre – *Halloween*, *Friday the 13th* and *Nightmare on Elm Street*, which they regard as being well made or original – and not others which were held to be formulaic or imitative. Some respondents preferred the funnier versions of the subgenre, while others said that they had to be in a particular frame of mind to watch slasher films.

Typically, many of those who stated that they liked slasher films made an attempt to argue against the criticisms made of the genre. A 39-year-old respondent argued:

> there is no predominance of females being killed. Most slasher films . . . have nearly equal numbers of male and female victims. I think an actual census of horror movie victims would show that females tend to be threatened but escape or are rescued; males tend to be killed. But people only notice the threats to the females and simply shrug off the male deaths.

Others recognised the genre's violence toward women, but chose to ignore it:

> there's definitely some sexist treatment of women going on but at the same time, I enjoy the films, sometimes despite the fact that I'm protesting all these naked female bodies and stupid women who can't do anything but scream. It's foolish when it comes down to it.

As this comment suggests, respondents themselves frequently recognised that their responses were contradictory. This extended to feelings about the victims themselves: one participant described her feelings about characters she referred to as 'the stereotypical bimbo': 'I tend to find that I don't mind these women being victims – they deserve to be killed off!'[8]

Participants were also invited to name up to ten of their favourite horror films. In total, 336 individual films were named by 107 of the participants. The ten most frequently listed favourite horror films were:

		No. of times listed
1.	*Hellraiser* (1987)	33
2.	*Alien* (1979)	30
3.	*Interview With the Vampire* (1995)	30
4.	*The Lost Boys* (1987)	22
5.	*Aliens* (1986)	21
6.	*Bram Stoker's Dracula* (1992)	19
7.	*The Evil Dead* (1982)	17
8.	*The Hunger* (1983)	17
9.	*The Thing* (1982)	17
10.	*Night of the Living Dead* (1968)	15

The twenty most frequently selected films confirm the favourite film type selections with four vampire films,[9] three supernatural/occult films,[10] two psychological thrillers[11] and three science-fiction/horror films[12] in the list. The list also contains three films adapted from the novels of Clive Barker,[13] and all three of the *Evil Dead* series.

Some films were undoubtedly selected because they were recent but, significantly, the majority are older. A number of the films most frequently selected have major female characters, a point that participants drew attention to when asked to explain their choice. By far the most frequently mentioned feature in the appeal of *Alien* (1979) was the enjoyment viewers obtained from watching a strong woman taking an active role. Many respondents felt that the representation of a strong, intelligent and resilient female was a major change from the vast majority of female roles they had previously seen. It has frequently been pointed out that this role was originally written as a male character and there has also been some criticism that Ripley (Sigourney Weaver) is stereotypically masculine. For some viewers, however, watching heroines who behave like heroes, in a masculine fashion, was itself attractive. In general, women appeared to enjoy strong, capable characters, regardless of sex, but were concerned that in the cinema few such characters are female. Other films with strong female leads, such as *Terminator 2* and *The Silence of the Lambs*, were also often named by women as favourites.

Issues of 'quality' were also frequently mentioned in the evaluation of particular films. Quality for these viewers signified several aspects of cinema, including high production values in art direction, set design and costumes. Acting was frequently mentioned as being crucial, with individual actors (in particular Peter Cushing, Christopher Lee and Vincent Price) singled out as giving convincing performances or having star appeal. In the main, however, the quality of a film was determined by plot and character development, in ways that parallel Janice Radway's findings about the interpretative activities of romance fiction readers.[14] Radway demonstrated how a group of women united by their reading preferences actively responded to romance fiction, using it to help themselves deal with their everyday lives. Although there are demographic differences between Radway's readers and the group of horror film viewers discussed here (in addition to the obvious difference of nationality, the horror film viewers are far more likely to be in full-time occupations), their reactions to their chosen cultural texts show strong similarities. Like the subjects of Radway's study, female horror fans judge the quality of films on the basis of the relationships which develop between the characters. This explains the particular liking for vampire films among this group of viewers, since many seemed to read them in a similar way to romance fiction, identifying the relationships between the vampires or between the vampire and its victim as a major source of pleasure. Like Radway's readers, these viewers chose to ignore the events and actions in the narrative that contradicted their reading of the heroine as strong and independent.[15]

For many viewers, the appeal of vampirism seems to be tied into a romanticisation of the past. The taste for Gothic horror is often linked to a liking for historical and costume dramas, with Hammer and other horror films providing a key source of images for this imagined past, which one 23-year-old respondent described as 'a stylish image of dark beauty . . . The classically Gothic full-length dresses and cloaks, the numerous high-ceilinged rooms full of dark wood and velvet curtains are now, without a doubt, for me synonymous with grace and charm'. A 41-year-old respondent commented that 'the vampire film is the closest the horror genre comes to the traditional romantic film. Vampires have most often been portrayed in literature and film as handsome, often foreign, exotic men who seem to have an uncanny knowledge of how to give pleasure. Not so different from the old ideal of a movie star: How do you think Valentino made it so big?' A 53-year-old participant suggested that 'tragic hero figures' such as Heathcliff or Lord Byron were similar to the 'magnetic vampire characters'.

Subtlety of horror was also mentioned as a reason for liking particular films or types of films (*The Haunting*, 1963, is commonly praised in this respect). The horror classics *Frankenstein* and *Dracula* were often cited as examples of 'quality' horror, along with films with a historical or costume-drama style and reflecting Gothic or Romantic themes. Quality in an individual film in a subgenre was given as a reason for liking that film when the subgenre was disliked as a whole. Lack of quality, defined in terms of weak or formulaic plots and stereotypical characters, was often cited as the main reason for not liking slasher films, which were regarded as boring and predictable. Viewers preferred to watch films they took to be imaginative, intelligent, literary or thought-provoking. Dislike was often expressed for films that revolved around excessive or gratuitous displays of violence, gore or other effects used to evoke revulsion in the audience. The women often preferred things left to their imaginations. A respondent in her early thirties claimed that 'those movies that allow me to use my imagination and offer the frame and some atmosphere are more scary to me than any other horror film'. Again, parallels can be identified with Radway's findings: lack of character development and relationships together with high levels of aggression and violence are very similar to the reasons that romance-fiction readers gave for defining romances as bad.[16]

For most respondents, the pleasures of viewing horror films did not include the violence inherent in many examples of the genre. A few expressed a delight in the more violent forms of horror, but women who claimed to enjoy the visceral thrills of watching violence were a small minority.[17] In the main, those who claimed to select horror films with gory special effects preferred such films to be over the top, unrealistic or comic. Bad special effects were enjoyed precisely because they *were* bad and unconvincing. If a gory or violent film was thought to have a good story with interesting characters and to be well made, however, some respondents who otherwise disliked this type of film might enjoy it. Female viewers appeared not to reject gore or violence *per se* so much as the way these elements were used in the film. Sexual and erotic themes, on the other hand, were important to many of the participants, particularly in vampire films. Although sexual violence is commonly disliked, vampires are the most popular form of horror-film monster, and blood is often mentioned as a crucial element. This may indicate that vampire films can function as a form of erotica for women, providing these viewers with sexual fantasy.

More generally, emotional or psychological responses were frequently deemed important in the enjoyment of a film. Tension and suspense were preferred over shock and revulsion. A writer in her forties declared: 'I have always enjoyed tense, thought-provoking films on what may be regarded as the edge of horror.' For a small number of women, being scared was identified as important (though equally as many claimed *not* to be scared by horror films). Generally, these viewers' discourses about their choices and tastes in horror films seemed to be at odds with the fact that horror films are widely regarded as low culture and viewed, as Jonathan Lake Crane observes, as 'the entertainment of the young, minorities, the working class, or the disenfranchised', and frequently criticised by mainstream critics and moral guardians.[18] In common with Radway's romance-fiction readers, these women cannot easily be viewed as ignorant, dull, or misguided consumers of mass culture, nor can they be viewed as the impressionable, bloodthirsty viewers which the moral guardians of society associate with horror cinema.[19]

For many of these habitual viewers, the taste for horror often began well before adolescence – several reported that their first experience of horror involved being enjoyably frightened by Disney-animated films and other dark children's films based on fairy tales – and has persisted long after. Horror films share the frequent representation of distortions of natural forms – supernatural monsters with a human face, for instance – with children's fiction, and these representations were often mentioned by participants as a continuing source of fascination, suggesting that these viewers continue to be simultaneously drawn to, and repelled by, similar representations to those that had engaged them in childhood.[20] Part of the appeal appears to be sympathy or empathy with monstrous creatures. A typical comment was provided by a respondent in her late thirties:

> When I was very little, I used to collect 'monster cards' and one I remember was called 'the gormless blob'. It was a huge heap of green slime with one eye in the middle of its

> head, it was hideously ugly but it lived on love. If it wasn't loved, it died. I had that card on my bedroom wall, near my bed and told it I loved it every night before I went to sleep . . . Monster films always make me cry – classic monsters such as Lon Chaney Jr., Karloff's monster, Charles Laughton's Hunchback, etc.

This empathy for the monster continues into adulthood and may be one of the reasons why some types of horror film – vampire films, versions of Frankenstein and films adapted from the work of Clive Barker, for example – are so popular with female viewers. Many respondents declared that they felt like loners or outsiders as children, describing themselves as 'school swot', 'introverted' or 'bookish', and their identification with the monster may be related to their not feeling part of a peer group.[21] Respondents reported that, as they got older, the very fact that they were fans contributed to their feelings of isolation. John Tulloch and Henry Jenkins describe the popular perception of the fan as other: 'The fan as extraterrestrial; the fan as excessive consumer; the fan as cultist; the fan as dangerous fanatic.'[22] In *Textual Poachers*, Jenkins observes that 'such representations isolate potential fans from others who share common interests and reading practices . . . [and] make it highly uncomfortable to speak publicly as a fan or to identify yourself even privately with fan cultural practices'.[23] This status as outsider – seeing themselves or being seen as a 'geek' or as belonging to a distinctive subculture – continues well into adulthood for some respondents.

Fascination with monstrosity is an important factor in the continuing appeal of horror for women. Although respondents mention many different kinds of monsters when describing what they like about horror films, vampires are by far the most frequently mentioned, often in terms of their sexual fascination for women. As a 24-year-old respondent puts it:

> I have a particular fondness for vampire films, a fascination with the vampire, really. It originated as a sexual feeling evoked in me by the vampire character, and an admiration of his/her style – the elegance of their costume and their aristocracy. As I got older this became a real hobby for me, really, and I began to read a lot to discover the psychology at work behind that. I wanted to understand the evolution of the vampire and to unravel the intrigue surrounding its sexuality.

This fascination for the vampire and its sexuality is typical of many participants, often related to the sexuality and appeal of the male stars playing the dark, handsome, exotic and charismatic vampire popularised by Bela Lugosi, Christopher Lee, Gary Oldman and Antonio Banderas. The homoerotic theme of *Interview With the Vampire* seemed to be no deterrent to its appeal to a female audience. The 24-year-old respondent quoted above describes her use of the film as erotica:

> I've hired vampire videos which I find particularly erotic and sat with my partner at the time watching them in a darkened room – *Interview With the Vampire* is one that I found particularly sexy, there's something intriguing about the homoeroticism between those beautiful young men. I didn't say anything but I think that my partner took pleasure in how I couldn't take my eyes off the screen, and obviously initiated something because of this.

Both film and fictional vampires are often portrayed as polygamous and bisexual and it would appear that for many viewers the vampire film reflects a sexual fantasy.[24] A number of respondents reported fantasising about becoming vampires themselves, and some fans wear vampire costumes, including fangs, on a regular basis.

The physical attraction of the identifiably human monster Pinhead was also a major factor in the appeal of the *Hellraiser* films, again illustrating the sexual fascination with monsters for the female horror fans.[25] Although the extreme levels of violence and excessive special effects render these films problematic for some viewers, others were eventually drawn to his human qualities. The artist respondent typifies this response:

> When I first saw Pinhead I think that he really did scare me . . . It wasn't until *Hellraiser* 3 that he showed any weakness at all, but to fans of the films I think that Pinhead finally revealing his hidden human depths was regarded merely as an insight into one of their favourite monsters. I'm certainly very fond of him now.

Clive Barker's source material was particularly well regarded for its sympathetic attitude to monsters. One respondent in her late thirties explained:

> Clive Barker's films are so beautiful, and his vision of the dark side is so complete. *Hellraiser* I and II and *Candyman* are scary, well written and beautifully filmed, but I feel his vision is most beautifully portrayed in *Nightbreed*, where the monsters are the good guys. I think this maybe a girlie film as most of the men I know don't like it much, but all the women do. A monster movie for people who love monsters.

This love of monsters was repeated by a 35-year-old respondent:

> I have always enjoyed the imagination of Clive Barker because he takes a very obvious joy in the supernatural, the macabre and the downright weird . . . I have never seen anyone else create quite such a variety of monsters. Some are ugly, some are beautiful, they are happy, confused and sad just like human beings.

Although many women felt it was socially unacceptable to express fantasies about stars or characters in horror films – perhaps because most of those surveyed were above the age at which fan attachments to stars are seen as acceptable – one 29-year-old respondent admitted to having crushes on horror film monsters, 'not only when in repose but when they change into their full monstrous forms, fangs bared, blood flowing . . . It is the entire image that I find attractive, not just the stars when they're looking human.' Such comments highlight a particular form of identification to emerge in this study – a 'subversive affinity' with the monster.

Many respondents also appear to have adopted deliberate interpretative strategies to accommodate the films' representations of women, either ignoring and making excuses for what they see as negative representations or condoning feminine behaviour in strong female characters. As one 24-year-old respondent explained,

> I think Ripley's strength in *Alien* is very female – a very female level of practicality that movies like *Predator* don't have. And I love the female lead in *Nightmare on Elm Street*. She knows what is going on and doesn't fall for all of the typical 'crazy female' coddling that everyone around her tries.

Other respondents excused the sexism of older horror films as reflecting a gender stereotype common at the time they were made, which one eighteen-year-old respondent called the 'pathetic female victim syndrome'. She added that 'there are a list of old horror films where the women have the upper hand, for example, they become vampires and men are attracted to them and led to their deaths which seems like justice to me!' A 29-year-old respondent agreed: 'men get the raw deal in horror – a women killed by a vampire tends to be seduced, a man is more likely to be savaged'. While these remarks do not indicate any depth of feminist belief or activism, they might suggest that the films fulfil some kind of revenge fantasy. Other respondents, however, did not overly concern themselves with issues of sexism and stereotyping, not allowing the representations of gender to overwhelm their viewing pleasures. As a nineteen-year-old participant said: 'I object to these women who scream every five seconds but I don't think women have to be the strong lead to make it a good film.'

On the evidence of their comments in this survey, female viewers of the horror film do not adopt purely masculine viewing positions, nor do they simply, as Clover suggests, respond to the literal level of the text.[26] When given the opportunity, as in *Alien*, female viewers strongly identify with the feminised hero because she is literally female. While Clover argues that 'the fact that we have in the killer a feminine male and in the main character a masculine female would seem to suggest a loosening of the category of the feminine', the participants' responses to films like *Alien* and *Hellraiser* suggests that for the female spectator the category of the feminine can be strengthened by adopting particular viewing strategies. Gendered identification for the female viewer may not be as fluid a process as Clover proposes it is for the male viewer.[27]

The similarities between these viewers' interpretative activities and the reading strategies of romance-fiction readers revealed in Radway's study suggest that the pleasures and responses of female horror fans may be categorised as feminine. But these female viewers do not react as might be expected: they do not flinch, block their view or turn away from the screen, nor do they appear as the emasculated viewers one might expect if they were adopting a male gaze or colluding with the male oppressor. This audience segment's preferences for Gothic horror film types and for the thrills and adrenalin rush of the shiver sensation combine with their liking for strong female characters and their most prevalent and frequently mentioned viewing pleasure, an erotic or romantic identification with vampires and other sympathetic or attractive monsters, to provide a distinctively feminine viewing strategy. Like the readers of feminine genres such as romance and historical fiction, these viewers exhibit a tendency to elide those narrative aspects of the films which conform to patriarchal repression or oppression of these characters. These feminine interpretative strategies suggest that if the horror film remains a predominantly masculine genre, it nevertheless continues to incorporate some of the feminine aspects integral to the literary forms of Gothic horror. Most significantly, perhaps, the pleasure that these viewers find in images of terror and gore and, in particular, in the body of the monster belies Linda Williams' assertion that the female spectator of the horror film can only refuse to look. In the words of the 24-year-old respondent:

> I was always touched by the immense tragedy and sorrow of the vampire, and I suppose enjoyed the vicarious pleasure of the female sexual excess and expression in [vampire] films. As a rather shy, mousy and introverted youngster it really filled a void in me. They were never so much role models, that style was far beyond me, but characters I could

> escape with into a fantasy world of glamour as I watched these films. I really found them arousing, exploring a sexual life which I had never had any contact with before – one that seemed otherworldly, and was glittering slick and soft focus on the screen, but beyond my imagination, confidence and certainty in real life.

Refusing to refuse to look is, for such viewers, an act of affinity with the monster more subversive than Williams imagined.

Notes

1 See, for instance, Barbara Creed, 'Horror and the monstrous-feminine: an imaginary abjection', in James Donald (ed.), *Fantasy and the Cinema* (London: British Films Institute, 1989, pp. 81–2, 87.
2 Linda Williams, 'When the woman looks', in Mary Ann Doane, Patricia Mellencamp and Linda Williams, (eds), *Revision: Feminist Essays in Film Analysis* (Washington, DC: American Film Institute, 1984), p. 89.
3 Jackie Stacey, *Star Gazing: Hollywood Cinema and Female Spectatorship* (London: Routledge, 1994).
4 Henry Jenkins, *Textual Poachers: Television Fans and Participatory Culture* (New York and London: Routledge, 1992).
5 Tanya Modleski, *Feminism Without Women* (London: Routledge, 1991); Liesbet van Zoonen, *Feminist Media Studies* (London: Sage Publications, 1994), pp. 128–9.
6 Brenda Dervin, 'The potential contribution of feminist scholarship to the field of communication', *Journal of Communication*, Autumn 1987, pp. 107–20.
7 Clover, *Men, Women and Chain Saws: Gender in the Modern Horror Film* (London: BFI Publishing, 1992), p. 66.
8 These ambivalent attitudes may be related to the response given to victims of domestic violence that they 'deserve it'. See Philip Schlesinger, R. Emerson Dobash, Russell P. Dobash, C. Kay Weaver, *Women Viewing Violence* (London: BFI Publishing, 1992).
9 *Interview with the Vampire*, *The Lost Boys*, *Bram Stoker's Dracula* and *The Hunger*.
10 *The Exorcist* (1973), *The Omen* (1976) and *The Haunting* (1963).
11 *The Silence of the Lambs* (1991) and *Psycho* (1960).
12 *Alien*, *Aliens* and *The Thing*.
13 *Hellraiser*, *Hellbound: Hellraiser II* (1988) and *Nightbreed* (1990).
14 Janice Radway, *Reading the Romance: Women, Patriarchy and Popular Literature* (Chapel Hill: University of North Carolina Press, 1984).
15 Ibid., p. 79.
16 Ibid., p. 159.
17 This aspect of horror film enjoyment is typified by a group of women in Brighton who formed 'Women Into Violent Movies' to watch horror, kung fu, and other similar films.
18 Jonathan Lake Crane, *Terror and Everyday Life: Singular Moments in the History of the Horror Film* (Thousand Oaks, California: Sage Publications, 1994), p. vii.
19 Ibid., p. 3.
20 Joanne Cantor and Mary Beth Oliver have described the kinds of material which frighten or otherwise affect children as varying with age. See Joanne Cantor and Mary Beth Oliver,

'Developmental differences in responses to horror', in James B. Weaver and Ron Tamborini (eds), *Horror Films: Current Research on Audience Preferences and Reactions* (Mahweh: New Jersey: Lawrence Erlbaum Associates, 1996), pp. 63–80.

21 Cantor and Oliver, 'Developmental differences', p. 71, discussing C. Hoffner and J. Cantor, 'Developmental differences in responses to a television character's appearance and behaviour', *Developmental Psychology* vol. 21, 1985, pp. 1065–1074.

22 John Tulloch and Henry Jenkins, *Science Fiction Audiences: Watching* Doctor Who *and* Star Trek (London/New York: Routledge, 1995), p. 4.

23 Jenkins, *Textual Poachers*, p. 19.

24 The Goth subculture too models a desired sexuality along similar lines.

25 Pinhead has become a pin-up and sex symbol in Japan, for instance.

26 Clover, *Men, Women and Chain Saws*, p. 54.

27 Ibid., pp. 62–3.

Bibliography

Adorno, Theodor and Max Horkheimer (1979) *Dialectic of Enlightenment*, London: New Left Books.

Altman, Rick (1999) *Film/Genre* London: BFI.

Ang, Ien (1989) 'Wanted Audiences: On the Politics of Empirical Audience Studies' in Ellen Seiter *et al.*, eds, *Remote Control: Television Audiences and Cultural Power* London: Routledge.

Barker, Martin, ed. (1984) *The Video Nasties: Freedom and Censorship in the Media* London: Pluto.

Benshoff, Harry (1997) *Monsters in the Closet: Homosexuality and the Horror Film* Manchester University Press.

Berenstein, Rhona (1996) *Attack of the Leading Ladies: Gender, Sexuality, and Spectatorship in Classic Horror Cinema* New York: Columbia University Press.

Biskind, Peter (1983) *Seeing is Believing: How Hollywood Taught Us to Stop Worrying and Love the Fifties* London: Pluto.

Bordwell, David (1985) *Narration and the Fiction Film* London: Routledge.

Bordwell, David, Janet Staiger and Kristin Thompson (1985) *The Classical Hollywood Cinema: Film Style and Mode of Production to 1960* New York: Columbia University Press.

Brunsdon, Charlotte (1997) *Screen Tastes: Soap Operas to Satellite Dishes* London: Routledge.

Butler, Ivan (1967) *Horror in the Cinema* New York: Paperback Library.

Carroll, Noël (1990) *The Philosophy of Horror: Or Paradoxes of the Heart* New York: Routledge.

Cawellti, John G. (1976) *Adventure, Mystery and Romance: Formula Stories as Art and Popular Culture* Chicago: University of Chicago Press.

Cherry, Brigid (1999) 'Refusing to Refuse to Look: Female Viewers of the Horror Film', in Melvyn Stokes and Richard Maltby, eds, *Identifying Hollywood's Audiences* London: BFI, pp. 187–203.

Clarens, Carlos (1967) *An Illustrated History of the Horror Film* London: Secker & Warburg.

Clover, Carol J. (1987) 'Her Body, Himself: Gender and the Slasher Film', in *Representations* 20 (Fall), pp. 205–28.

Clover, Carol J. (1992) *Men, Women and Chain Saws: Gender in the Modern Horror Film*, London: BFI.

Crane, Jonathan Lake (1994) *Terror and Everyday Life: Singular Moments in the History of the Horror Film* Thousand Oaks: Sage.

Creed, Barbara (1986) 'Horror and the Monstrous-Feminine: An Imaginary Abjection', in *Screen*, 27 (1) January–February, pp. 44–70.

Creed, Barbara (1987) 'From Here to Modernity: Feminism and Postmodernism', in *Screen* 28 (2), pp. 47–67.

Creed, Barbara (1993) *The Monstrous-Feminine: Film, Feminism, Psychoanalysis* London: Routledge.

Dika, Vera (1990) *Games of Terror:* Halloween, Friday the 13th, *and the Films of the Stalker Cycle* Rutherford, N.J.: Fairleigh Dickinson University Press.

Dillard, R. H. W. (1976) *Horror Films* London: Monarch Press.

Doherty, Thomas (1988) *Teenagers and Teenpics: The Juvenilization of American Movies in the 1950s* London: Unwin Hyman.

Donald, James (1989) *Fantasy and the Cinema* London: BFI.

Dyer, Richard (1988) 'Children of the Night: Vampirism as Homosexuality, Homosexuality as Vampirism', in Susannah Radstone, ed., *Sweet Dreams: Sexuality, Gender, and Popular Fiction* London: Lawrence and Wishart, pp. 47–72.

Elsaesser, Thomas (1989) 'Social Mobility and the Fantastic: German Silent Cinema', in James Donald, ed., *Fantasy and the Cinema* London: BFI.

Erb, Cynthia (1998) *Tracking King Kong* Detroit: Wayne State University Press.

Everson, William K. (1974) *Classics of the Horror Film* London: Citadel.

Freeland, Cynthia (1999) *The Naked and the Undead: Evil and the Appeal of Horror* Boulder, Colorado.: Westview Press.

Gelder, Ken, ed. (2000) *The Horror Reader* London: Routledge.

Grant, Barry K., ed. (1984) *Planks of Reason: Essays on the Horror Film* Metuchen, N.J.: Scarecrow Press.

Grant, Barry K., ed. (1984) *The Dread of Difference: Gender and the Horror Film* Austin: University of Texas Press.

Greenberg, Harvey R. (1975) *Movies on Your Mind* New York: Dutton, 1975.

Gunning, Tom (1990) 'The Cinema of Attractions: Early Film, its Spectator and the Avant-Garde', in Thomas Elsaesser, ed., *Early Cinema: Space, Frame, Narrative* London: BFI.

Halberstam, Judith (1995) *Skin Shows: Gothic Horror and the Technology of Monsters* Durham, N.C.: Duke University Press.

Handling, Piers ed. (1983) *The Shape of Rage: The Films of David Cronenberg* Toronto: General.

Hawkins, Joan C. (1999) 'Sleaze Mania, Euro–trash, and High Art: The Place of European Art Films in American Low Culture', in *Film Quarterly* 53 (2), Winter, pp. 14–29.

Hawkins, Joan C. (2000) '"See it from the Beginning": Hitchcock's Reconstruction of Film History', in *The Hitchcock Annual* pp. 13–30.

Hogan, David J. (1986) *Dark Romance: Sex and Death in the Horror Film* Jefferson, N.C.: McFarland.

Hollows, Joanne (1995) 'Mass Culture Theory and Political Economy', in Joanne Hollows and Mark Jancovich, eds, *Approaches to Popular Film* Manchester University Press.

Hutchings, Peter (1993) *Hammer and Beyond: The British Horror Film* Manchester University Press.

Hutchings, Peter (1995) 'Genre Theory and Criticism', in Joanne Hollows and Mark Jancovich, eds, *Approaches to Popular Film* Manchester University Press.

Jancovich, Mark (1992) *Horror*, London: Batsford.

Jancovich, Mark (1996) *Rational Fears: American Horror in the 1950s* Manchester University Press.

Jancovich, Mark (2000) 'A Real Shocker: Authencity, Genre and the Struggle for Distinction', in *Continuum: Journal of Media and Cultural Studies* 14 (2), pp. 23–35.

Jancovich, Mark 'Cult Fictions: Cult Movies, Subcultural Capital and the Production of Cultural Distinctions', in *Cultural Studies*, forthcoming.

Jancovich, Mark (2001) 'Genre and the Audience: Generic Classifications and Cultural Distinctions in the Mediation of *The Silence of the Lambs*', in Melvyn Stokes and Richard Maltby, eds, *Hollywood Spectatorship: Changing Perceptions of Cinema Audiences*, London: BFI.

Kawin, Bruce (1984) 'The Mummy's Pool' in Barry K. Grant, ed., *Planks of Reason: Essays on the Horror Film* Metuchen: Scarecrow Press, pp. 3–20.

Kitses, Jim (1969) *Horizon's West* London: Thames and Hudson/BFI.

Klinger, Barbara (1994) *Melodrama and Meaning: History, Culture and the Films of Douglas Sirk*, Bloomington, Ind. Indiana University Press.

Kracauer, Siegfried (1947) *From Caligari to Hitler: A Psychological History of the German Film* Princeton: Princeton University Press.

Lévi-Strauss, Claude (1968) *Structural Anthropology* London: Allen Lane.

Macdonald, Dwight (1963) *Against the American Grain*, London: Gollancz.

Maltby, Richard and Ian Craven (1995) *Hollywood Cinema* Oxford: Blackwell.

Naremore, James (1995–6) 'American Film Noir: The History of An Idea', in *Film Quarterly*, 49 (2), Winter, pp. 12–28.

Neale, Stephen (1980) *Genre* London: BFI.

Neale, Stephen (1981) '*Halloween*: Suspense, Aggression and the Look', in *Framework* 14, pp. 25–29.

Neale, Stephen (1990) 'Questions of Genre', in *Screen* 31 (4), Spring, pp. 45–66.

Neale, Stephen (1999) *Genre and Hollywood*, London: Routledge.

Newman, Kim (1988) *Nightmare Movies, The New Edition: A Critical History of the Horror Film*, 1968–88 London: Bloomsbury.

O'Flinn, Paul (1983) 'Production and Reproduction: The Case of *Frankenstein*, in Literature and History, 9 (2), Autumn, pp. 194–213.

Paul, William (1994) *Laughing Screaming: Modern Horror and Comedy* New York: Columbia University Press.

Pinedo, Isabel Cristina (1997) *Recreational Terror* New York: State University of New York Press.

Pirie, David (1973) *A Heritage of Horror: The English Gothic Cinema 1946–1972* London: Gordon Fraser.

Prawer, S. S. (1980) *Caligari's Children: The Film as Tale of Terror* New York: Da Capo.

Punter, David (1980) *The Literature of Terror* London: Longmans.

Ross, Andrew (1989) *No Respect: Intellectuals and Popular Culture* New York: Routledge.

Russell, David J. (1998) 'Monster Roundup: Reintegrating the Horror Genre', in Nick Browne, ed., *Refiguring American Film Genres: Theory and History* Berkeley: University of California Press.

Sarris, Andrew (1976) 'Towards a Theory of Film History', in Bill Nichols, ed., *Movies and Methods* Berkeley: University of California Press.

Siegal, J. E. (1972) *Val Lewton: The Reality of Terror* London: Secker and Warburg.

Skal, David J. (1993) *Hollywood Gothic: The Tangled Web of Dracula from Novel to Stage to Screen* New York: W. W. Norton.

Skal, David J. (1993) *The Monster Show: A Cultural History of Horror* New York: W. W. Norton.

Staiger, Janet (1992) *Interpreting Films: Studies in the Historical Reception of American Cinema* Princeton: Princeton University Press.

Telotte, J. P. (1988) *Dreams of Darkness: Fantasy and the Films of Val Lewton* Urbana: University of Illinois Press.

Tudor, Andrew (1986) 'Genre', in Barry K. Grant, ed., *The Film Genre Reader* Austin: University of Texas Press.

Tudor, Andrew (1989) *Monsters and Mad Scientists: A Cultural History of the Horror Movie*, Oxford: Blackwell.

Tudor, Andrew (1997) 'Why Horror? The Peculiar Pleasures of a Popular Genre', in *Cultural Studies* 11 (3), pp. 443–63.

Twitchell, James B. (1985) *Dreadful Pleasures: An Anatomy of Modern Horror*, New York: Oxford University Press.

Waller, Gregory A. (1986) *The Living and the Undead: From Bram Stoker's Dracula to Romero's Night of the Living Dead* Urbana: University of Illinois Press.

Waller, Gregory A. (1987) *American Horrors: Essays on the Modern American Horror Film* Urbana: University of Illinois Press.

Weaver, Tom (1993) 'Poverty Row Horrors! Monogram, PRC and the Republic Horror Films of the Forties' Jefferson, N.C.: McFarland.

Williams, Linda (1984) 'When the Woman Looks', in Mary Ann Doane, Patricia Mellencamp, and Linda Williams, eds, *Re-Vision: Essays in Feminist Criticism* Frederick, Md.: University Publications of America, pp. 83–99.

Williams, Linda (1994). 'Learning to Scream', in *Sight and Sound*, December, pp. 14–17.

Williams, Tony (1996) *Hearths of Darkness: The Family in the American Horror Film* Madison, N.J.: Fairleigh Dickinson University Press.

Wood, Robin (1976) *Personal Views: Explorations in Film* London: Gordon Fraser.

Wood, Robin (1986) *Hollywood from Vietnam to Reagan* New York: Columbia University Press.

Wood, Robin and Richard Lippe, eds (1979) *American Nightmare: Essays on the Horror Film* Toronto: Festival of Festivals.

Index